THE FENWAY EFFECT

THE FENWAY EFFECT

EFFECT

A CULTURAL HISTORY of the
BOSTON RED SOX

DAVID KRELL

University of Nebraska Press | Lincoln

The University of Nebraska Press is part of a land-grant institution with campuses and programs on the past, present, and future homelands of the Pawnee, Ponca, Otoe-Missouria, Omaha, Dakota, Lakota, Kaw, Cheyenne, and Arapaho Peoples, as well as those of the relocated Ho-Chunk, Sac and Fox, and Iowa Peoples.

Library of Congress Cataloging-in-Publication Data
Names: Krell, David, 1967– author.
Title: The Fenway effect: a cultural history
of the Boston Red Sox / David Krell.
Description: Lincoln: University of Nebraska Press,
[2024] | Includes bibliographical references and index.
Identifiers: LCCN 2023033208
ISBN 9781496232335 (hardback)
ISBN 9781496239655 (epub)
ISBN 9781496239662 (pdf)
Subjects: LCSH: Boston Red Sox (Baseball team)—
History. | Fenway Park (Boston, Mass.)—History. |
BISAC: SPORTS & RECREATION / Baseball / History
Classification: LCC GV875.B62 K74 2024 | DDC
796.357/640974461—dc23/eng/20230828
LC record available at https://lccn.loc.gov/2023033208

Designed and set in Lyon Text by L. Welch.

On April 15, 2013, and for several days
afterward, the Greater Boston area
was in the hearts and prayers of good-hearted
people around the world.

The Boston Marathon bombing
killed 3 people and injured
more than 260 near the finish line.
Some required amputations.

The two terrorists responsible also killed
an MIT police officer during the manhunt.

This book is dedicated to the
victims, survivors, and
first responders of that time.
And their families and friends.

Stay strong.

Contents

Acknowledgments ix

Introduction xiii

Part 1. Boston Strong

1. April 15, 2013 3

2. Never Give Up! The Incredible
   Story of the Jimmy Fund 11

3. A Chance to Excel: Josh Gibson, Satchel Paige,
   and Ted Williams's Hall of Fame Speech 25

Part 2. History and Tradition

4. Songs of the Sox 37

5. Hi Neighbor! Curt Gowdy,
   Narragansett Beer, and the Red Sox 45

6. Where Red Sox History Began: The First
   Game at Huntington Avenue Grounds 54

Part 3. Hollywood and the Red Sox

7. Reel Red Sox 65

8. The Ballad of Sam "Mayday" Malone 76

9. A Little Roller up along First: Game Six,
   Curb Your Enthusiasm, and the
   Dignity of Bill Buckner 87

Part 4. Heartbreaks and Happiness

10. Hope for Tomorrow: American Optimism,
    Cultural Revolutions, and Game Six of
    the 1975 World Series 101

11. Out of Sight, Baby: The Sixties and the Sox 112

12. Worthy Rivals: The Red Sox and the Yankees 129

Part 5. Icons

13. A Man Called Yastrzemski 145

14. Tom Seaver's Last Hurrah 155

15. Location, Location, Location: The Tales
     and Travails of the Citgo Sign 167

16. Of Sluggers and Statues 178

Part 6. Voices of the Fans

17. Go Sox! The Fans Speak Out 189

     Notes 207

     Selected Bibliography 233

     Index 235

Acknowledgments

As always, I'm grateful for the generosity of librarians, scholars, and archivists who protect baseball's history.

Cassidy Lent at the National Baseball Hall of Fame and Museum's A. Bartlett Giamatti Research Center did a yeoman's job in fulfilling my research requests concerning Red Sox history. It was a challenging yet worthwhile task to pore through hundreds of newspaper clippings on various Red Sox notables for confirming information, selecting quotes, and getting background information.

Research services team leader Amber De Angelis runs an extraordinary squad of librarians at the Boston Public Library's main branch at 700 Boylston Street. Going through decades-old microfilm of Boston newspapers in the Washington Room to chronicle the tremendously rich cultural history of the Red Sox was like walking through time.

Molly Riportella of the Walpole Public Library deserves recognition for helping me track down a *Walpole Times* article with a great quote from Carl Yastrzemski on the day that the Red Sox retired his number. Paula Kepich of the Carnegie Library of Pittsburgh, Kelly Dunnagan of the Louisville Free Public Library, and Dr. Thomas Aiello at Valdosta State University tried to track down the original source of an article that I found in Josh Gibson's Hall of Fame file. It appears that the original is lost to history, which is explained in an endnote to chapter 3.

In New York City, the main branch of the New York Public Library at Fifth Avenue and Forty-Second Street was a popular destination during my research. The library's access to the ProQuest database allowed me to easily access and download articles from the *Boston Globe* and *New York Times* archives. Additionally, the NYPL's gargantuan collection of New York City's newspapers on microfilm proved invaluable for the chapter about the Red Sox–Yankees rivalry. Newspapers.com was also a valuable resource.

Acknowledgments

David McCarthy clarified information regarding the statues of Ted Williams, and Al Nipper gave me some great background on Tom Seaver during the pitcher's brief tenure with the Red Sox. For the chapter on the Jimmy Fund, I had the privilege of talking with the daughters of Einar Gustafson, the original "Jimmy." Lynn MacLeod and Lisa Patti opened their hearts and shared their memories, as did Thomas Farber regarding his father, Dr. Sidney Farber, a cornerstone of the Jimmy Fund for decades and a pioneer in cancer research.

Mark Hellendrung shared some terrific information about the history, demise, and revival of Narragansett Beer. Jim Crooks, the company's resident historian, gave me some valuable background. My appreciation to Brooke Cure for setting up these connections. Also, Brian Schade represents the view of the Narragansett memorabilia collector. It's a terrific niche in breweriana.

Bruce Wells provided much-needed perspective regarding the Citgo sign from an oil history perspective. Alison Frazee's insight as a preservationist was formidable. Eddie Bruckner gave an artist's view, and Arthur Krim, an urban historian, is a noted source. Warren Thayer recalled his days at Boston University with the sign as a location identifier. Our conversations were great complements to the research through newspaper articles.

University of Maryland architecture professor Brian Kelly shared a copy of Jean Labatut's landmark essay "Monuments and Memorials," which I used as a guidepost for the chapter about the statues at Fenway Park. I took Professor Kelly's Introduction to Architecture course as an elective more than thirty-five years ago, and the lessons of analysis have remained with me ever since.

Photographs are critical. Special thanks to Jack Baker, Kristin Parker, and Aaron Schmidt in the Boston Public Library's Special Collections Department. Bob Cullum was gracious in granting the necessary and separate permission to use photos from the Leslie Jones Collection housed at the BPL. John Horne at the National Baseball Hall of Fame and Museum deserves applause for finding a photo of Babe Ruth in his pitching days. Matt Lutts from the Associated Press was his usual effective self in cycling through the red tape required for photo licensing.

I'm appreciative of honest appraisals from Lisa Bloomfield, Art Carine, and Gabriel Lipker during the editing stage, before I submitted the manuscript. Later, the University of Nebraska Press paired me with Maureen Creamer Bemko, an outstanding copy editor whose suggestions were exemplary. I had worked with Maureen on my UNP book *1962: Baseball and America in the Time of JFK.*

One chapter belongs to the fans. Members of Red Sox Nation are proud, passionate, and devoted, so I wanted a chapter acknowledging the emotional impact of the team. Generosity does not begin to describe their involvement in this project. Responses to my questions went on for several pages, leading to the very difficult decision of what to cut and what to keep.

Chronicling their experiences, memories, and insights was a revelation. Their generosity, inspiring. Seeing the Red Sox through the perspectives of folks who have been at Fenway Park dozens of times—hundreds for some—provided the four Cs, which were great companions during my research: color, context, clarity, and compassion.

The fans deserve praise, as do the people who put me in touch with some of them. My thanks to Marty Appel, John Bennett, Eric Burckhardt, Julia Claire, Dan Cleary, Donna Cohen, Michael Dillon, Thomas Farber, Alison Frazee, Donna Halper, Howard Homonoff, Mark Hoyle, MaryEllen Kelly, Ron Kercheville, Joshua Krumholz, Joe LeBritton, Karl Lindholm, Barbara Mantegani, Scott Melesky, Antonio Tobias Mendez, Max Nadoraski, Bill Nowlin, John Pearson, Mark Peloquin, Amy Polacko, Larry Ruttman, Brian Schade, Mel Seibolt, Jim Smith, David Starr, Gabrielle Starr, Gary Stockbridge, John Tierney, and Clayton Trutor.

I'm also grateful for the generosity of Donna Cohen and her family for letting me sit in their section close to the Fenway Park field on Opening Day in 2023. The Cohens' season tickets have been in the family for decades.

Finally, thanks to Rob Taylor for having confidence in me and this project. Kudos and appreciation go to Rob, Sara Springsteen, Rosemary Sekora, and their colleagues on the editorial, production, and marketing teams at the University of Nebraska Press.

Introduction

Baseball is a tribal endeavor marked by pride in a team's lineage. Examples are abundant.

Yankees fans point to more than two dozen World Series titles. There are Lou Gehrig's "luckiest man" speech, Mickey Mantle's Triple Crown season, and Reggie Jackson hitting three home runs in a World Series game. Babe Ruth hit sixty home runs in 1927, a Major League record broken by Roger Maris with sixty-one in 1961. Although National Leaguers have since bested Maris, his sixty-one homers stood as the benchmark for the American League until Aaron Judge hit sixty-two in 2022. Another Yankee.

Milwaukeeans and Atlantans lay claim to Hank Aaron, a Braves icon who broke Ruth's career home run record of 714 and ended his career with 755. Barry Bonds surpassed him, totaling 762. In 2023 Aaron still held the career RBI record.

Willie Mays is a hero to Giants fans who saw him play at the Polo Grounds and others who called Candlestick Park his home. The Say Hey Kid led the Major Leagues in slugging percentage four times—twice in New York, twice in San Francisco.

Cubs fans can warm their hearts on Chicago's icy winter nights with reminders of Ernie Banks's two MVP Awards, Kiki Cuyler's four seasons leading the National League in stolen bases, and the famed Tinker-Evers-Chance double-play combination.

Dodgers fans count Sandy Koufax among the greatest pitchers ever, evidenced by the powerful lefty winning three Cy Young Awards, topping the Majors in strikeouts four times, and throwing four no-hitters, including a perfect game.

In western Pennsylvania, Pirates history boasts eight-time National League batting average leader Honus Wagner, twelve-time All-Star Roberto Clemente, and the "We Are Family" season of 1979 capped by a comeback against the Orioles in the World Series after being down three games to one.

Being a Red Sox fan is more than just a roster of accomplishments, though.

It's more than Ted Williams being the last .400 hitter.

It's more than Carl Yastrzemski winning the Triple Crown.

It's more than Fred Lynn winning Rookie of the Year and Most Valuable Player in the same season.

It's more than Roger Clemens notching twenty strikeouts in one game.

It's more than the World Series title in 2004 breaking the so-called Curse of the Bambino—a theory positing that the trade of Babe Ruth to the Yankees caused the lack of World Series titles for several decades.

Being a Red Sox fan is a state of mind enveloping a New Englander in a protective sense of belonging from cradle to grave, creating memories that resonate with the steadiness of a metronome in high-definition clarity, and keeping the team's lore alive through generations.

Sox fandom is rooted. Deeply.

It runs across classes and persists through generations, creating a bond with the Red Sox, Fenway Park, and fellow fans no matter your station in life. The accountant from Peabody. The contractor from Newton. The real estate appraiser from Medford. The electrician from Dorchester. The banker from Brookline. The nurse from Sudbury. The attorney from Needham. The teacher from Roxbury. The mechanic from Marlboro.

They cheer in victory, mourn in loss, and remain in steadfast devotion. Their energy, passion, and bond are as noticeable as the Green Monster at Red Sox home games.

Membership in Red Sox Nation requires being a hopeful romantic who neither betrays loyalty nor surrenders hope in the direst of circumstances. Bostonians have learned to endure in baseball matters.

And life.

Fenway Park was their lodestar after the Boston Marathon bombing in 2013. David "Big Papi" Ortiz declared before a home game, "This is our fucking city!" It left no doubt that Boston's power resides in the hearts, minds, and souls of the people. Boston Strong, indeed.

But there have already been tremendous narratives and documentaries concerning the Red Sox. So why walk where so many others have trod?

Answer: I didn't. I wrote a different kind of book.

My curiosity is fixed in the team's cultural impact. I trace my interest in that culture to my sophomore year in high school: 1982. That year NBC premiered two Boston-based shows in prime time. On *St. Elsewhere*, Howie Mandel played Dr. Wayne Fiscus, an emergency room doctor prone to wearing a Red Sox cap during his shifts at St. Eligius Hospital. *Cheers* revolved around the patrons and staff at the eponymous Boston watering hole owned by former Red Sox relief pitcher Sam "Mayday" Malone. Dialogue featured Sam's career and the Red Sox throughout the show's eleven-year run, particularly in the first two seasons.[1]

Nearly forty years later, my interest revived because of COVID-19. During the early days of the pandemic when politicians and doctors strongly suggested that we stay inside, I screened all 273 episodes of *Cheers* to construct a biography of Malone, a fictional character, for the Society for American Baseball Research Biography Project.

Rewatching the episodes reminded me of the depths of detail that the *Cheers* producers employed, using verisimilitude as a device placing the show in realism, whether it was Coach and Carla playing Red Sox trivia or Sam recalling when he struck out Norm Cash, Al Kaline, and Bill Freehan with the tying run on second base. These are conversations one would expect in a Boston bar owned by a former Red Sox player.

That experience got me thinking about other cultural touchstones that belong to the Red Sox.

Why did the link between Narragansett Beer and the Red Sox break?

What's the architectural significance of *The Teammates*—the statue of Bobby Doerr, Johnny Pesky, Ted Williams, and Dom DiMaggio—outside Fenway Park?

What's the story behind Bill Buckner's redemption on *Curb Your Enthusiasm*?

How does Tom Seaver's experience with the Red Sox fit into the 1980s aura of nostalgia?

It was quite a journey of discovery.

Introduction

Before Opening Day in 2023, I walked outside Fenway Park and soaked in the ambience of excitement, renewal, and hopefulness as somebody played a remix of Belinda Carlisle's 1980s song "Heaven Is a Place on Earth." For Red Sox fans, that place is Fenway Park. Down 10-4 against the Orioles going into the bottom of the eighth, Boston rallied for five runs in the next two innings. Alas, the game ended with a 10-9 loss.

As fans headed toward the exit, an organist's version of "Will You Still Love Me Tomorrow?" blared through the speakers. Red Sox fans can easily respond with another song title—"I Love You Always Forever."

Go Sox!

PART 1

Boston Strong

1

April 15, 2013

"This is our fucking city!"

When David Ortiz made his pregame declaration of urban pride on April 20, 2013, five days after the Boston Marathon bombing, he let Red Sox fans know that their beloved baseball team is more than just twenty-five athletic avatars for entertainment, distraction, and catharsis in the spring, summer, and hopefully an extended postseason in the fall. During the aftermath of the bombing, the Red Sox gave a reason to congregate, to cheer, and to look forward with possibility.

There was no better person to provide encouragement for them than the man everyone called "Big Papi."

Ortiz's moment on April 20 is a cornerstone of Red Sox culture, which has proven time and time again—and continues to do so—that the team and its fans form the bedrock of a community that is rich in its legacy, colorful in its members, and optimistic in its outlook.

The Dominican-born slugger—who has an infectious, Santa-like positivity about him, with a smile that could light up Boston Harbor on a foggy day in October—reminded everyone at Fenway Park that they all belong to the same family. Ortiz's statement in full: "This jersey that we wear today, it doesn't say Red Sox. It says Boston. We want to thank you Mayor Menino, Governor Patrick, the whole police department for the great job that they did this past week. This is our fucking city! And nobody's going to dictate our freedom. Stay strong."[1]

The last sentence honored "Boston Strong," the two-word slogan embraced after the April 15 attack in which two homemade pressure cooker bombs killed 3 people near the marathon's finish line on Boylston Street—twenty-three-year-old Lingzi Lu, twenty-nine-year-old Krystle Marie Campbell, eight-year-old Martin Richard—and wounded more than 260. Several victims had to have amputations.

As has been the custom on Marathon Day—also called Patriots Day—

the Red Sox played a home game that started in the late morning. Boston's 3–2 victory, which happened in storybook fashion on an RBI double by Mike Napoli in the bottom of the ninth inning, had been finished for about forty-five minutes when the bombs detonated at 2:49 p.m.

The bombers, later identified as brothers Tamerlan Tsarnaev and Dzhokar Tsarnaev, both in their twenties, also shot and killed Sean Collier, a twenty-seven-year-old MIT campus police officer, in his parked police car as they evaded a manhunt conducted by local, state, and federal law enforcement agencies for four days. Their strategy was simple but effective. Hiding in plain sight and detonating the devices toward the end of the marathon course at Copley Square was not difficult for the Tsarnaev brothers because of the Boston Marathon's considerable drawing power. "This isn't Russia or Cuba," stated Kevin G. Miles, a retired FBI bomb technician. "You're not going to be able to check everybody's bag, everybody's pocketbook on a massive event like this."[2]

From Somerville to Southie, fear and revenge fueled conversations.

"I hope they give these bastards the death penalty" was a likely comment from a TD Garden maintenance worker gulping from a bottle of Narragansett Beer at Sullivan's Tap; a Massachusetts General Hospital X-ray technician munching on a slice with mushrooms complemented by a Diet Coke from Nino's Pizza; or an MIT sophomore ordering a cup of joe at—where else?—the Dunkin' Donuts outlet in the Stratton Student Center.

Comments to the contrary were unthinkable. Violence directed at innocent people had turned Boylston Street into a war zone; carnage replaced joy in a twelve-second span. Vengeance may belong to God according to the Bible—as in the verses Hebrews 10:30, Deuteronomy 32:35, and Romans 12:17—but this was not a time for sermonizing by do-gooders when victims were grappling with the loss of limbs and long, grueling recoveries. Bostonians needed the bombers either captured or killed. The former option was fine. The latter, preferred.

One victim came to represent "Boston Strong," though reluctantly at first: Jeff Bauman.

Near the finish line with a homemade sign to cheer his girlfriend, Erin Hurley, Bauman became famous worldwide because of a photograph taken by an Associated Press photographer after the bombing. Charles Krupa captured Bauman being helped to safety by Carlos Arredondo, a cowboy-hat-wearing Good Samaritan who rushed from across the street; Boston emergency medical technician Paul Mitchell also assisted as first responder Devin Wang pushed Bauman in a wheelchair.[3]

Bauman's legs suffered tremendous damage during the bombing, forcing doctors to perform a double amputation. After awakening, he told a friend that he saw one of the bombers. His detailed description of Tamerlan Tsarnaev to the FBI proved crucial in narrowing the list of suspects.

Three weeks after the bombing, Bauman was the Boston Bruins fan banner captain before a Maple Leafs–Bruins playoff game. Hurley wheeled him onto a carpet laid on the ice so he could wave a flag with the words "Boston Strong" written in Bruins gold on a black background.[4] In another three weeks, Arredondo and Bauman threw out the first pitches at a Phillies–Red Sox game. Bauman's battery mate was Jarrod Saltalamacchia. David Ortiz caught Arredondo's toss.

Jake Gyllenhaal starred as Bauman in the 2017 movie *Stronger*—based on Bauman's autobiography of the same name—which revolved around his relationships with family, friends, and Hurley throughout his incremental, heartbreaking, but ultimately successful recovery. During the filming of the movie in 2016, Bauman ventured to the Fenway Park mound again, this time with his portrayer, to inaugurate a Blue Jays–Red Sox game. Bauman's partner for this moment was Hanley Ramirez; Ortiz repeated his catching duty for Gyllenhaal.

A touching scene in *Stronger* takes place in the corridors of Fenway Park when a crowd swarms around Bauman. One by one, people tell him how he inspired them, including a brother of a soldier who was killed by an IED—presumably in Iraq—and a third grader who wrote a report about him for a class. Bauman gladly hears their stories and humbly accepts their praises in this critical story point—he has come to accept that he symbolizes strength just by living his life.

The 2016 film *Patriots Day* recounts the bombing and manhunt, capped by footage of the pregame ceremony on April 20, 2013; Ortiz's speech; snippets of interviews with victims and members of law enforcement;

and pictures of the four victims. Directed by Peter Berg and starring Mark Wahlberg as BPD sergeant Tommy Saunders, a fictional character serving as a composite for officers involved in the investigation, *Patriots Day* got high praise from Boston police commissioner Ed Davis, who was among the honorees highlighted before the game. "I think they nailed it," said Davis at a panel event coinciding with the film's premiere in December 2016. "They squeezed an enormous amount of detail into two hours."[5]

Before the attack, the Boston Marathon's most notorious incident happened in 1980, when Rosie Ruiz cheated by claiming to be the women's winner. It was later discovered that she didn't run the full course. Four years later, the marathon got national exposure in prime time—or at least an homage—when Dr. Philip Chandler, a character played by Denzel Washington on NBC's *St. Elsewhere*, ran the course alone in the middle of winter.[6]

Carnage caused by the terrorists on April 15, 2013, placed the marathon on the roster of violent acts that America had suffered on its soil. Four presidents have been assassinated: Abraham Lincoln, James A. Garfield, William McKinley, and John F. Kennedy. There was an attempt on Franklin Roosevelt's life in his first year in office.

Gerald Ford survived two attempts in one month. Ronald Reagan, with his presidency less than three months old, was shot; he survived and served two terms.

The Japanese attack on Pearl Harbor led to America's involvement in the Pacific theater in World War II. In 1954 four Puerto Rican nationalists shot and wounded four members of Congress on the floor of the House of Representatives.

Six people died and more than a thousand were injured during the explosion of a van bomb in a World Trade Center parking garage in 1993. Eight years later, the Twin Towers collapsed after terrorists hijacked two planes and flew them into the structures that had come to define New York City since their opening in 1973. Nearly 3,000 people died; 343 deaths belonged to the FDNY.

As part of the same plot, terrorists hijacked a plane and flew it into the Pentagon; on United Flight 93, passengers fought terrorists until the jet crashed in an open field in Pennsylvania. There were no survivors in either incident.

Sports might seem meaningless to some in the wake of terrorism or disaster. It's a false premise.

The praise-laden introductions of Bauman at Fenway Park and TD Garden brought thousands of people together, if only for a few moments, to remind us of the goodness in the hearts and souls of people.

Further, the games themselves, like other leisure activities, are necessary for a community's emotional bonding. President Franklin Roosevelt urged Major League Baseball commissioner Kenesaw Mountain Landis to continue the operations of the Major Leagues in the early days of World War II. The president's missive became known as the "green light letter." For Roosevelt, it was integral to keeping morale high on the home front: "I honestly feel that it would be best for the country to keep baseball going. There will be fewer people unemployed and everybody will work longer hours and harder than ever before. And that means that they ought to have a chance for recreation and for taking their minds off their work even more than before."[7]

A strong earthquake just before Game Three of the Giants versus A's World Series in 1989 only postponed the game; it didn't cancel the series. Oakland won in a four-game sweep.

Mike Piazza's game-winning home run in the Braves-Mets game on September 21, 2001, gave New Yorkers a moment of positive excitement after ten days of rage, frustration, worry, and vengeance occupying their minds after the 9/11 attacks.

At Fenway Park, the crowd of 35,152 on April 20, 2013, had tremendous enthusiasm as Boston aimed to get back to its emotional baseline of rhythms and routines. "I thought about how important it was to put a city back together, go back to normal, and show terrorists they're not going to prevail," said the BPD's Davis, who admitted that he questioned whether to go to the game.[8]

Indeed, it was an opportunity for Bostonians to release their pent-up emotions, given the news celebrated on the night of April 19—Dzhokar, the younger of the two bombers, had surrendered after an hours-long standoff with the FBI, Boston Police Department, and Watertown Police

Department that played out at 67 Franklin Street in Watertown. David Henneberry, the homeowner, had alerted the cops that someone was hiding under the tarp covering his boat, landlocked in the driveway.

Tamerlan had died on April 18 from injuries sustained in a shootout with Watertown cops; Dzhokar stole an SUV and ran over him in a failed attempt to kill the cops subduing his brother.

One terrorist was dead. The other faced the death penalty. Time to move forward. Ortiz's stature warranted a pregame speech to reinforce the tone of resilience now that feelings of vengeance had been dimmed by liberation from the terrorism threat. Beginning his Major League journey with the Minnesota Twins in 1997, Ortiz had been released after six seasons and signed with the Red Sox on January 22, 2003. He became an offensive force, though an Achilles heel injury sidelined him in 2012 and reduced his playing time to ninety games. He batted .318 with twenty-three home runs and sixty RBIs. Boston finished in last place in the American League East without their star, twenty-six games behind the Yankees.

But he wasn't quite ready to play when the team opened the 2013 season on the road in Yankee Stadium. Rehabilitating his injury with the Pawtucket Red Sox—Boston's Triple-A team—Ortiz needed to prove his Achilles problem was not a hindrance. And so he did. On April 11, Pawtucket beat the Rochester Red Wings 5–4. Ortiz scored a run, knocked in a run, and went two-for-three; his mobility was determinative. "I feel fine," stated the ballplayer. "That's the important thing to be able to run around the bases and be able to move around and be able to do that with freedom, without hesitation."[9]

Ortiz had a one-for-four day against Rochester two days later, notching two RBIs and scoring a run. Although the slugger didn't give any interviews or statements, Pawtucket skipper Gary DiSarcina validated his progress. "He knows his body better than anyone," remarked DiSarcina, who had played with the Angels from 1989 to 2000 and made the All-Star team in 1995. "He's rehabbed before. He knows how many at-bats he needs to be able to get out of here and be with his teammates in Boston."

It looked promising for Red Sox fans. "As far as I know, he hasn't come up with any issues and is progressing," continued DiSarcina.[10] When Boston's front office reinstated Ortiz, Red Sox Nation anticipated his presence at Fenway Park with the eagerness of a Revere kid at Garfield Elementary School on the last day before Christmas break. And for good reason. Now in the twilight of his career, "Big Papi" had an outstanding résumé, including two World Series rings and 332 home runs with the Red Sox. Combining those numbers with his stats in a Twins uniform, he had 401 career round-trippers. Ortiz led the American League in homers once. In RBIs, twice. He also led the Majors in one of those massive RBI seasons.[11]

The April 20 game was the seventh in a seven-game winning streak, which included a three-hitter by Clay Buchholz against the Tampa Bay Rays. Buchholz was also the starting pitcher on April 20.

Through four innings, the teams were scoreless. That changed in the top of the fifth, when Lorenzo Cain led off with a double off Buchholz, went to third on Mike Moustakas's fly ball to Red Sox center fielder Jacoby Ellsbury, and scored on Jeff Francoeur's single.

Royals right-hander James Shields protected Kansas City's 1-0 lead in the bottom of the fifth, but the Red Sox tied the game an inning later with some old-fashioned, move-the-runner offense. Ellsbury's lead-off single set the tone. Shane Victorino sacrificed him to second with a bunt; catcher Salvador Pérez fielded it and threw to Eric Hosmer at first base. Dustin Pedroia's grounder to third baseman Moustakas allowed Ellsbury to move to third base, and Ortiz the orator knocked him home with a single.

The Royals responded with a run in the top of the seventh.

Kansas City manager Ned Yost sent Aaron Crow to start the bottom of the inning. It did not begin well for the visitors. Crow hit Daniel Nava with a pitch and Will Middlebrooks singled. Pérez picked Nava off second base for the first out, but Moustakas's error gave Stephen Drew first base; Jarrod Saltalamacchia pinch-hit for David Ross. Yost sent in Tim Collins, who got Saltalamacchia out on a pop-up to Moustakas and retired Ellsbury on a fly ball to right fielder Francoeur.

Boston leaped ahead with three runs in the bottom of the eighth. The rally began when Red Sox skipper John Farrell sent Jonny Gomes to pinch-hit for Victorino. Gomes doubled. Pedroia walked, raising the hopes that the need—almost a craving—for Red Sox fans to celebrate a victory after a harrowing five days would be fulfilled. Alas, it happened, but not immediately.

Ortiz grounded to Royals shortstop Alcides Escobar for a double play; Gomes moved to third base. Yost relieved Collins with Kelvin Herrera, who walked Mike Napoli; Nava crushed a three-run homer to make the score 4–2.

Buchholz pitched for eight innings, striking out six and scattering eight hits; Andrew Bailey replaced him in the top of the ninth. Cain closed Boston's margin to 4–3 with a lead-off home run—his fourth hit on a four-for-four day—and Kansas City pecked away at Bailey.

A fly ball to Ellsbury in center field retired Moustakas, but Francoeur singled. Bailey whiffed Pérez for the second out, then walked George Kottaras—a pinch hitter substituting for Chris Getz—and Elliot Johnson then performed pinch-running duties. But Alex Gordon's groundout to shortstop Drew secured the win, ended the rally, and began the healing for Boston.

After the game, Buchholz noted the mood among the players: "Not since 9/11, I can't imagine how those guys felt going out there and playing the first time after that happened, but I think this was probably as close as it could be to feeling that way, knowing that all we wanted to do was get through this game with a 'W' today and the fashion that we did was awesome."[12]

Boston's victory gave Buchholz a 4-0 record; he finished at 12-1, emblematic of the team's success in 2013. The Red Sox took two of three from the rival Yankees to begin the season and ended it by beating the St. Louis Cardinals in six games to win the World Series.

But no matter how many World Series titles enter the Red Sox annals, no matter how many All-Stars wear Red Sox jerseys, no matter how many Hall of Famers have a Red Sox cap on their likenesses depicted on their plaques, the events of April 15, 2013, and subsequent days will be permanent reminders of Boston's vulnerability, endurance, and toughness.

So will the stories of Jeff Bauman and other survivors.

So will the actions of first responders and volunteers.

So will the words of David Ortiz.

2

Never Give Up!

The Incredible Story of the Jimmy Fund

The Bible is chock-full of verses encouraging charitableness.

"Whoever is generous to the poor lends to the Lord, and he will repay him for his deed."[1]

"But if anyone has the world's goods and sees his brother in need, yet closes his heart against him, how does God's love abide in him?"[2]

"Each one must give as he has decided in his heart, not reluctantly or under compulsion, for God loves a cheerful giver."[3]

Celebrities attach their fame to a cause for the same purpose, thereby increasing the likelihood of awareness, empathy, and donations. Danny Thomas founded St. Jude Children's Hospital. Jerry Lewis's annual Muscular Dystrophy Association telethon was a Labor Day staple for decades.

Their involvement may be prompted by suffering from the ailment that the charity seeks to defeat. Or at least moderate. Oscar winner and seven-time Emmy Award winner Mary Tyler Moore, a Type 1 diabetic, became the celebrity spokesperson for the Juvenile Diabetes Research Foundation. Yul Brynner's posthumous antismoking TV commercial for the American Cancer Society arose from an interview that the Russian-born star did for ABC's *Good Morning America* nine months before passing away from lung cancer on October 10, 1985, at the age of sixty-five. The commercial first aired on February 19, 1986.[4]

The Jimmy Fund has the Boston Red Sox. Not just one player. The entire organization.

1947

A chance meeting created the seedlings for what would become a signature charity in Boston. Members of the Variety Club of New England—comprising theater and entertainment industry executives—had the opportunity to visit the Children's Medical Center. William Koster, the club's executive director, met with two doctors who envisioned a research center dedicated to children's cancer—Dr. Sidney Farber and his assistant, Dr. George Foley. And so, the Children's Cancer Research Foundation was born.

1948

When the Jimmy Fund began, there was a different baseball sponsor. It was the same year that Milton Berle emerged as TV's first star when he debuted as the host of NBC's *Texaco Star Theater*; President Harry Truman ordered the desegregation of U.S. military forces; Laurence Olivier gave an Oscar-winning performance in the title role of *Hamlet*; Satchel Paige won the American League Rookie of the Year Award at forty-two years old; David Ben-Gurion became the first prime minister of the newly formed, independent State of Israel; and Rudolf Dassler founded Puma to rival Adidas, the sportswear company founded by his brother, Adi Dassler.

The Jimmy Fund is named after the alias of a cancer patient at Children's Hospital in Boston—a child introduced to the public on the May 22, 1948, episode of the NBC radio show *Truth or Consequences*, hosted by Ralph Edwards. The boy had "an intestinal tumor that had spread to the lymph glands."[5]

To protect his identity, "Jimmy" served as his moniker, and whether intended or not, it stuck with the public. Immediately. Hence, the Jimmy Fund was created as a fundraising vehicle for the hospital's cancer research. Intrigued, Koster took on the role of the Jimmy Fund's executive director; his fundraising was estimated at more than $52 million when he died in 1978.[6]

In his hospital room, Jimmy met with the players and manager, Billy Southworth, from his favorite team—the Boston Braves. "Jimmy's eyes almost popped out of his head," described the *Boston Globe* when Johnny Sain came into Jimmy's room.[7] Sain, the young patient's favorite player, had won twenty games in 1946 and twenty-one in 1947; he was on his way to lead the Major Leagues in victories, games started, complete games, and innings pitched in 1948. The Braves lost the '48 World Series to the Cleveland Indians in six games.

There were several gifts for the patient, including "a tailor-made Braves uniform" and a bat autographed by Earl Torgeson. Additionally, Jimmy learned that he'd be getting a television, which was a luxury item in the late 1940s.[8]

Besides Sain and Southworth, Jimmy's other visitors during the broadcast were Torgeson, Bob Elliott, Eddie Stanky, Jeff Heath, Warren Spahn, Phil Masi, Alvin Dark, Jim Russell, and Tommy Holmes. But there was something else—two season passes. Jimmy went to the following day's doubleheader against the Chicago Cubs; Boston won both contests.[9]

The *Truth or Consequences* broadcast had a viral impact around Boston. Less than a week later came an announcement for a June 11 exhibition game at Marblehead High School.[10] About forty miles from Boston, a twenty-inch trout was the biggest fish caught in a children's fishing derby in Ayer at the end of May. But the contestants agreed that Jimmy should get the trophy.[11]

An exhibition between amateur teams—South Shore League's Milton Merchants and Boston Parks Department's Linehan Club—was announced to raise money. The venue: South Boston Stadium, the city's largest public park.[12] Brookline's Cypress Street Playground had a softball doubleheader fundraiser the night after July 4.[13] The Boston Army Base raised $175 by passing the hat because it couldn't charge an admission fee for its games at Columbus Park.[14]

A controversy brewed during the first couple of months of the Jimmy Fund's existence when Somerville's board of aldermen claimed that a carnival run by Endy Brothers—the third-biggest carnival in the United States—ripped off its customers. Under the agreement, the Jimmy Fund was entitled to $1,500 in addition to 20 percent of sales exceeding $12,000 in gross revenue. The carnival claimed, inexplicably, that the information regarding gross revenue was unavailable. In turn, the board mandated that Endy Brothers shut down its operation and then revoked the carnival's license, labeling the operation "a public nuisance where the people are being milked far in excess of the benefit to be given the Jimmy Fund."[15]

The football world got involved, too. Boston's NFL team—the Yanks—had played an exhibition game against the Bears in '46 and drew thirty-seven thousand, the biggest crowd for a professional football game in the city. A plan for a 1947 exhibition never got off the ground.[16] Inspired, the Braves hosted the New York Yankees and Brooklyn Dodgers of the All-America Football Conference at Braves Field for an exhibition game on August 21 to raise money.

The Yankees won 14-7. Attendance exceeded fourteen thousand.[17]

In late October, as Braves fans celebrated a fantastic season but mourned losing to the Indians in the World Series, the Jimmy Fund had reportedly received a bounty of more than $225,000. Support was incredible—forty thousand letters and ten thousand telegrams expressing kindness, empathy, and dedication to furthering cancer research.

Joe Cifre, president of the Variety Club's New England chapter, was a key part of this success. He credited "showmanship" and the *Truth or Consequences* broadcast with the foundation for the Jimmy Fund. That happened because of George Swartz, a Boston insurance broker with connections to entertainment. Swartz had lobbied Edwards for the radio segment.

Expounding on the importance of awareness regarding leukemia as well as money to treat and eventually find a cure, Cifre explained, "It's not like heart trouble—with that all you do is take your digitalis, be careful not to run up and down stairs more than once a year, and let somebody else shovel the snow. They have to shoot you then before you'll die. Leukemia, so far, has been incurable."[18]

Regarding the allotment of funds, Cifre explained that general gifts to hospitals get distributed among departments. The Jimmy Fund ensured that the money raised went straight to the Children's Cancer Research Foundation.[19]

1951

Students at Plymouth High School had started a fundraising operation to help send packages to Europe through CARE—Cooperative for American Remittances to Europe—for people suffering and looking to rebuild after the destruction of World War II. They raised $1,000. The following year, they had more than $1,000 to give to Natick's Amputee Veterans' Recreation Home. At the end of the 1950-51 school year, Plymouth's students showed their kindness once again in raising more than $1,000 and donating it to the Jimmy Fund.[20]

1953

At a January luncheon honoring New England's state chairmen of the Jimmy Fund and their cochairs, the attendees learned that 1952 fund-raising efforts had yielded more than $370,000.[21]

Three months later, the Red Sox stepped into the breach caused by Braves owner Lou Perini moving his team to Milwaukee.[22]

In August, Ted Williams returned to Boston after his second stint as a Marine pilot during wartime. He had given up three years to serve his country during World War II. During the Korean War, he played six games in 1952 before returning to the military and thirty-seven games in 1953 after his service concluded.

Williams was a strong public advocate for the Jimmy Fund. He agreed to a dinner in his honor—which included getting the Variety Club's Distinguished Service Medal and the City of Boston Korean War Medal—only if it served as a fundraiser. Ted Kennedy gave $50,000 on behalf of his family. "Ted Williams is not a new friend and may we through him welcome the Red Sox into our fold," said Dr. Farber, who pioneered research backed by the Jimmy Fund. "I'd like to say just two things about our Foundation," he continued. "We've never turned away a child. As long as a child is alive the term 'incurable disease' may not be used."[23]

In his speech, Williams talked about the importance of donating and making life better for the youngest victims and their families afflicted by horrible circumstances. Having returned from battle, he knew the value of freedom and the cost of it: "All the bullets and all the bombs that explode all over the world won't leave the impact—when all is said and done—of a dollar bill dropped in the Jimmy Fund pot by a warm heart and a willing hand."[24]

Williams and Farber would become synonymous with the Jimmy Fund. In Williams's case, it was not a publicity matter. He didn't want photographers and reporters tagging along to write about his visits, but patients and staff were aware of his involvement.

1956

A profile of Williams highlighted his avoidance of the spotlight regarding his visits to cancer patients. But they went beyond handholding and storytelling. One kid wanted to grow up and be a baseball announcer. Williams arranged for Red Sox broadcaster Curt Gowdy to visit him at the hospital. It was estimated that Williams's efforts resulted in donations totaling more than $250,000.

Additionally, Williams went to the public directly. A report in January claimed that an annual two-week drive during the previous September included visits to drive-in theaters with Jimmy Fund containers. Amount raised: $29,000. Visits with patients to sixteen police stations added $16,000.[25] Williams also offered the bat that he had used for his two thousandth hit and the ball together as a prize for a letter-writing contest to raise money for the Jimmy Fund. The woman who won, Mrs. Eugene Covert, donated them to the National Baseball Hall of Fame and Museum in Cooperstown, New York, where they have remained.[26]

In June, Williams became the fund's general chairman.[27]

1957

Sam Howard served as the Braves' bat boy for the exhibition game against the Red Sox on July 22. Described as "an odd-jobs man whose first thought is for the crippled and ill," the forty-nine-year-old resident of Newburyport got an invitation when the Braves visited their old hometown to raise money for the Jimmy Fund. He had wanted to see the game from the grandstands; Perini sought him out and offered the honor.

His friendship with the Braves' owner went back to 1950; Sam and his assistant, Joseph Morse, had bought tickets for a disabled kid from a boardinghouse to see a Braves doubleheader on Labor Day. Howard wrote to Perini and explained the situation, but Perini refunded the money and granted a request to have the kid, Bobby, sit in the owner's box. Generosity didn't end there. Perini allowed Bobby to go on the field, gave him a ball and glove autographed by the team, and invited him to the clubhouse. "Johnny Sain held the little boy in his lap," said Howard. "What a thrill for him and me. And Mrs. Perini entertained him in the box seat like her own child."[28]

1963

Since the *Truth or Consequences* broadcast, fundraising efforts had yielded $8 million. Federal government grants amounted to a yearly figure of $2 million.[29]

On December 9 more than 1,400 donors showed up for a gala event in the Statler Hilton celebrating the fund's fifteenth anniversary and learned that the Children's Cancer Research Foundation was set for a massive expansion that would elevate the facility to being a primary place of care known around the world thanks to the Jimmy Fund. Boisfeuillet Jones, a special assistant for health and medical affairs in the federal Health, Education, and Welfare Department, underscored the public-private link in his speech: "Medical research is, in fact, a partnership among scientists in their scholarly environment, supporters through voluntary efforts and the Federal government."[30]

1967

The Red Sox donated a portion of their World Series money to the Jimmy Fund.[31]

1972

An exhibition game for the Jimmy Fund had been planned between the Red Sox and Expos, but a reported "schedule conflict" negated the latter squad's availability. The Texas Rangers pinch-hit. It was somewhat ironic. Since 1969 Ted Williams had managed the team known as the Washington Senators until moving to the Lone Star State and changing the moniker after the 1971 season. Williams's last season at the helm of a Major League squad would be 1972.

Red Sox owner Tom Yawkey praised the legendary player and his avoidance of the spotlight regarding the patients: "Ted does more for those kids than therapy. He has a way with them—a magnetic personality. But he would never allow it to be publicized."[32]

Yawkey also emphasized the everyday travails of life paling next to the grim plight that families suffer when a child has cancer. "This is when you put your sense of values in their proper perspective. You see these children who will never reach adulthood, and you realize that winning a pennant is so unimportant by comparison."[33]

1974

The Children's Cancer Research Foundation changed its name to honor Dr. Farber. It's now called the Sidney Farber Cancer Center.[34]

1975

Koster, the longtime executive director of the Variety Club of New England, revealed the origins of the Jimmy Fund. He and his fellow volunteers had held a raffle in 1947 for three cars—Cadillac, Ford, Chevy. With $47,000 in the kitty, they approached Dr. Sidney Farber with this substantive donation. It was Dr. Farber who suggested that the club members start a foundation for the Children's Cancer Research Center. Dr. Farber also suggested the name Jimmy Fund.[35]

1977

Dr. Norman Jaffe explained the progress of medical research thanks to Dr. Farber's dedication combined with the Jimmy Fund's financial success. Whereas children were once likely doomed if they had acute leukemia, Dr. Jaffe explained that remissions now happen in 60 percent of the cases. Their length ranged "from 3½ months to three years. In fact, we've been able to stop the disease, if caught early[,] in 50–60 percent of the cases."[36]

1978

William Koster passed away. Williams commended the tireless advocate: "I know of no one in my lifetime who was dedicated to a project of any kind as Bill Koster was to the Jimmy Fund."[37]

1983

The Charles A. Dana Foundation was honored for its support of the Jimmy Fund. The center was renamed Dana-Farber Cancer Institute.[38]

1998

Globe sports reporter Dan Shaughnessy revealed Jimmy's identity nearly fifty years to the date after the *Truth or Consequences* broadcast. Shaughnessy's front-page story explained that Carl Einar Gustafson was the boy who met the Boston Braves a half century ago.

And he was alive.

Shaughnessy's sleuthing revealed that Gustafson, known to friends and family as Einar, had become a truck driver; married his high school sweetheart; had three daughters; grew to be six feet, five inches tall; and still had the Braves jersey that Southworth had bestowed upon him. Gustafson's first wife, Karen, had died of cancer in 1986. A second marriage happened in 1989.[39]

Gustafson brought to light the harsh reality of being in a hospital with other kids whose path was fatal. "I didn't know much," he said in Shaughnessy's piece. "I saw quite a few kids go in and then the curtain would be pulled around the bed and the doctors were doing something and then they'd pull the curtain back and the kid would be sleeping. But then they'd pull the curtain back again and the kid would be gone. I saw a lot of that stuff."[40]

2001

Einar Gustafson passed away.

2013

Opening Day at Fenway Park honored the sixtieth anniversary of the relationship between the Red Sox and the Jimmy Fund. Former chairman of the Jimmy Fund and Red Sox player Mike Andrews—he stepped down from the fund in 2009—recounted a gut-wrenching experience from 1967 that still affected him nearly fifty years later. After substituting for a player who couldn't meet with a twelve-year-old patient, Andrews learned the boy's fate from Koster, who told him, "I really appreciate you doing that. We just sent him home. There's no more we can do for him. He's not going to make it."[41]

2016

Red Sox president Larry Lucchino, a non-Hodgkin lymphoma survivor who was treated at Dana-Farber in the mid-1980s, took on the responsibility of being the Jimmy Fund's public spokesperson. With a history of chemotherapy and a bone marrow transplant, Lucchino had a patient's insight. His business sense complemented his personal experience—thirteen years as a trustee at Dana-Farber plus chairmanship of its Trustee Development Committee.[42]

2023

The Jimmy Fund marked its seventy-fifth anniversary since the *Truth or Consequences* broadcast.

Dr. Farber's son Thomas underscores the team's link. "Red Sox Nation extends from Connecticut to Maine. No other team has the single-mindedness with a charity that the Red Sox have with the Jimmy Fund. Boston was a small city in the 1940s, very parochial. The people that first supported my father's idea for a hospital were the sports teams. I think people in the 1940s and 1950s were staggered by the idea that children died of cancer. It came as a kind of terrible revelation.

"My father had enormous compassion. It was remarkable. What he wanted to do was spare people from misery. He believed you could stop some of the suffering with scientific research.

"A lot of his physical strength was spent not just for the hospital and patients, but flying in DC-3 planes across the country to Washington to lobby senators and congressmen in a wealthy, post–World War II world. A lot of his lifeblood was spent making that happen. Though he didn't make it a big deal, he was one of 14 children of immigrants. My grandfather had a great vision of social service. He owned a small business and he believed in social justice, helping everyone who needed to be helped.

"My father's manifestation of that impulse was medical care. He didn't want to fight battles about socialized medicine or doctors being rich. My mother took on the responsibility of raising four children. She empowered my father to go after his dream."[43]

Lynn MacLeod, one of Gustafson's daughters, recalls:

"The Jimmy Fund has always been part of our family. Dad had surgical scars on his abdomen that initially drew my attention as a young child. He explained that he had been sick when he was 12 years old but had gotten better. My dad would never boast and we children would never dream of going around telling people that he was the original Jimmy—that would be bragging and boasting. Of course, all his childhood friends and their families in his hometown of New Sweden, Maine, knew.

"It is amazing to me how much that community helped my dad's family. If somebody had a reliable car and was heading south to Boston, then you could catch a ride with them or by bus. Driving back and forth to Boston was quite an undertaking in 1948! I think what a blessing he was born in that small northern community when he took ill because those close-knit Swedes cared and took care of their neighbors—I am not so sure in today's society that could ever be duplicated.

"Dad was never a complainer but he did convey how lonesome and scared he was in that hospital bed. Nobody said the word cancer to him. He was just 'sick.' His family would visit as much as they possibly could throughout this time. As a mother myself to a son, I could not even imagine having to leave my child 500 miles away in a hospital bed for a whole year—how absolutely gut wrenching that must have been for my grandparents Bror and Lillian! But unfortunately, as small potato farmers, they had to continue working the farm and try to make a living. Dad said he saw his father cry for the first time during this period. This was the era that children were seen and not heard. The word 'cancer' was never spoken.

"But miraculously with the experimental treatments and the care he received from the kind nursing staff, he survived! He was able to return home after a year's time and kept an annual checkup schedule at the hospital. I do know that his mother wrote letters faithfully to Dr. Farber during this time.

"Eventually, the checkups tapered off as he married and started a family. Dr. Farber had become a father figure to him and was very respected and revered by his family, which included his sisters, Phyllis and Sandra. I have a memory as a small child in the early 1970s meeting Dr. Farber at his office in Boston, so I know there was continued communication between the two men.

"In 1998, as the 50th anniversary of the Jimmy Fund approached, my Dad's older sister, Phyllis Clauson, was struck with the thought that the Jimmy Fund should know that 'Jimmy' was still alive! She included a note with her yearly contribution stating that fact. That of course started the ball rolling with interviews and news articles—especially an interview with Dan Shaughnessy of the *Boston Globe*.

"The next few years were an exciting time for Dad as he was introduced to the public as Jimmy. I was amazed at how well he handled his instant 'fame' with all his appearances at charity events and various functions and Red Sox games. He really was a natural speaker! He tried his best to attend every function he could even while still working full-time as a long-haul trucker.

"If he was needed, then he somehow made it work and got to that event. I saw up close and in person how many cancer victims and their families wanted to meet with him. He gave them such hope and spark—he had survived childhood cancer so they could too! I will never forget the happiness and positive vibes surrounding these meetings! He had lost his wife Karen in 1986 from cancer and being 'Jimmy' truly gave him a new lease on life. He squeezed a lot in those three short years and I know in my heart that if Dad were alive today he would still be attending these events and helping the Jimmy Fund in any manner that he could!

"If people ask me if I believe in miracles my answer is yes! My family and grandchildren are living proof."[44]

Lisa Patti, another daughter, says that her father's initial prognosis was grim:

"I was around 12 years old when my dad told us about being sick with cancer as a child. I remember being just a little older than he was at the age of getting sick. Dad said he had a lot of stomach pain and was brought to a hospital in Bangor, Maine.

"He had an appendectomy at the age of eleven. After returning home to New Sweden, Maine, the pain was still present. His parents then brought him to a hospital in Boston for evaluation. Keep in mind, back in those days, Route 95 had barely been started to be built. It was a long trip that he made multiple times.

"Dad said he was told he had cancer, non-Hodgkin's lymphoma, and was not expected to live. He was placed in a ward with other children with curtains placed between the beds. He would frequently wake up and see a bed had become empty as a child had died.

"Most of the time his parents would not be with him. His older sister, Phyllis, was a nursing student and would visit him when she could. One can only imagine the fear of not having your parents with you constantly.

"Dad said he became very friendly with Dr. Farber who 'took a shine to him.' He was chosen by this doctor to be the spokesperson for the children who were sick with cancer as he was outspoken. He was called 'Jimmy' to protect his identity.

"A radio-thon was started to raise money to buy a television for the children in the hospital. During this, Dad was interviewed. He was asked who his favorite baseball team was and player. As a surprise to him, the Boston Braves came to visit him and the other children!

"Dad was asked by the Braves to not only attend one of their games but was also able to throw out a pitch and was given one of their official uniforms. Dad always kept that uniform. It was stored for years in a chest. My Aunt Phyllis (Clauson) annually donated to the Jimmy Fund which had been established in 1948. One year, she casually included a note saying that her brother was still alive. She was contacted by someone from the Jimmy Fund and asked if Dad would want to be interviewed.

"She called Dad and of course he said yes. He was asked multiple questions to prove that he was the original 'Jimmy.' Apparently over the years, several people had come forward and proclaimed they were 'Jimmy.'

"Obviously, Dad was able to give factual information. We also had medical records of Dad being tested annually for several years after his groundbreaking chemotherapy. We also had the Boston Braves uniform! Our family has since donated that uniform to the hospital and it is part of the Jimmy Fund history.

"A lovely woman named Karen Cummings who worked for the Jimmy Fund reached out to Dad. She wanted to know if he would be interested in stepping forward and speaking about his ties with Dr. Sidney Farber and how he became 'Jimmy.' Dad could not be more pleased!

"Dad could not turn down any requests to speak at multiple Jimmy Fund fundraisers or events. He was interviewed by *People* magazine, made a television commercial, and got to meet the legendary Ted Williams. He was so happy to be able to do anything for the Jimmy Fund!

"When the news came out that Dad was still alive, he was invited to throw a pitch at a Boston Red Sox game. Our family was so honored to be there. That was truly an amazing time for Dad.

"I feel that Dad enjoyed going to and speaking at various JF events and never turned down a request to do so. We never talked about Dad being the original 'Jimmy.' He was so grateful to be alive. He felt claiming to be Jimmy was boastful and he was not that type of person. If it wasn't for Dr. Farber and his efforts, he would not be alive.

"What is Dad's legacy? Hope! He wanted to show people that he was alive! He wanted to show cancer victims that if he could live with early onset of chemotherapy back in the 1940's, they certainly now have a better chance. He loved to visit the children at the hospital and could not believe how much medical research and technology had improved. Hope, never give up!"[45]

3

A Chance to Excel

Josh Gibson, Satchel Paige, and
Ted Williams's Hall of Fame Speech

An advertising campaign for a famous stock brokerage once boasted of its financial prowess with the tagline "When E. F. Hutton talks, people listen."

The same principle goes for Ted Williams regarding baseball.

A template of batting excellence, Williams—who wore a Red Sox uniform for his entire nineteen-year career in the Major Leagues and sacrificed three full seasons to serve as a Marine pilot in World War II and most of one season in the Korean War—retired in 1960 with outstanding credentials, including a .344 batting average, 521 home runs, and two MVP Awards. His career slugging percentage of .482 leads the Majors. In 1941 Williams batted .406; he is the last Major Leaguer to crack the .400 barrier.

Williams's knowledge reflected in his managing as well. He took the helm of the Washington Senators in 1969 and brought them from a team average of .224 to .251 in one season; Washington's record improved from 65-96 and last place to 86-76 for a fourth-place finish in the newly formed American League East.

Breaking down the essence of being a keen-eyed batter using physiology and physics for the best chances of hitting the baseball, Williams coauthored *The Science of Hitting* with sportswriter John Underwood in 1970. Practice is the cornerstone of success, according to Williams. "I said I hit until the blisters bled, and I did; it was something I forced myself to do to build up those hard, tough calluses," wrote the slugger. "I doubt you'd see as many calluses today. Most players hit with those golf gloves, to begin with, but more important, they don't take as much batting practice—as much *extra* batting practice and that's how you learn.

Part of the problem is there just isn't enough time. It used to be we'd have thirty-three or thirty-four players practicing in the spring; today it's more like forty-five. A guy doesn't get in the batting cage often enough and doesn't stay there long enough."[1]

Williams's appreciation for baseball skills went beyond scripting thoughts about adjusting stances, waiting for good pitches, and batting techniques. Way beyond.

On July 25, 1966, Williams, whose fantastic exploits at the professional level dated back to FDR's second term, took a colossal leap toward social progress when he raised an issue that hadn't been discussed by someone of his stature in a public setting to any significant degree. Compounding the importance of his words was the setting—his induction speech at the Baseball Hall of Fame in Cooperstown, New York.

"Baseball gives every American boy a chance to excel, not just to be as good as someone else, but to be better than someone else," stated Williams. "This is the nature of man and the name of the game. And I've always been a very lucky guy to have worn a baseball uniform. To have struck out or hit a tape-measure home run. And I hope that someday, the names of Satchel Paige and Josh Gibson in some way can be added as a symbol of the great Negro players that are not here only because they were not given a chance."[2]

It was a striking admonition of baseball's power structure. Negro Leaguers of the highest caliber deserved consideration for Hall of Fame membership. Full stop. Sadly, baseball's track record on progress was below the Mendoza Line. More like Joe Shlabotnik than Joe DiMaggio.

Baseball's first Black player in the Major Leagues was Moses Fleetwood Walker, who played for the 1884 Toledo Blue Hens in the American Association, along with his brother Weldy. But there was an unspoken mandate afterward banning Black players from joining the ranks of the Major Leagues. The slow climb toward integration began a couple of months after Alfred Eisenstadt photographed a spontaneous kiss between a sailor and a female reveler in Times Square on V-J Day. With World War II ending, the country seemed poised to turn a corner toward the ideals of freedom that we claimed to espouse. We talked the talk. It was time to walk the walk. So thought Brooklyn Dodgers general manager Branch Rickey, though his was a lone voice among the sixteen ball clubs.

Jackie Robinson signed with the Dodgers in late October 1945 after one season with the Kansas City Monarchs in the Negro Leagues and became the first Black player in the modern era (post-1900). Rickey sent him to the Triple-A Montreal Royals of the International League; Montreal won the 1946 Little World Series. Robinson led the IL with a .349 batting average and .468 on-base percentage; his Major League debut happened on April 15, 1947, in a 5-3 Dodgers victory against the Boston Braves.

Cleveland Indians owner Bill Veeck signed Larry Doby three months later and brought Satchel Paige to the team in 1948. Six years earlier, Paige had noted his skepticism about integration in baseball, citing the restrictions on dining and lodging in the South: "All the nice statements in the world from both sides aren't going to knock out Jim Crow."[3]

Hank Thompson has a double entry in this area of baseball—he broke the color barrier for the St. Louis Browns less than two weeks after Doby's achievement in Cleveland in 1947 and did the same for the New York Giants in 1949.

Other teams were tortoiselike on the integration path.

The Cubs broke with their colorless past in 1953; Ernie Banks's first game was in September. The Yankees didn't integrate until 1955 with Elston Howard. In 1957 John Kennedy was the first Black player for the Phillies. Ozzie Virgil led the way for the Tigers in 1958.

Red Sox owner Tom Yawkey was the last in the Major Leagues to sign a Black player, Pumpsie Green in 1959, marking the end of baseball's journey challenging the outdated, unfair, and impractical status quo. Boston could have been at the forefront of integration instead of lagging. The day after America laid Franklin Delano Roosevelt—who had just begun his fourth term as president—to rest, Jackie Robinson joined Marvin Williams and Sam Jethroe for a tryout at Fenway Park on April 16, 1945.

Boston City Council member Isadore Muchnick had lobbied for the inclusion of Negro League players for the Braves and Red Sox. He saw the result of his efforts when the trio took the field under the watchful, critical eyes of Red Sox skipper Joe Cronin. *Pittsburgh Courier* scribe Wendell Smith also attended.

The tryout lasted about as long as it takes for a B-movie plot to go from boy-meets-girl to boy-gets-girl to boy-loses-girl to boy-wins-girl-back. Ninety minutes. The Red Sox remained an all-white team.[4] Steadfast as a maple tree in a Brookline backyard, Yawkey refused to sign Black players until Green and received no substantive admonishment, formal or otherwise, during the decades hence as Green's name became the answer to a trivia question.

In 2018 Boston acknowledged Yawkey's lackluster record on race and integration by restoring the name of Jersey Street outside Fenway Park, replacing the Yawkey Way moniker that had stood for more than forty years. It started a long, painful road toward substantive recognition of wrongful attitudes. Williams had praised Yawkey in his Hall of Fame speech, but that was confined to his experiences in the player-owner relationship, not the front office's decisions on whom to hire.

Racial progress moved glacially at Fenway Park while America trekked forward in other areas. Suburbia had expanded in the 1950s, prompting a massive exodus from apartment buildings in claustrophobic cities to cookie-cutter homes in spacious neighborhoods. TV, once found only in the province of the wealthy, had become a mass medium as much a staple in the home as an oven.

A month after Jackie Robinson won Rookie of the Year in 1947, air force test pilot Chuck Yeager broke the sound barrier and took the X-1 to twenty-five thousand feet. By the time Green suited up for the Red Sox in 1959, NASA had selected its first astronauts for space exploration.

But NASA had no Black astronauts; Guion Bluford broke the space agency's color line when he went on the Space Shuttle *Challenger* in 1983.

There were also no Black managers in the Major Leagues. That wouldn't happen until 1975 with Frank Robinson as the Indians' player-manager. The Fortune 500 didn't get its first Black CEO until 1987.

Given the country's cultural zeitgeist on race in the mid-1960s, Williams's brief statement was timely. The civil rights movement had picked up some speed beginning with Martin Luther King Jr. leading the Montgomery bus boycott that began in 1955, then escalated again with King's

"I Have a Dream" speech during the March on Washington in 1963. A year later, President Lyndon Johnson signed the Civil Rights Act into law. The Voting Rights Act followed.

In 1966 Emmett Ashford became the first Black Major League umpire; Constance Baker Motley got confirmed by the Senate to be the first Black female judge on the federal bench; and Robert Weaver led the Department of Housing and Urban Development, which made him the first Black cabinet member.

Williams's call for inclusion also complemented racial barriers being broken on TV in the 1960s. Bill Cosby had debuted in *I Spy* the year before and won an Emmy for Outstanding Lead Actor each of the three years that the show was on the air. He was the first Black actor to win in that category. Greg Morris starred as electronics genius Barney Collier on *Mission: Impossible*, which premiered in 1966. William Shatner and Nichelle Nichols had the first interracial kiss on TV in a 1968 episode of *Star Trek*.

Also in '68, Harry Belafonte held hands with Petula Clark during a song on her NBC special, inciting horrors from narrow-minded viewers and those ready to dip a toe into the waters of racial tolerance but not dive into them.

Had Williams not made his concise but potent declaration, the void of Hall of Fame membership among Negro Leaguers might have been delayed even further than Paige's induction in 1971, which was hardly a smooth operation. The press release from the Office of Commissioner Bowie Kuhn on February 9 lit the kindling of controversy by announcing, "A bronze plaque listing his achievements will be hung in the National Museum, as part of a new exhibit commemorating the contributions of the Negro leagues to baseball."[5]

Exhibit? It was a hedge. Baseball's executive tier had long lacked the *menschkeit* to acknowledge superior talent in the Negro Leagues. Players like Paige weren't Cooperstown-worthy in the Hall of Fame paradigm because they didn't play the requisite ten seasons in the Major Leagues for membership. But that was an unfair barometer. Many stars were either retired or too old to follow the path that Robinson began. Their output was undeniable, however.

Turkey Stearnes stopped playing in 1940, leaving the game with a .349 career batting average. Mule Suttles batted .340 lifetime and retired in 1944. Biz Mackey—who later tutored Roy Campanella in the intricacies of the catcher position—retired at the age of fifty with a .328 average. His first season was 1920. His last was 1947, when he played thirty games with the Newark Eagles. But an opportunity in the Major Leagues was not going to somebody born in the nineteenth century.

Keeping the Negro Leaguers out of the Hall of Fame because of the ten-year rule was circular logic underscoring a "separate but equal" mindset, a cornerstone of racism knocked down in the 1954 U.S. Supreme Court decision *Brown v. Board of Education of Topeka*. Kuhn admitted, "Technically, you'd have to say he's not in the Hall of Fame. But I've often said the Hall of Fame isn't a building but a state of mind. The important thing is how the public views Satchel Paige, and I know how I view him."[6]

Apparently, the commissioner viewed one of the game's greatest pitchers as unqualified to have his plaque in the same area occupied by Bob Feller, Cy Young, and Grover Cleveland Alexander. Paige, as was his wont, rolled with it. "As far as I am concerned, I'm in the Hall of Fame. I don't know nothing about no Negro section. I'm proud to be in it. Wherever they put me is all right with me." Addressing the heart of the issue, Paige said, "I don't feel segregated."[7]

In July 1971 Kuhn and National Baseball Hall of Fame and Museum president Paul Kirk jointly announced that Paige would be on equal footing with other Hall of Famers. Again, Paige showed no animus for the previous decision. Gratitude abounded. "I was just going along with the program, and I didn't have no kick or no say when they put me in that separate wing," revealed the legendary hurler. "But getting into the real Hall of Fame is the greatest thing that ever happened to me in baseball."[8]

Calls for Paige to enter the Hall of Fame dated back to at least 1964. Joe Williams of the *New York World-Telegram and Sun* concurred with Paige's old boss Bill Veeck, who spoke at a gathering of Boston baseball writers and deemed Paige's qualifications worthy of consideration by the sportswriters who vote on Hall of Fame membership. It was unfair, Williams wrote, to say that Paige and his peers didn't meet the criteria for time spent in the Major Leagues. "Because Jim Crow wouldn't let him, that's why," wrote Williams.[9]

Paige stopped pitching in the Majors in 1953, then played with the Triple-A Miami Marlins in the International League from 1956 to 1958, compiling a 31-22 record. In 1961 he pitched three innings for another Triple-A team, the Portland Beavers in the Pacific Coast League.

Mostly as a promotional stunt, Paige returned for one game with the Kansas City Athletics in 1965 and pitched three innings. His last professional outing on record was a two-inning performance in 1966 with the Peninsula Grays in the Class A Carolina League.

When Paige died in 1982, Seattle Mariners manager Rene Lachemann recalled catching for the legend as a nineteen-year-old backstop during warm-ups and batting practice. "He had tremendous control. He moved the ball wherever he wanted it. His ball sank pretty good. I felt he could still get a lot of people out with his stuff. And I know a lot of guys in the major leagues right now who aren't throwing as hard as Satchel did back then."[10]

Besides his ball playing, Paige was known for his colorful personality. His signature quote: "Don't look back. Something might be gaining on you." It inspired the title for a 1981 ABC biographical TV movie, *Don't Look Back*, starring Lou Gossett Jr. as Paige.

Perhaps the quote referred to his age.

A Paige hallmark was keeping the press confused. He never answered questions concretely regarding his birthdate, though the commonly accepted version is that Paige was forty-two years old when he debuted with the Cleveland Indians in 1948 and won Rookie of the Year. When Paige signed with Cleveland, he said that his birthplace was Mobile, Alabama, and his birthdate was September 18, 1908.[11] Upon joining the Browns in 1952, he said it was February 8, 1908.[12]

Paige was in good company with the age gag. Legendary comedian Jack Benny—who found success in radio, film, TV, and personal appearances—jested about being thirty-nine years old, a running joke throughout his career along with others, including being stingy, playing the violin badly, having a polar bear named Carmichael in the basement of his Beverly Hills home, and owning a broken-down Maxwell car. Benny's proclaimed age was a bedrock of twentieth-century popular culture, inspiring Dean Martin to introduce the Waukegan, Illinois, native as the "Satchel Paige of comedy" during *The Dean Martin Celebrity Roast* honoring Johnny Carson in 1973.

According to the Baseball Reference website, Paige debuted with the Birmingham Black Barons of the Negro National League in 1927, finishing with a 7-2 record and three shutouts through ten games started and twenty games played.

But Paige's confidence about his personal information being undecipherable proved costly in 1948 when somebody met his $500 challenge to prove that he played in professional baseball before 1927.[13] In 1946 sportswriter Dan Daniel noted that Paige may have been pitching in 1920.[14]

When Josh Gibson got elected to the Hall of Fame in 1972—along with fellow Negro Leaguer Buck Leonard—praise was plentiful regarding the man whom Wendell Smith called "six feet four and 220 pounds of dynamite."[15] Paige offered, "Josh was the greatest hitter I ever pitched to, and I pitched to everybody. There's been some great hitters—Williams, DiMaggio, Musial, Mays, Mantle. But none of them was as great as Josh. I used to get Williams out with my screwball on the outside. Musial, the same thing. DiMaggio, with my sidearm stuff. Mays, he's no Josh. I got Mays with a fastball on his letters. Mantle had to bunt me. But Josh, I had to throw sidearm curves to Josh, break it on the outside corner and pray. Break it inside, he'd just rip it."[16]

Gibson is credited on his Hall of Fame plaque as having bashed nearly eight hundred home runs.

How many of these homers came in exhibitions or barnstorming games remains an evolving point of scholarship among baseball historians. Baseball Reference gives Gibson credit for 165 home runs and a .374 lifetime batting average in his career with the Pittsburgh Crawfords and Homestead Grays.

In the 1996 HBO TV movie *Soul of the Game*—a highly significant entry on the cable network's 1990s roster of docudramas about Black history—a postscript credits Gibson with 972 home runs.[17] Starring Delroy Lindo as Satchel Paige, Mykelti Williamson as Josh Gibson, and Blair

Underwood as Jackie Robinson, *Soul of the Game* takes place in 1945 as the trio competes in the Negro Leagues and anticipates who will break baseball's color line.

Also in 1996, the Negro Leagues got more attention from the merchandising arena when General Mills put photos of Gibson, Paige, and Cool Papa Bell on Wheaties boxes. The City of Pittsburgh gave a permanent honor to Gibson that year with a historical marker in the Hill District explaining his significance to baseball.

In 2020 Major League Baseball took another step toward reconciliation with its ugly past regarding race when Commissioner Rob Manfred announced that Negro League statistics would be incorporated into MLB stats. Baseball Reference has adjusted its tallies accordingly.[18] New scholarship will perhaps reveal more information about the Negro Leagues, making the players' credentials even more pronounced.

But the road to recognition began in 1966, when a former Red Sox slugger took the spotlight that shone upon him during a career highpoint and selflessly directed it toward Paige, Gibson, and their brethren.

PART 2

History and Tradition

4

Songs of the Sox

In *The Godfather Part II*, Hyman Roth laments the lack of a tangible honor for Moe Greene's conception of Las Vegas: "This was a great man, a man with vision and guts, and there isn't even a plaque or a signpost or a statue of him in that town."[1]

Michael McGreevy's death at the age of seventy-seven in 1943 prompted a similar oratory from columnist Dave Egan in the *Boston Daily Record*. Egan's advocacy for this legendary Boston baseball fan nicknamed "Nuf Ced" included recognition at not only Braves Field and Fenway Park but also the highest echelons of baseball. "It was he, most of all, who by his enthusiasm popularized baseball and helped make it the national sport, so I think that old Nuf Ced deserves a special niche for himself in the Hall of Fame with [Christy Mathewson] and [John] McGraw and Cy Young and Nap Lajoie and so many of his old friends," stated Egan.[2]

McGreevy, who donated his massive collection of baseball memorabilia and photos to the Boston Public Library, founded the Red Sox fan group known as the Royal Rooters during the team's early years. His nickname germinated from his declaration "Nuf Ced"—a shortened version of "Enough Said," which became a trademark of ending arguments and maintaining order at his Boston bar. Egan acknowledged this oft-told lore but also mentioned another possible origin: McGreevy using the two-word statement as an authoritative declaration at the end of his tales. The bar's moniker, Third Base, denoted a baseball theme and a double entendre; third base is the last stop before home.[3]

In McGreevy's obituary, the *Boston Evening American* called him a "leading figure" during the first World Series, between the Pittsburgh Pirates and the Boston Americans, in 1903; Boston's American League team wouldn't be known as the Red Sox until 1907. McGreevy enjoyed prominence during the Red Sox reign yielding four World Series titles in the 1910s and in Boston Braves circles as well.[4] Although the bar owner initially endorsed the Braves with his legendary spirit, he allegedly turned away his National League fandom when New York Giants manager John McGraw refused the opportunity to match his club against the Americans for the 1904 World Series.

McGraw targeted AL president Ban Johnson. "I have not forgotten its boast when it entered New York last year," said the fiery manager. It promised to put the National league [sic] club in this city out of business by June. That was the American league [sic] idea of sportsmanship then. Never while I am manager of the New York club and while this club holds the pennant, will I consent to enter into a haphazard box office game with Ban Johnson & Co."[5]

And so the Red Sox became the sole beneficiary of McGreevy's passion for the national pastime in Boston.

The Royal Rooters inspired fans with music, playing instruments and singing for the crowd. McGreevy's presence was resolute. But the barkeep famous for ceasing clashes in his saloon and leading his fellow American League baseball fans—first at Huntington Avenue Grounds and then at Fenway Park—showed impeccable guidance even before the American League and the Boston club were born in 1901.

When the Baltimore Orioles—National League champions—hosted the Boston Beaneaters for an important three-game series at the end of the 1897 season, McGreevy spearheaded the migration of fans to the Old Line State. Estimated to be "at least 300 men from Boston and vicinity," these fans were not passive tourists content to sit quietly and see their team battle one of the toughest nines in baseball. "About half of them were seated just back of the Boston bench, wearing badges and loaded with massive tin horns," reported the *Boston Globe*. "They opened their cheering chorus before the game started, and, encouraged by Congressman [John 'Honey Fitz'] Fitzgerald, worked like hired men to the end, much to the disgust of the sensitive Baltimoreans, who think it wrong to cheer for the 'other fellows.'"[6]

Beyond shouts of approval, there were cheers, including, "Hit her up, hit her up, hit her up again. B-O-S-T-O-N."[7]

A lengthier one from the visitors was:

"B-O-S-T-O-N, Boston! Boston!!
"Rah! rah!! rah!!!
"Rocket, racket,
"Siz, boom, whiz,
"Champions, champions, here dey is."[8]

Deriding the invaders, the *Baltimore Sun* chronicled the fans' behavior: "The Cape Cod contingent also carried horns and bazoos and horse fiddles and instruments for making various hideous sounds in addition to their college 'rah, rah.'"[9]

Boston's 6-4 win delighted supporters and earned plaudits in the *Sun*, which noted that the Beaneaters "put up a game which has seldom been surpassed, if equaled, at Union Park." In addition, Baltimoreans likely read with some regret the *Sun*'s account of the visiting fans overshadowing their counterparts in noise levels and, by implication, excitement.[10]

At the corner of Eutaw and Baltimore Streets that night, one could enter the Eutaw House, where the Beaneaters stayed, and hear a brass band strike the first note at 8:00 p.m. and play for four hours. It was more than a celebration, though. Fitzgerald hired the band for the following afternoon to complement McGreevy's group and combat whatever the Orioles fans would bring to the ballpark. "I feel sure that everyone in Baltimore will be out tomorrow with a fish horn, so I thought the band would help us out," said the Boston politico.[11] It was observed that these musicians paid homage to their hosts during the third game of the series by performing "My Maryland, My Maryland" in addition to "Yankee Doodle."[12]

McGreevy and his cohorts garnered significant notice for their passion and pride in the ball club during the series. Although the level of their actions may have been foreign, if not annoying, to the regular Union Park dwellers, it was a fact that the cheers and songs expressing their loyalty were harbingers of the tools that organists and screen operators later used on grander scales to rally hometown crowds. The *Sun* declared, "The Bostonians are staunch and loyal rooters and their pets [fans] will not lack encouragement and noise—that much is certain."[13] The *Baltimore American* concurred: "The Boston rooters, however, did their noblest in holding up their end of the line and everybody knew they were on hand.

Their whistles and horns were heard at regular intervals in a chorus of salutes as the players walked to and from the bench."[14]

Boston split the remaining two games against Baltimore and won two out of three against the Brooklyn Bridegrooms to finish 1897 with a 93-39-3 record atop the NL. Baltimore ended the season two games behind Boston.

Although McGreevy is a bedrock of Red Sox fandom, he returned to the fold of the Braves and showed his pride during the 1914 World Series. Pushing aside ill will generated by McGraw's insults ten years earlier, the man nicknamed Nuf Ced had plenty to say about the "Miracle Braves" as they swept the Philadelphia Athletics in four games. Still, something was missing. "He did so in a superior manner and it was noted that he did not sing 'Tessie' with his old-time fervor," recounted Egan. "He recaptured his form, however, as the Red Sox of Bill Carrigan came back in 1915 and '16 and '18, and he raised the royal rooters [sic] to the stature of a nationally-known organization."[15]

"Tessie" refers to a song from the Broadway show *The Silver Slipper*. It became a signature of the Royal Rooters; a 1903 World Series souvenir card from the group bore the name of McGreevy and his bar in addition to the lyrics of the chorus:

"Tessie, you make me feel so badly, why don't you turn around.

"Tessie, you know I love you madly, babe, my heart weighs about a pound.

"Don't blame me if I ever doubt you, you know I wouldn't live without you.

"Tessie, you are the only, only, only, -ly."[16]

The punk rock group Dropkick Murphys rewrote the lyrics for their 2004 version, which pays homage to McGreevy along with Jake Stahl, Bill Dinneen, and Cy Young. Beyond respecting the strong-as-Samson lineage of the Red Sox, the modification had value from a creative standpoint because the original lyrics reflected a woman singing to her pet parakeet. But this wasn't the first time that the lyrics had been changed—the Royal Rooters altered them to frustrate Pirates star Honus Wagner in '03: "Honus, why do you hit so badly?"

Matt Kelly, the Dropkick Murphys drummer, grew up a little more than fifty miles from Fenway Park. His dedication dated back to his 1980s childhood. "I think the moment that cemented me as a lifelong Sox fan was the '86 World Series," said Kelly. "I was 10 and the whole neighborhood was abuzz, and the Red Sox getting knocked out sort of did it for me. I always liked an underdog."[17]

Reviving "Tessie" undoubtedly pleased the ghosts of McGreevy and his clan and perhaps also baseball's fates. The Red Sox won the 2004 World Series.

Also in 2004, The Standells played their signature Red Sox song "Dirty Water" at Fenway Park before Game Two of the World Series. Maybe music has more power than just to entertain and inspire, after all.

Four decades prior, The Standells had capitalized on the popularity of The Beatles, which began on a mass scale with the release of their first album in 1963 and skyrocketed when they appeared on *The Ed Sullivan Show* for their first appearance in the United States, on February 9, 1964.[18] Bands composed of young men were suddenly blue-chip assets for record companies, concert arenas, and radio stations. The Zombies, The Kinks, The Animals, The Dave Clark Five, The Rolling Stones, The Yardbirds, The Who, Herman's Hermits, Gerry & the Pacemakers, Chad & Jeremy, The Monkees, and The Beach Boys joined the quartet of Liverpudlians named Ringo Starr, George Harrison, Paul McCartney, and John Lennon in dominating popular music in the 1960s.

The Standells didn't get to perform in the Ed Sullivan Theater—located in Manhattan on Broadway between West Fifty-Third and West Fifty-Fourth Streets—but they got terrific prime-time exposure a little more than a year after The Beatles' historic appearance when they appeared as themselves on an episode of *The Munsters* and sang "I Wanna Hold Your Hand."

To Red Sox fans, that TV performance may be a nice piece of nostalgia in the group's history, but the song "Dirty Water"—which also got released in 1965—hits closer to home even though Boston had not been visited by any member of the group. The song's lyrics encompass Boston elements, including the pollution in the Charles River referenced in the song's title.

In 1998 the connection between "Dirty Water" and the Red Sox began with the team's home opener—a landmark day at Fenway Park. Down 7-2 against the Seattle Mariners, Boston closed the gap to 7-5 in the bottom of the ninth. Then Mo Vaughn went yard with a grand slam to win the game.

"Dirty Water" entertained the crowd afterward. It started a tradition of the song being played after every Red Sox victory.[19]

A year after the Cinderella season of 1967, the Val Perry Trio recorded Judy Harbison's ode to Ken "Hawk" Harrelson: "Don't Walk the Hawk."

Boston's misfortunes attributed to the trade of Babe Ruth inspired early twenty-first-century offerings before the World Series victory in 2004. Joe Pickering Jr. wrote the song "Babe Ruth's Curse." *Curse of the Bambino* premiered at the Lyric Stage in 2001, charting the team's epic journey with a script by David Kruh and music by Steven Bergman. Both are credited with the songs' lyrics. The 2004 World Series is incorporated into a revision.

But another song is the sonic emblem for the Red Sox, igniting a Pavlovian response among the home crowd at Fenway Park: "Sweet Caroline." During the chorus, the fans repeat the line "So good" three times and imitate the trumpet's three-note highlight by singing "Bah! Bah! Bah!" in a moment of togetherness that defines Red Sox Nation. Joy courses through the crowd; hymns perform the same function at churches and synagogues.

This is evidenced in *Ted 2*—the 2015 sequel to the 2012 movie *Ted*—when the title character, a talking, pot-smoking, foul-mouthed teddy bear, tries to evade capture by a kidnapper named Donny, who had unsuccessfully tried in the first movie to snatch this child's toy that inexplicably can walk, talk, and feel emotions. Donny wants Ted for his kid.

When he tracks Ted to the New York Comic Con, the teddy bear hides among a stack of his generic likenesses. Donny uses "Sweet Caroline" to identify Ted, knowing that any true Red Sox fan cannot help but shout out "Bah! Bah! Bah!" The ruse works. A chase begins, though Ted is rescued by his friend, John, who had received Ted as a Christmas gift in 1985.

It was an accepted part of Red Sox history that Neil Diamond wrote "Sweet Caroline" to honor the daughter of President John F. Kennedy and Jacqueline Kennedy. Diamond recorded the song in 1969, six years after President Kennedy was assassinated in Dallas. But in 2014 the Brooklyn native stated that his wife was the inspiration for the lyrics. Her two-syllable name—Marsha—did not fit the music, so Diamond went with a three-syllable moniker. "It was last minute," admitted the singer-songwriter on NBC's *Today*. "The whole thing took about a half hour. It took about a half hour to write it."[20] Diamond also said that he recalled Caroline Kennedy's name from a book that he owned. So, even though he did not write it for the daughter of the thirty-fifth president of the United States, her fame led to her name being used.

Diamond had songwriting success before "Sweet Caroline," most prominently with The Monkees. "I'm a Believer" was a No. 1 hit on the *Billboard* rankings; "A Little Bit Me, a Little Bit You" reached the No. 2 slot. But "Sweet Caroline" has become a cultural icon thanks to the Red Sox adopting it as part of the Fenway Park experience. That began nearly thirty years after the song's 1969 release.

In 1997 Amy Tobey's domain at Fenway Park included selecting the music at Red Sox games. Knowing that her peers had blasted "Sweet Caroline" to entertain crowds for "other sporting events," Tobey selected it when the Red Sox were ahead of their competition. But it didn't get played for every home game.[21]

She chose "Sweet Caroline" not because of its appeal or lightheartedness but because "someone she knew had just had a baby named Caroline." The song did not get traction immediately. Dr. Charles Steinberg changed the paradigm in 2002. As executive vice president of public affairs, Steinberg saw the "transformative powers" of Diamond's music and lyrics, then chose the middle of eighth inning for placement in the ballpark's sonic rotation.[22]

Fenway Park does not, however, have a monopoly on "Sweet Caroline." Iowa State University adopted it in 2006 for the Cyclones football games at Jack Trice Stadium, thanks to athletics department staffer Mary Pink. In a 2018 interview, Pink did not credit Fenway Park as a cause and could not pinpoint the inspiration for using Diamond's tune.[23]

In 2008 the University of Pittsburgh incorporated indicators to reflect its identity when the song is played during football games at the end of the third quarter and thousands of Panthers sing in unison. "Let's go

Pitt!" replaces "Bah! Bah! Bah!" Additionally, "Go Pitt!" takes over "So good" in triplicate.[24]

"Sweet Caroline" unified Bostonians after the Boston Marathon bombing.

On April 15, 2013, they clung to each other figuratively and literally as newscasters informed the world about the detonation of two homemade pressure cooker bombs close to the finish line of the Boston Marathon. The day after the capture of Dzhokhar Tsarnaev, Neil Diamond wore a Red Sox cap and appeared at Fenway Park to lead the crowd of 35,152 at the Royals–Red Sox game on April 20 and accompany the recording of his voice in a cathartic moment. Red Sox fans brandished "Boston Strong" signs and the American flag. Diamond also appeared with the cast of his biographical play *A Beautiful Noise* at Fenway Park to coincide with the show's Boston premiere in 2022.

During the bombing's aftermath, "Sweet Caroline" exemplified the kinship of baseball when it was played at a most unlikely location to honor Boston—Yankee Stadium.

It happened at the end of the third inning of the Diamondbacks versus Yankees game on April 16. Any Red Sox fan would have doubted, scoffed at, or looked askance at such a display in any other instance. You might as well have declared that the Kennedy family had made a sizable donation to the Massachusetts Republican Party, that the Celtics had changed the color of their uniforms from green and white to blue and gold, or that Tom Brady is an overrated, overpaid, overhyped quarterback.

There was a circle on the stadium screen depicting the Yankees and Red Sox logos inside it and bordered by the words "NEW YORK STANDS WITH BOSTON *** PRAY FOR BOSTON." The Yankee Entertainment and Sports (YES) Network cameras captured it along with the crowd's rather passive response to the song.[25]

Their reaction to "Sweet Caroline"—or lack thereof—is understandable, though.

It's a Boston thing.

5

Hi Neighbor!

Curt Gowdy, Narragansett Beer, and the Red Sox

Once upon a few decades in the mid- to late twentieth century, Narragansett Beer was synonymous with the Boston Red Sox.

Founded in 1890 by six German immigrants in Cranston, Rhode Island, Narragansett eclipsed the competition within ten years to become New England's top beer brand. Transportation technology proved to be a boon for the Rhode Island company's growth. "In the early 1900's, we tapped into the New York/New Haven/Hartford Railroad line that ran right through the brewery," states the company's website. "We were able to start building refrigerated railroad cars to help get our beer to many other cities quickly and without it spoiling."[1]

Prohibition ceased beer production. In response to the Eighteenth Amendment, which took effect in the fall of 1919, Narragansett began making sodas.[2] The repeal in 1933 returned it to making beer; two years later, the invention of the beer can offered brewers a new, practical way to sell their products.[3]

Narragansett escalated its promotion in 1944 by sponsoring Boston Braves radio broadcasts, which made the brewer a trailblazer—the first North American team broadcast sponsored by an alcohol company.[4] The Narragansett Baseball Network included radio stations in the New England states, plus TV stations WNAC and WBZ in Boston; WJAR broadcast to the Providence TV market. A Red Sox sponsorship followed in 1946, reinforcing Narragansett's stature as a New England fixture.

Curt Gowdy is linked to Narragansett and the Red Sox, a common occurrence with sportscasters as radio shifted from novelty item to mass medium.

Beginning his broadcasting career in his home state of Wyoming in the 1940s, Gowdy went to Oklahoma City and had landed in New York by the end of the decade. After working with Mel Allen for radio and TV broadcasts of Yankees games, Gowdy focused on an opening in the Boston radio market caused by a shift in the Braves–Red Sox paradigm. Jim Britt had been the announcer for both teams during their home stands, but a plan for them to have separate personnel in 1951 placed Britt with the Braves and created an opening on the broadcasts of Boston's AL team.

Gowdy took initiative during the Yankees' last road trip in 1950, introducing himself to Red Sox general manager Joe Cronin, who said that he could get the New York radio broadcasts "clearer than Boston" at his summer home on Cape Cod.

"The job itself represented the realization of all my ambitions," wrote Gowdy in his autobiography. "At the time there were only sixteen major league teams. To be the top announcer for one of them was the answer to a sports broadcaster's prayer." Gowdy had a guardian angel in addition to Cronin. Yankees owner Dan Topping worked with his counterpart, Tom Yawkey, to ensure that the Red Sox hired Gowdy because a switch in the sponsor or radio station could sever Gowdy's association with the Yankees.[5]

"Hi Neighbor! Have a 'Gansett!"—Gowdy's friendly invitation and conversational timbre—began the Red Sox broadcasts from 1951 to 1965, providing a cultural touchstone for New England in a progressive and sometimes volatile period. America went through the Korean War, rock and roll's birth, 3-D movies, the Soviet Union's launch of Sputnik and beginning of the space race, JFK's assassination, and The Beatles igniting a "British Invasion" of music during Gowdy's tenure as a Red Sox broadcaster.

When the Braves decamped for Milwaukee in 1953, Gowdy became the signature voice for baseball in Boston and the sonic background for Red Sox fans, whether they were Cambridge newlyweds picnicking in Boston Common, a Lexington family of five vacationing at Cape Cod, recent Boston College graduates barbecuing in Brighton, Salem high school students working at Canobie Lake Park, Wellesley police officers patrolling in their cars, or bar patrons having one for the road in Charlestown.

Donna Halper was born in Boston's Dorchester section, a predominantly Jewish, working-class neighborhood. When she was eight years old, her family moved to Roslindale, a middle-class section, mostly Irish and Italian. She grew up listening to Gowdy's announcing and got a primer for her later career as a disc jockey in radio.

"I remember listening to him and his then sidekick Bob Murphy; they were storytellers and they had great chemistry. I did not know that they knew each other from their minor league days in Oklahoma—I just thought they were friends who loved baseball. Both guys could make even a losing team (which the Sox often were back then) sound interesting. Curt Gowdy was a masterful play-by-play announcer, and I'm so glad I had a chance to hear him when I was a kid and still learning the ins and outs of the game.

"He was conversational, and no matter what was happening on the field, he always made it sound interesting. I do remember how he handled the commercials. Atlantic and Narragansett were two of the sponsors and he especially did the beer commercials with enthusiasm. But as I said, his style was so friendly that it almost didn't seem like a commercial. It just fit into the rhythm of calling the game."[6]

Gowdy was there when Clyde Vollmer hit three home runs in one game in 1951 and when Norm Zauchin did it in 1955.

Gowdy was there when the Red Sox had an astounding 17-3 stretch over twenty games in July 1953.

Gowdy was there when Mel Parnell threw a no-hitter in 1956, the first in thirty-three years for the Red Sox; when Earl Wilson and Bill Monbouquette threw two of MLB's five no-hitters in 1962; and when Dave Morehead threw one in 1965, the last for the Red Sox until Hideo Nomo's no-no thirty-six years later.

Gowdy was there when Pumpsie Green took the field in 1959, making Boston the last team in the Major Leagues to break the color line.

Gowdy was there when Ted Williams crushed home run number 521, in the last at bat of his career, in 1960.[7]

Gowdy was there when Carl Yastrzemski went five-for-five and hit for the cycle in 1965.

Ascending to the national broadcasting ranks in 1966, Gowdy joined NBC for the *Game of the Week*. Time was the primary factor for the change.

With a wife and young kids at home, Gowdy decided that another year of road trips with the Red Sox would be a burden on them. "I didn't do it for money," he explained in 2000. "I really didn't. I didn't do it for national fame or anything. I just thought it would be better for my family."[8]

It's not as if he was unknown coast to coast; NBC had hired Gowdy for the World Series from 1958 to 1964. But this new deal secured his nationwide status on a weekly basis.

Baseball fans welcomed Gowdy's announcing the World Series from 1966 to 1975, one of the national pastime's most colorful periods. The Orioles surprised the baseball world when they swept the Dodgers in 1966. Three years later, they lost in another upset when the "Miracle Mets" won the series in five games. The A's won three consecutive championships. The Reds beat the Red Sox in seven games, marked by the epic battle in Game Six won by Boston on Carlton Fisk's body language telepathically urging a ball to stay fair as it sails over the Green Monster in the bottom of the twelfth inning.

Gowdy also was a fixture for the Super Bowl, Rose Bowl, and Orange Bowl. His ABC show *The American Sportsman* celebrated the outdoors and lasted more than twenty years: 1965 to 1986. Mobil sponsored *The Way It Was*, Gowdy's nostalgia-based PBS show airing five seasons, from 1974 to 1978, and featuring guests such as peers Dick Enberg, Mel Allen, Red Barber, and Don Dunphy in addition to Joe Louis, Joe DiMaggio, Willie Mays, Don Newcombe, Duke Snider, and Cookie Lavagetto.

Those who remember Gowdy may say that his conversational tone accounted for his success, making viewers feel as if they knew him. But he pointed to another factor. "Homework," he said in a 1972 profile for New York's *Daily News*. "Sports fans today are damned sophisticated and many know the sport as well, or even better, than the broadcaster. When a guy gets on the air, he surer than hell better know what he's talking about. You can't con an audience. They know when you're unprepared or trying to fake it. You've got to be honest."[9]

In the hearts and minds of New Englanders who recall the voice that constituted a cornerstone of their baseball fandom, Gowdy's other accomplishments—many, famed, and distinguished though they may be—stand in the shadow of being the voice of the Red Sox for a decade and a half.

Just as baseball was not Gowdy's only source of employment, it was not the only sport with Narragansett sponsorship. A large sign with a clock and the company's slogan "Hi Neighbor!" topped Boston Garden for a terrific identifier with the storied Celtics teams that won eleven NBA championships in the 1950s and 1960s.

When Narragansett got a new owner—Falstaff Brewing Company—in 1975, the legendary link between the regional beer icon and a beloved baseball institution ceased. Falstaff dissolved the connection to New England altogether in 1982, when it moved production to Fort Wayne, Indiana; a revival effort for the Rhode Island operation failed a year later.[10]

Two decades had passed when serendipity intervened. Mark Hellendrung, an executive with Nantucket Nectars for "close to a decade," had been contemplating a career move. "I was in a bar one night with a buddy. And keep in mind this is 2002 or so and we didn't have all the great options that we have today. I said, 'Hey, do you have any other beers available here?' And all of a sudden, some older guy down at the end of the bar said, 'Give the kid a 'Gansett.' The next thing you know, the whole bar is talking about Narragansett Beer and history and stories and family and who used to work there. I didn't even know they still made it. The next thing you know, we're sitting here drinking it. There was just this great passion for it. I wonder if we could bring this back. This is our beer. We gotta do this."[11]

Pabst owned Narragansett at the time, fending off suitors with similar visions of polishing a beloved brand relegated to old-timers waxing nostalgic about the glory days. But Hellendrung had a magic arrow in his quiver. Pabst CEO Brian Kovalchuk's kids liked Nantucket Nectars, which got the entrepreneur an invitation.[12] In 2005 Hellendrung bought the Narragansett brand, restored production to its geographic birthright, and revived the name in New England.[13]

A former Narragansett brewmaster, Bill Anderson, provided the formulas that created a gateway to the past and matched with the revival's nostalgia-rich marketing.[14]

Brian Schade is the owner of Vintage Beer Collectibles and a dedicated Red Sox fan.

"It's interesting, because I look at the revival of today's craft beer market, where many smaller towns and cities have their own breweries or brewpubs to mimic that of the olden days," he stated. "In the early 1900s, up to Prohibition, there were so many small breweries in so many small towns in states all across the country. Many of those breweries, however, went under because of Prohibition and how long it lasted. The ones that were able to survive and start making beer again became more regional because many of those local breweries were gone. Narragansett, at one time, became the number one brand in the New England region.

"Just like many things 'back in the day' there is that nostalgia for older brands and products that people used, especially when they sponsor another brand—the Boston Red Sox. Whether it was parents or grandparents taking their kids or grandkids to games, or simply talking about 'their day' in the back yard sharing a beer, it's hard not to talk about Narragansett or even share one.

"The collecting world of breweriana is strong right now and isn't showing any signs of slowing down. Narragansett items are still very collectible, especially if you can find collectibles that advertise both Narragansett *and* the Red Sox. Now, with that said, the value of those collectibles comes down to many factors. Rarity, condition, and subject matter.

"As you got farther away from the 1930s and '40s, items started to get made from cheaper materials like plastic and/or were mass produced. There are still many items from the '50s, '60s and '70s that can command high prices, but typically if one were to own something that hardly no one else has and it's made of something like glass, metal, or wood, and the subject matter is just cool to look at, it will most likely fetch a lot of money. If it attracts both breweriana collectors and baseball collectors, your audience of potential buyers becomes larger.

"I have always been a sucker for tin signs and trays. I look at them like I look at fine art. The craftsmanship of the artist that came up with the scene and how they made the trays and signs is remarkable. Even with all the technology that industries have today, they can't duplicate the look of what was produced back then.

"Back in that era, I think the region was very community oriented. It's not that New England was any different than other locations in the United States, I just think Narragansett came up with a great slogan— 'Hi Neighbor!' It's also a little bit more. It's actually 'Hi Neighbor, have a Gansett!' What I feel helped the slogan stick in many people's minds was that legendary Boston Red Sox announcer Curt Gowdy used to say it all throughout his broadcasts.

"Narragansett is a legendary beer for that region and I'm glad to see it revived. I'm not sure it will have the hold it once had but if it has its niche, it's great. It will be sustained if it continues to make a quality product. There is a lot of competition in the Northeast when it comes to breweries.

"It's all about the love of beer! Americans have a long love affair with beer. It's a popular drink that can be associated with lots of memories. People can recall sitting on their back porch, or fishing, or at a baseball game, and remember the beer that they drank. They don't necessarily recall the brand [of] shirt they wore or the detergent that cleaned their clothes. I also get a lot of customers with the same namesake of the brewery. In addition, many old breweries were named after the founder's last name. Because of that, I get a lot of people who contact me through my website looking for breweriana that advertises their last names.

"For example, there was a brewery out of Pennsylvania called the Seitz Brewing Co. and there is this gentleman that stays in contact with me in case I get anything from that brewery. He is not related to the family of the founder but just likes to see his name on old advertising. It's the same for myself. In Spokane, Washington, there was the B. Schade Brewing Co. I collect anything from that brewery I can get my hands on, even though I am not a descendant of the family.

"My dad was actually a Phillies fan since we lived about an hour outside of Philadelphia in a very small town called Kutztown. But for me, I like American history and I love the sport of baseball. The game is so unique in many ways. Take the combination of those two things and a visit to Fenway Park, and you create a life-long, die-hard fan.

"I literally cannot explain the feeling I felt the first time I stepped foot into Fenway Park. All I can say is that it was magical, in a sense. The love of American history, the love of baseball and then the American history that occurred in that stadium was just overwhelming. It started about 25 years ago and it was simply a family vacation and a bucket list item."[15]

Hellendrung's insights below reveal Narragansett's emotional, historical, and economical ties to New England.

What does Narragansett Beer mean to the New England community?

"Narragansett Beer means a lot of different things to many people. To some it's generational pride as their relatives worked at the brewery, to some it's a reminder of a memorable time or place in their lives while for others it's a comeback, small company story in a sea of mega-brands and commercialization."

Narragansett Beer is part of the cultural heritage of the Red Sox. At one time, it was synonymous. How important is that to you and why?

"It's hard to deny the foundational importance of Narragansett's relationship with the Red Sox. For nearly two generations, New Englanders were greeted with 'Hi Neighbor, Have a Gansett' with every broadcast."

Why do you think Narragansett Beer still has a nostalgic hold among New Englanders? How does its long association with the Red Sox factor into this, if at all?

"I think most people yearn for a sense of place and belonging, especially as the pace of change continues to accelerate. Narragansett Beer is a company and a brand that respects that sense of place and works hard to foster it."

How do you want to educate the next generation of Red Sox fans about the link between Narragansett Beer and the Red Sox?

"Unfortunately, it gets harder to communicate the relevance each year because of the relationships that Budweiser and now Sam Adams spend a lot of money for. But it's obviously a huge part of our history and we continue to tell the story."

What's your greatest accomplishment since the revival of Narragansett Beer? What do you want to accomplish going forward?

"The building of our brewery taproom on the Providence waterfront must be our greatest accomplishment. It took over a decade to grow the company, find the ideal location, and survive the COVID interruptions to complete the construction. It is so gratifying to walk into the taproom and see the appreciation of the great beers that head brewer Lee Lord is brewing."

Take us through the history of Narragansett Beer and its revival. What were the reasons for the revival and what were the biggest challenges?

"Wow, it's been 18 years of challenges, that's a whole book unto itself. The revival was important to me and many others in that the brand/beer deserved a much better fate than the demise it was experiencing. The emotional ties that it had to so many people made it important to resuscitate."

What are the prominent values of your company and how do you further them? Is regional pride involved?

"How do you market the beer along with those values? Our values are like the three words above: community, authenticity, and timelessness. We work to incorporate that into everything we do, from our packaging and social media communications to the way we designed the new taproom for community engagement."

What is the most important archival find that you've made in researching Narragansett Beer? Is it a picture of an advertisement? A piece of memorabilia?

"That's nearly impossible to answer because it's a constant discovery. We found a Narragansett bottle from the early 1900s onsite during excavation of our brewery in Providence, how serendipitous is that?! Listening to Curt Gowdy promote our new advertising campaign on an old 45 [record] or our recent discovery of original Newport Jazz Fest advertising from the 1950s is just as amazing."

What are the three words that you want people to think of when they see or hear the words "Narragansett Beer"?

"Community, authenticity, and timelessness."[16]

6

Where Red Sox History Began

The First Game at Huntington Avenue Grounds

Fenway Park's synonymy with Boston is a fact ranking with death and taxes in certainty.

The parody film trailer "Boston Accent" on a 2016 episode of *Late Night with Seth Meyers* honors hallmarks of Boston-set movies, including mentions of neighboring cities, different types of local accents, and images of the stadium that's been the Red Sox's home field since 1912. "See the movie that is being hailed as chock-full of aerial shots of Fenway Park," invites the narrator.

Before Fenway Park became a cultural touchstone, Boston's AL ball club played on a spot now occupied by Northeastern University. A statue of Cy Young adorns the campus, reminding students, staff, and visitors of his magnitude, including a perfect game thrown for the squad then known as the Americans on May 5, 1904. Unveiled nearly ninety years later, on September 23, 1993, the likeness of Major League Baseball's career leader in wins—511—is near the area that used to be the pitcher's mound at Fenway Park's predecessor.

Huntington Avenue Grounds.

Before inaugurating their turf on May 8—with Cy Young as the starting pitcher—the Americans, part of the nascent eight-team American League in 1901, began the season with a ten-game road trip. They lost the first two games against the Baltimore Orioles, then split a four-game series against the Philadelphia Athletics. With a 2-4 record, the Americans went to Washington and dropped the first game of a four-game series against the Senators but rebounded to take the next three contests and bring home a .500 record to face the Athletics again.

Boston was abuzz. New team. New league. New home.

On the morning of the maiden game for Huntington Avenue Grounds, the *Boston Evening Record* reported that the site's "transformation . . . into a fine looking ball field has been nothing short of marvellous [*sic*]. It certainly looked like anything but a ball field six weeks ago, and the transformation has been accomplished in spite of the most adverse weather conditions possible."[1]

The *Boston Daily Advertiser* concurred in its game account: "It was the first time that baseball has been played on these grounds and their adaptability to the game reflects much credit on the management. It was not long ago that they resembled anything but a ball field." Even though the ground was "a trifle soft," which added to the burden of fielding balls hit to the outfield, the *Advertiser* avoided criticism of the ballpark's design, construction, or grass: "Misjudgments of ground hits were not due to the condition of the grounds."[2]

But there was a challenge for even the most powerful batter. "The infield was well sodded and the outfield was reasonably hard for filled land. The fences are beyond the ambition of any batsman," explained W. S. Barnes Jr. in the *Boston Morning Journal*.[3]

A home opener inspires a team's fan base with a clean slate of games to attend and, in turn, to feel part of a congregation that has no boundary on religion, gender, age, income, wealth, education, ethnicity, or social status. A ballpark's debut elevates the excitement. Usually containing more embellishments than a team's previous homes, a new facility cements the bond between the team and its fans by using grandeur in size, design, and accessories.

But a new ballpark coinciding with a new team ratchets up the emotional timbre to a gargantuan level.

Mother Nature cooperated for the seminal event, giving Boston a beautiful day for christening its new baseball site.[4] Fanfare abounded. This homecoming had the anticipation of Christmas morning, excitement of July Fourth fireworks, and camaraderie of a family reunion combined. The crowd surpassed expectations—an estimated eleven thousand people showed up compared to ten thousand foreseen—and Boston's hometown attendees welcomed their team with "the greetings extended national heroes." Besides verbal expressions of affection, the crowd had another way of showing approval. "A few horns made harsh noises, but the spirit impelling them changed the grating sounds into sweet music," reported the *Boston Post*.[5]

Such was the excess attendance that the teams adhered to an ad hoc rule taking into account the people on the ground, in areas roped off in left field and right field: a batter got three bases for hitting a ball into that crowd.[6]

Charles Somers owned the Americans and beamed with pride as his new ball-playing facility—a showplace, really—filled the hearts of fans embracing a new team and a new era in baseball. A Clevelander who had filled his bank account with profits from his family's coal concerns, Somers had only recently begun his tenure as an owner and a key figure of the American League, affirmed by his baseball roots as a fan.

His beloved Cleveland Spiders—along with the Baltimore Orioles, Washington Senators, and Louisville Colonels—met their demise after the 1899 season as the National League condensed from a twelve-team operation to an octet. Western League president Ban Johnson lured the coal investor to use his sooted bounty and participate on an ownership level. Somers and a Cleveland hatmaker, John Kilfoyl, bought the Grand Rapids Furniture Makers—which had been the Columbus Senators until moving in the middle of the 1899 campaign—and transplanted the team to Cleveland with a moniker redubbing (the Lake Shores) for Johnson's new enterprise in the Minor Leagues: the American League.

This Minor League entity lasted one season, after which Johnson stated that it would be a Major League entity beginning in 1901. The Buffalo Bisons had moved to Boston, but a viable owner was not to be found, so Somers took the opportunity. He also reached into his pockets to help bolster other AL team owners, feeling that it would be good for baseball since a rising tide lifts all ships; assistance was approximated at $1 million.[7] Somers only had a one-season stay in Boston. Henry J. Killilea bought the team, and Somers returned to familiar territory: co-owning the Cleveland ball club.

But on May 8, 1901, Somers's status as a Boston hero was secure. The fans waved American flags in their approval of a new place to cheer and, on what they hoped would be rare occasions, commiserate regarding the exploits of their new team. Neither question nor quarrel arose regarding the efficacy of Huntington Avenue Grounds as a home for baseball playing: "The superiority of the park could be taken in with one sweep of the eye," declared the *Post*. "The perfectly level field and the large grand stand [*sic*] had an exceedingly inviting appearance."[8]

Americans player-manager Jimmie Collins got a raucous welcome exceeding the shouts and applause for his teammates, sounds that "could have been heard blocks away" as the players took their turns at bat. "[But] when it came to Collins's turn the noise redoubled in force. Handclapping was reinforced by thundering yells and howls." There were more than noisy, positive utterances for the team's leader, though. The Brigham's Hotel gave him "a basket of roses," and the Royal Rooters offered a four-foot-high horseshoe of cut flowers.[9]

Collins was a hometown hero. He began his career with the National League's Boston Beaneaters in 1895 then got released to the Louisville Colonels in mid-May.[10] There was a catch—the Beaneaters had the legal power to recall him, if desired. And so, they did. Collins, a formidable third baseman, became a fixture in the lineup:

1896: 84 games, .296 batting average
1897: 134 games, .346 batting average
1898: 152 games, .328 batting average[11]
1899: 151 games, .277 batting average
1900: 142 games, .304 batting average

After traveling to Cleveland on February 28 for a conversation with Somers, Collins reportedly promised that he wouldn't sign a contract without talking to the Beaneaters. His time frame was a week at the maximum.[12] But two days later, he signed with the Americans.[13] While respecting Beaneaters owners Arthur Soden, William Conant, and James Billings for their relationship while he played, Collins noted his output and previous exchanges with the front office, where he "often asked them for more money, knowing that I was worth it, but until now they have turned a deaf ear to all my requests, and so it is the same with many others."[14]

Collins played most of the rest of his career with the Americans/Red Sox, leaving for the A's in the middle of the 1907 season—a result of a trade for John Knight—and retiring in 1908 with a .294 career batting average, two American League pennants, and a World Series championship.

Philadelphia star Nap Lajoie received weighty accolades at the opening of Huntington Avenue Grounds as well, though he was a cornerstone of the visiting team. This benefit was accorded to the blue-chip ballplayer not merely because of his prowess but more because he grew up in Woonsocket, Rhode Island, about fifty miles away and played for the Fall River Indians in the New England League five years before this occasion. Roughly the same distance separated Fall River from Boston.

With the Indians, Lajoie put up Jupiterian figures of a .429 batting average with a .726 slugging percentage before the Philadelphia Phillies bought his services and those of Phil Geier in early August 1896. Lajoie left Fall River in style, going three-for-six with two runs scored in an 18–3 victory over the Pawtucket Phenoms. Geier had a banner day, too, scoring three runs and bashing two hits in six times at bat.[15]

A bona fide star with the Phillies, Lajoie racked up averages of .326, .361, .324, .378, and .337. He led the National League in slugging percentage in 1897; his doubles and RBI stats topped the NL the following year. Bostonians feared what Lajoie could do with a bat. As well they should have. In 1901 he led both leagues in runs scored, hits, doubles, batting average, on-base percentage, and slugging percentage. He topped the NL in homers and RBIs.

Contingents from Lajoie's hometown plus knowledgeable Massachusetts baseball followers remembering his Fall River days fueled shouts of approval. But there was also a bit of tension, if not danger, associated with Lajoie. He had left the Phillies for the crosstown A's before the 1901 season, igniting a legal firestorm over the decision, which Phillies fans considered to be disloyal abandonment and the team's front office judged to be illegal.[16]

The following year, the Supreme Court of Pennsylvania ruled that Lajoie could play only for the Phillies, which A's manager Connie Mack learned during the Opening Day game against the Orioles; the ruling sent his star player to the bench. But there was a loophole—the injunction banning Lajoie applied only to the Commonwealth of Pennsylvania.

Lajoie got traded to Cleveland—where he was under the auspices of Somers—and refrained from playing on road trips to Philadelphia.

There was no rest for the weary on this home opener date. Staying in New York overnight after the last game with Washington, Collins et al. went directly from the Back Bay train station to Huntington Avenue Grounds with large appetites—they had no time to eat before the game against the A's.[17] In their rush, they left their bats at the station. They had to use the opposition's lumber, but a good craftsman never blames his tools. Boston's batsmen didn't need to.

Philadelphia righty Bill Bernhard, a new addition to the lineup after two seasons and a 21-17 record with the crosstown Phillies, got pounded for twenty-two hits in a 12-4 victory for the Americans.

Boston's lineup blessed the new home with four runs in the bottom of the first inning.

Tommy Dowd started the action with a lead-off single. Charlie Hemphill followed with a bunt single; Bernhard retired Chick Stahl, which moved the runners over. Player-manager Collins singled, scoring Dowd and advancing Hemphill to third base. Buck Freeman accounted for the other three scores with a homer, marking the beginning of an outstanding day for the Americans' first baseman—three-for-five with five RBIs and a run scored.

Acknowledging Freeman's feat of hitting the ball to deep center field, the *Boston Traveler* reported, "It showed clearly that home runs are possible, even if the ball doesn't go anywhere near the fence, to say nothing about going over it."[18]

Freddy Parent grounded out to A's third baseman Lave Cross for the second out; it looked like the Americans might bat around the order when Hobe Ferris, their number seven hitter, singled off Bernhard. Lou Criger's swat and A's right fielder Jack Hayden's error gave more reason for the hometown crowd to cheer, but Criger failed in his attempt to reach second base safely for a double.

Boston notched its fifth run on back-to-back-to-back singles by Young, Dowd, and Hemphill, "a master of the bunt art," repeating his feat in the bottom of the second inning followed by Stahl's sacrifice fly to A's left fielder Dave Fultz.[19] Their sixth run came an inning later when Ferris got a two-out hit, but Hayden couldn't handle the ball and his errant throw escaped the clutches of A's catcher Doc Powers, allowing Ferris to cross the plate safely.

They magnified the score to 9-0 in the bottom of the fourth.

Hemphill got his third hit of the day, a lead-off triple. Stahl banged a base hit by hitting a ground ball to first baseman Socks Seybold and winning the race to the bag when Bernhard didn't make it there to cover. Bernhard resumed by getting Collins out on a fly ball to Fultz in left field, which scored Hemphill for the home team's seventh run; Boston's player-manager exercised discretion from the second half of his hyphenated title and selected Charlie Jones to replace Stahl on the base paths after the player "complained of a strained side, but it was found that he had fractured a rib."[20]

Freeman notched his second hit, a triple, to score Jones for Boston's eighth run. It would have been a home run except for the ground rule about limiting the batter to a triple for a ball going into the crowd. Up next was Parent, who got all the way to third when third baseman Cross fielded a ground ball and commenced a rundown to catch Freeman between himself and Powers at the plate. Parent notched the home team's ninth run when Ferris singled; Criger's ground ball to Bernhard ended the punishment.[21]

Young began the Americans' half of the fifth inning with a triple and scored the tenth run when Dowd also bashed a three-bagger off Bernhard. Hemphill flew out; Dowd scored and inflated the padding to eleven runs.

Handling the Philadelphia lineup with aplomb, Young kept Mack's men scoreless through six innings. The visitors prevented a shutout with a run in the seventh when Hayden knocked in Harry Lochhead. Their other three runs came an inning later—Seybold tripled home Fultz and Lajoie, then scored when Cross smacked a fly ball to Jones in center field.

The Americans responded with their final run. Hemphill doubled, advanced when Jones made an out, and scored on Collins's second hit of the afternoon.[22]

According to the Boston press, Bernhard was lackluster. But Philadelphia's woes did not solely belong to his domain—his teammates had an absence of prowess on offense or defense, prompting the descriptor "amateurish in the extreme" from Barnes's report in the *Morning Journal* regarding the latter task.[23]

Freeman's outstanding game signaled what was to come for the slugger in his first year with Boston. It's arguable whether 1901 was his best season, but there's a strong case—he batted .339, drew 30 walks, knocked in 114 runs, and hit 15 home runs.

Two years earlier, Freeman led the NL with twenty-five home runs for the Washington Senators. He batted .301 for the Boston Beaneaters in 1901, then joined the Americans and hit .318 with 122 RBIs in 1902. But he had nearly ninety more opportunities in the batter's box. In 1902 and 1903, he led both leagues in RBIs. His thirteen homers were also the most in both leagues in 1903.[24] The following year, he led both leagues in triples. His last season was 1907; he played in four games.

Cy Young was already a legend before signing with the Americans in early March, ahead of the team's inaugural season.[25] He led the Major Leagues in wins twice, shutouts three times, and strikeouts once during his nine-year stay with the Cleveland Spiders. His best year was 1892. In addition to being the wins leader, he surpassed his fellow hurlers in win-loss percentage and ERA.

After two more years in the National League with St. Louis—known as the Perfectos in 1899, then shifting to the Cardinals moniker in 1900—Young had a 286-169 record and another season leading both leagues in shutouts. He prospered further in Boston, topping the Majors twice again in wins: thirty-three in 1901, thirty-two in 1902. His twenty-eight notches in 1903 led the American League but placed him third overall behind Giants aces Joe McGinnity and Christy Mathewson.

During the first World Series, initially a best-of-nine combat, Young got two victories against the Pittsburgh Pirates to lead the Americans to the 1903 championship. Additionally, his ERA was astonishing. In five of his eight seasons with Boston, Young kept it below 2.00 and didn't go higher than 2.15 except for 1906, when it was 3.19. In 1901 he had the lowest ERA of any pitcher.

Young's output tapered off toward the end of his career. He went to the Cleveland Naps in a trade before the 1909 season; Boston got Charlie

Chech, Jack Ryan, and $12,500. After going 19-15 for the Naps, Young had a 7-10 record in 1910. Cleveland released him the following August with a 3-4 record. He joined the Boston Rustlers, went 4-5, and closed out his outstanding tenure as a premier pitcher with a career tally of 511-315. His victory total is unlikely to ever be surpassed.

Denton True "Cy" Young—so nicknamed because the speed of his fastball was compared to a cyclone—holds the Major League records for career wins, losses, games started, complete games, and innings pitched. Of course, his unparalleled odyssey on the mound meant more opportunities for the opposition, so Young also leads in hits and runs allowed.

For Red Sox Nation, Young's effort on May 8, 1901, ranks as one of the most important because it began one of the richest legacies in baseball and American culture. The devotion, idolatry, and goodwill felt by Somers, Young, Collins, Freeman, and other members of Boston's nascent ball club that day continue with every home opener at Fenway Park, which replaced Huntington Avenue Grounds eleven years later.

PART 3

Hollywood and the Red Sox

7

Reel Red Sox

Red Sox chronicles have been the stuff of legend, passed down from generation to generation like a precious family heirloom. Hollywood has tapped into this rich resource with enough compelling stories, colorful characters, and provocative pathos to keep one entertained during a paralyzing Nor'easter while counting the days until the home opener at Fenway Park.

Fear Strikes Out

Mental illness was decades away from being seen as a matter-of-fact topic rather than a shameful or embarrassing one when *Fear Strikes Out*, a 1957 film, penetrated the cause, depth, and aftermath of Jimmy Piersall's internal horror manifesting in a public breakdown during a Red Sox game.

Based on Piersall's 1955 autobiography of the same title, *Fear Strikes Out* charts a hopeful but challenging journey and reveals that playing for the Red Sox was more about pleasing his father than achieving a personal goal. But John Piersall is never satisfied by his son's success. There's always another rung to climb as far as he's concerned, so he drives the young ballplayer to excel and uses disappointment rather than intimidation or approval as leverage in their rather shabby apartment in Waterbury, Connecticut.

It's the Red Sox or bust for the working-class patriarch.

When the younger Piersall is on his way with the team's Eastern League outfit in Scranton and shows promise of being a Major Leaguer, his third-place ranking for the league's batting average neither impresses nor inspires his father. It's not first place.

Piersall batted .281 for the 1948 Scranton Red Sox, then got elevated from Class A to Triple-A and joined the Louisville Colonels in the American Association. His stay lasted nearly two full seasons, resulting in averages of .271 and .255 before the Red Sox called him up to the show—along with Fred Hatfield of the Double-A Birmingham Barons in the

Double-A Southern Association—at the end of August to supplement the lineup during the 1950 pennant race.[1]

Playing as a substitute, Piersall began his Major League career with appearances in six games in 1950. He got on base six times in eleven plate appearances—four walks, two hits—and scored four times.

The Red Sox finished in third place, four games behind the first-place Yankees.

Piersall returned to Louisville in 1951. After seventeen games and a .310 average, he packed his bags with orders for Birmingham, where he crushed SA pitching for a .342 average, eighty-three RBIs, and one hundred runs scored. In 1952 the Red Sox brought him back to the Majors.

Anthony Perkins portrays Piersall on his harrowing journey toward a mental collapse.[2] He's overenthusiastic during the early days with the Red Sox, but it's later discovered that his behavior is the consequence of a mental illness; genetics may be a factor. During a scene involving his parents—played by Karl Malden and Norma Moore—it's subtly mentioned that Mary Piersall had spent time in an asylum in the past.

The turning point in *Fear Strikes Out* comes when Piersall climbs the backstop fence after hitting an inside-the-park home run. Electroconvulsive therapy, hospitalization, counseling, and lithium guide him back to ball playing.

Boston Globe sportswriter Hy Hurwitz lamented that the film ends with Piersall returning to the ball club after psychiatric treatment, stopping short of depicting his subsequent rebound.[3] The ending was dramatically sound, but Hurwitz had a point. Piersall delivered a productive season against American League pitchers in 1953, playing in all but three games and hitting .272 with fifty-two RBIs and seventy-six runs scored. He placed third—tying with Dave Philley of the Philadelphia Athletics—in triples, ninth in plate appearances, tenth in hits, and tenth in at bats.

But the most relevant critic of *Fear Strikes Out* was Piersall himself. "The movie was a fantasy world by Hollywood," stated the two-time All-Star in 1994. "They rewrote the whole script. My relationship with my father was nothing like that. And I never climbed the screen."[4] In his 1984 autobiography, Piersall—who retired in 1967 with a .272 lifetime average—wrote, "They made my father out to be a real bastard, one who was trying to drive me to a mental breakdown. Well, he wasn't. I have never blamed my father for that breakdown. My father and I actually had a good relationship.

"They also had him coming to visit me in the sanitarium. He never did that. He wasn't supposed to, according to the doctors. But that's the way they showed it. The whole movie was filled with things that simply had not happened in my life.

"When the movie came out, I took one look at it and said, 'horseshit.' It was not about the Jimmy Piersall I knew."[5]

But in 2000 Joe Ginsberg, who played for the Tigers during Piersall's early days with the Red Sox, confirmed the screen-climbing incident happening during a game and Piersall wanting the crowd to cheer. George Kell, a Red Sox teammate, said that Piersall climbed the backstop screen to confront fans who were heckling him.[6]

ABC's 1970s powerhouse sitcom *Happy Days*, initially set in 1956 and revolving around the teenage middle child of a middle-class family in Milwaukee, acknowledged Piersall's challenges with a nod toward the breakdown scene. When Richie Cunningham reveals to his parents that he recently saw a psychiatrist to deal with his teen angst, his father, Howard, says, "I mean, look, they helped that baseball player . . . uh . . . uh . . . Jimmy Piersall. He . . . he doesn't climb up backstops anymore."[7]

As is the custom with biographical films, *Fear Strikes Out* takes dramatic license. Joe Cronin was the Red Sox's general manager, for instance, not the skipper, but he was involved in the decision to move Piersall to the infield.[8] In the film, Piersall's position change disappoints both *père* and *fils*.[9] Piersall later played for the Indians, Senators, Mets, and Angels. After retiring from ball playing, he became a broadcaster.

In the book, Piersall begins with an explanation about wanting to speak for his fellow patients, a revolutionary act at the time. "The best way to help us get well and stay well is to treat us like human beings—as I've been treated," wrote Piersall. "We don't have to talk about our sickness in whispers or prowl about on the edge of society with our hands to our ears to block out the whispers of others. We have nothing to be ashamed of. All we want is to be understood by those who have never been where we have. There is no better therapy than understanding."[10]

Even if the film version is factually incorrect in parts, it serves the same purpose.

Fever Pitch

A lust-driven man getting together with a pragmatic-minded woman is a storytelling template dating back to Bathsheba and King David. Bathsheba bargained with the ruler to ensure that their son, Solomon, would ascend to the throne of the king of Israel after David's passing instead of one of his sons by other wives.

Lust does not necessarily equal sex, though.

George Bailey felt increasingly claustrophobic in Bedford Falls as his wanderlust gnawed at him until he married Mary Hatch in *It's a Wonderful Life*.

Ralph Kramden's pursuit of wealth through get-rich-quick schemes was a cornerstone of *The Honeymooners*. They never panned out, but Ralph's wife, Alice, forgave him time and time again.

David Addison and Maddie Hayes at the Blue Moon Detective Agency in *Moonlighting*, Sam Malone and Diane Chambers at the Boston bar downstairs from Melville's in *Cheers*, Tim the "Tool Man" and Jill Taylor at home after Tim hosts his fix-it TV show sponsored by Binford Tools in *Home Improvement*, Pete Mitchell and Charlotte Blackwood at Air Station Miramar in *Top Gun*, and Dr. Doug Ross and Nurse Carol Hathaway at Cook County General Hospital in ER are other notable examples.

Ben Wrightman and Lindsey Meeks deserve inclusion in these vaunted ranks of popular culture, especially for Red Sox fans. In *Fever Pitch*, a 2005 romantic comedy based loosely on a novel by Nick Hornby, Boston is the setting for a burgeoning, passionate relationship between Ben, a likable schoolteacher whose fervor for the Red Sox extends to having Yankees toilet paper, and Lindsey, a marketing executive whose demeanor is welcoming if not completely understanding of the team's hold on her beau.

Jimmy Fallon and Drew Barrymore play the lead characters.

It begins with a meet cute. Ben takes students from his math class to meet someone who employs math skills in everyday scenarios at work. Cupid blesses him with Lindsey—an adorable, composed, and accessible woman on an upward career trajectory in marketing—to be that person. And so, a romance begins with several dates. Ben is smitten, deeply enough to make a proposal that will bring him and Lindsey even closer: he asks her to be his date for Opening Day at Fenway Park.

Ben's lust is Red Sox fandom. But he's not just any New Englander donning a jersey, plunking a dollar in a Jimmy Fund box, and singing "Sweet Caroline." The ball club is Ben's bedrock. It has been ever since his uncle took him to his first Red Sox game. When the uncle died, Ben inherited his season tickets and continued the devotion to the point of absurdity for an outsider but nirvana for a Red Sox fan. Ben's apartment, as Lindsey points out, looks like a gift shop. Red Sox paraphernalia is everywhere.

But it's not just filled with merchandise. Ben honors Red Sox history with an advertisement for the Jimmy Fund, a facsimile of a Fenway Park scoreboard, and a framed picture of the 1970 *Sports Illustrated* cover with Tony Conigliaro and his black eye after getting beaned by Angels pitcher Jack Hamilton in 1967.

So deep is Ben's devotion that he crosses himself in the morning, kisses the fingers on his right hand, and touches the picture. It's a subtle, tender moment showing the everlasting effect of that tragic moment in Red Sox history.

Lindsey honors the passion by attending Red Sox games and being incorporated into Ben's "summer family." A baseball novice, she soon gets absorbed in the lore, love, and labor of being a fan. But there's a cost. She works all day, goes to the games at night, and they make love afterward. Being a fan at Ben's level is exhausting, causing her to slip up at work.

The inevitable breakup happens when Ben sacrifices his tickets to a Yankees–Red Sox game to attend a party with Lindsey. Down seven runs in the bottom of the ninth inning, the Red Sox mount an epic comeback. Although the night ended with spectacular sex, Ben blames Lindsey for his missing the game; she separates from him like a space shuttle from a booster rocket.

Ben, crestfallen, deepens his misery by repeatedly playing a video recording of the Bill Buckner error from the 1986 World Series. His friends rescue him from the doldrums, but Ben realizes that he needs to make a bold statement to show Lindsey how much he cares for her—

sell his season tickets. When Lindsey finds out, she bolts from a party celebrating her promotion and heads to Fenway Park for the playoff game against the Yankees; Ben is completing the sale with the husband of one of Lindsey's friends.

Lindsey jumps onto the field during the game and sprints toward Ben's seats. Startled by this show of affection, which will result in Lindsey getting arrested, Ben can think of only one thing to ask. "The outfield—the grass—is it spongy?" Lindsey tears up the contract and reveals the strength of their relationship: "You love me enough to sell your tickets. I love you enough not to let you."

Fever Pitch had a touch of wonder about it. Filmed during 2004, narration and a montage tagged on to the ending explain subsequent events culminating in the Red Sox winning their first World Series since 1918. Fallon and Barrymore went to St. Louis and celebrated on the field at Busch Stadium after the Red Sox beat the Cardinals in Game Four to complete the sweep; *Fever Pitch* used a clip of them as part of the montage.

The lead actors had a likability factor that makes audiences smile whenever they're on-screen. Fallon banked the currency of goodwill from his stint on *Saturday Night Live* highlighted by coanchoring the "Weekend Update" segment with Tina Fey. She had the persona of a high school valedictorian. His was the goofy, welcoming version of the guy deemed Most Popular.

Fallon, who appeared on SNL from 1998 to 2004, had a roster of characters, including Nick Burns, a condescending IT support worker; Sully, a loudmouth Boston teen with his girlfriend Denise; and Joey Mack, an obnoxious radio host from Saugerties, New York, in the morning drive slot. After starring in several movies, Fallon took over *Late Night* hosting duties from Conan O'Brien on NBC and fulfilled a prophecy—his junior high school yearbook predicted that he would host the show one day. He became the host of *The Tonight Show* in 2014.

Barrymore brought sweetness and generosity to her portrayal of Lindsey, complementing a résumé that's a gold standard for diversity of stories. Action. Thriller. Drama. Romantic Comedy. Slapstick. Barrymore has done it all.

Praise was plentiful.

David Germain of the Associated Press said that Barrymore "is at her most likable" and Fallon had an "understated charm and cheeriness."[11] Forrest Hartman of Gannett described Fallon as "a competent and entertaining leading man." Regarding the female lead, he declared, "Barrymore has nothing to prove, as she's been cranking out likable romantic comedies for years, but she is in typically solid form."[12]

Christopher Smith of the *Bangor Daily News* wrote, "Throughout, the writing is solid and often clever, the chemistry between Barrymore and Fallon is undeniable, you come to care for the characters, which is key, and the robust, wholly unbelievable ending is earned."[13] Fallon has a "lightness and tenderness that's quite winning" and Barrymore is "equally charming" were the endorsements in the *Los Angeles Times*.[14]

Fever Pitch emblemizes the heart, soul, and endurance of Red Sox Nation. Even Yankees fans might tip their hats to Ben's commitment.

The Town

Entertainers, no matter how successful, often honor their hometowns.

In his live album *Sinatra at the Sands*, Frank Sinatra joked about growing up in Hoboken, New Jersey. Fellow Garden State native Lou Costello invoked Paterson in his movies with Bud Abbott. Any fan of Jack Benny knew that the perpetual thirty-nine-year-old grew up in Waukegan, Illinois. Lucille Ball's hometown of Jamestown, New York, was part of Lucy Ricardo's biography in *I Love Lucy*. Tom Selleck wore a Detroit Tigers hat on *Magnum, P.I.* to reflect his roots.

Ben Affleck's bond with Boston heightened when the Cambridge native cowrote and costarred in the 1997 film *Good Will Hunting*, for which he won the Oscar for Best Original Screenplay with childhood friend Matt Damon. Ten years later, he directed his first film—*Gone Baby Gone*, a mystery set in Boston and based on the novel of the same name by Dennis Lehane; Affleck's brother, Casey, was the lead actor.

In 2010 Affleck debuted his second film as a helmsman—*The Town*. Based on Chuck Hogan's 2004 novel *Prince of Thieves*, this awesome heist tale also uses Boston as the setting. But the thieves' target of Fenway Park may give Red Sox fans a twinge of the heart. Affleck—also the film's cowriter with Peter Craig and Aaron Stockard—stars as Doug MacRay, one part of a bank-robbing quartet. "I promised that I wouldn't actually show the real way money was brought in and out of Fenway Park," said the actor.[15]

A brief scene between Doug and one of his partners, James "Jem" Coughlin, who has served a nine-year prison term, summarizes the matter-of-fact way that they grew up. After the group's first bank job in the story, Doug starts dating the assistant manager, Claire Keesey. Because the robbers were masked, Claire doesn't know Doug's true identity until later in the story. When Doug finds out that Claire was assaulted, vengeance inspires him to go to Jem. "I need your help. I can't tell you what it is. You can never ask me about it later. And we're gonna hurt some people." Jem pauses a moment, then responds, "Whose car we gonna take?"

They find out who was responsible; Jem shoots the culprit in both legs. Jeremy Renner plays Jem. Rebecca Hall plays Claire. Jon Hamm plays Adam Frawley, the FBI agent pursuing the thieves. According to Frawley, Boston has the highest number of bank robberies per capita—four hundred—more than anywhere in the world. Charlestown, a one-square-mile part of Boston, is the incubator for nine out of ten area bank robbers.

For Doug, thievery is not only part of a neighborhood legacy—it's the family business. Currently in prison, Doug's father used to work for Fergie, a local mobster using a flower shop as a front, until he wanted to break away and begin his own criminal enterprise. To Doug's horror, Fergie reveals his revenge—he had the father chemically castrated and got Doug's mom hooked on drugs. She hanged herself with a wire. Doug had no idea; he always thought she had abandoned the family.

Like the Shaw Memorial Elms in Boston Common, Affleck's connection to the area is deeply rooted. "Not only is he literally the patron saint of Boston, but he's also perfectly cast in the role," noted Hamm, the Emmy-winning star of *Mad Men*.[16] Titus Welliver, who played Frawley's partner at the FBI, confirmed the adoration bestowed upon Affleck: "It's like walking through London with one of the Beatles."[17]

Affleck chose the story not only because of his affinity and affection for the locale but also because of an artistic goal. "We're just not used to all this attention," explained the filmmaker of his Boston-area compadres. "With 'Gone Baby Gone,' I knew that city. I wanted to show the city that's different from the one on the postcards. I wanted to show the multiethnic city. I wanted to show Dorchester; no one knows anything about Dorchester. These neighborhoods are really interesting. I did Southie, Dorchester, and Charlestown."[18]

Viewers of *The Town* may sense a confining tone when a car chase on narrow Charlestown streets follows a bank robbery. It's amplified later when the Fenway Park heist—after a four-game series with the Yankees and estimated to be a haul of more than $3 million in cash—takes place within the interior of the hallowed baseball site. The story ends with Doug's other two partners—Albert Magloan and Desmond Elden—getting killed during the robbery, which has brought in Frawley, a swarm of his fellow agents, and a SWAT team.

Jem escapes but is killed during a gunfight with a cop. Doug kills Fergie, who conceived the ballpark robbery. Afterward Doug buries some of the loot in Claire's garden for her to find. By this time, she knows Doug is a bank robber. She says something in code during a phone conversation to warn him that the FBI is waiting at her apartment. He escapes; she uses the money to build a skating rink in honor of Doug's mother. Doug had a potential NHL career when he was younger but traded in skates for skullduggery.

Renner got high praise for his performance, as did Affleck for his directing and acting. New York's *Daily News* said that Renner "charges every scene with a feral power" and shows "a mixture of efficiency and jovial homeboyness."[19] The Associated Press stated that *The Town* "may not have the emotional heft of 'Gone Baby Gone.' . . . What it has instead, though, is a greater technical complexity, a larger scope, and the promise of a director who's well on his way to establishing a distinctive vision and voice."[20]

Though ignored two years later for an Oscar nomination for directing *Argo*—which he also starred in—Affleck won the Critics Choice Award, Golden Globe Award, and Directors Guild of America Award for Best Director for that film. *Argo* did win the Oscar for Best Picture, Best Writing in an Adapted Screenplay, and Best Film Editing. It also won the Golden Globe for Best Motion Picture.

Game 6

The template of a story taking place in one day—and/or night—has been used to great effect by screenwriters, perhaps most prominently in *High Noon*. To instruct and inspire the next generation of filmmakers, scholars have used these films as educational fodder. *12 Angry Men*, *Three O'clock High*, *Die Hard*, *Dog Day Afternoon*, *Airport*, and *Draft Day* will likely be prominent on a syllabus, which may also include *Glengarry Glen Ross*, a film based on the play of the same name featuring events at a real estate office taking place over the course of one evening and the following morning.

Game 6 is an independent film in this genre. Starring Michael Keaton as famous playwright Nicky Rogan, this 2005 film revolves around Nicky's day leading up to the debut of his latest play. He has a tryst with his mistress, who's one of his steadfast financial backers; a chance meeting with his daughter, Laurel, in a cab; a visit with his father; a discussion with a fellow playwright who's eccentric and insecure; a cordial but somewhat tense conversation with his divorce-seeking wife; and encounters with advertisements for the latest edition of *New York* magazine, featuring a cover story about Broadway's nastiest critic—Steven Schwimmer. Though acclaimed and successful, Nicky fears him.

But the play and Schwimmer—played by Robert Downey Jr.—do not totally dominate Nicky's thoughts. *Game 6* takes place on October 25, 1986. Nicky's beloved Boston Red Sox are on the verge of a catharsis—a cleansing of sixty-eight years of emotional debris with a win against the New York Mets.

Rather than seeing the play, Nicky spends his time in a Manhattan bar among Mets fans, who are witnessing a year of destiny for the Red Sox. Wade Boggs hit .357. Jim Rice hit .324. Roger Clemens racked up twenty-four wins against four losses. Oil Can Boyd went 16-10; Bruce Hurst offered a 13-8 record. After a grueling seven-game American League play-off against the California Angels—which included two games decided in eleven innings—the Red Sox won the first two games of the World Series at Shea Stadium. The Mets took the next two; Boston won Game Five.

With the Red Sox up 5-3 in the bottom of the tenth, Nicky is understandably optimistic when Calvin Schiraldi retires the first two batters—Wally

Backman and Keith Hernandez—on fly balls to the outfield. Optimism quickly turns to worry when Gary Carter and Kevin Mitchell both hit singles; Carter scores on Ray Knight's single, which sends Mitchell to third base.

Bob Stanley relieves Schiraldi and throws a wild pitch that scores Mitchell, making the score 5-5 and putting Knight on third. Then disaster strikes. Mookie Wilson's ground ball goes through Bill Buckner's legs. Knight scores the winning run to tie the World Series at three games apiece; New York wins the deciding game two nights later.

Frustrated, Nicky seeks revenge. Schwimmer is his target. Or outlet, at least.

Tracking the critic to his loft, Nicky sees him about to have sex with Laurel. They had met at the theater after the performance, but Schwimmer disguised himself with a massive gray wig and makeup covering a huge birthmark on his face; he refused to tell Laurel his name even in their actions about to precede sex. Now she knows everything; Schwimmer is subjected to anger by both Nicky and his daughter. The tension is defused when Schwimmer reveals that he grew up on Boylston Street. A true Red Sox fan. Both critic and playwright begin to bond over the night's misery. A bonus: Schwimmer loved Nicky's play.

Ty Burr of the *Boston Globe* gave *Game 6* high marks: "a small, lovingly overwritten comic drama about fate, failure, and primal longing. To put it in words a Sox fan would understand, the movie hurts good."[21]

8

The Ballad of
Sam "Mayday" Malone

Brashness, thy name is Malone.

Sam "Mayday" Malone was the lead character on the NBC sitcom *Cheers*, which ran from 1982 to 1993, won twenty-eight Emmy Awards, and revolved around his sports bar named Cheers at 112½ Beacon Street near Boston Common and downstairs from Melville's Seafood Restaurant.[1]

Ted Danson plays Sam, whose tenure with the Red Sox bullpen in the 1970s gives him local celebrity status. Success with women earns him idolatry from the bar regulars. It would have put Casanova to shame—Sam refers to himself as the "Cy Young of skirt chasers," once dated Miss Tennessee, and claims to have slept with more than a thousand women.[2] The Lothario archetype was prominent on NBC's Thursday night lineup in the 1980s. *Night Court* had Dan Fielding; *L.A. Law* had Arnie Becker; and *Cheers* had Malone, a recovering alcoholic whose mammoth taste for sexual conquest did not lessen when he gave up drinking.

Created by James Burrows, Glen Charles, and Les Charles, *Cheers* is largely a "unity of place" show with most scenes taking place in the bar. Writing, acting, and directing—Burrows helmed 240 of 273 episodes—were stellar efforts that brought laughter with an occasional dose of pathos in its eleven-year run.[3]

Until *Cheers*, Boston had been underrepresented on prime-time television. Perhaps the most well-known example was *Banacek*, starring George Peppard as an insurance investigator plagued with seven-figure claims to resolve. The NBC *Wednesday Mystery Movie* anthology aired seventeen episodes of the show from 1972 to 1974. Some establishing shots and the scenes accompanying the theme song were filmed in Boston, but producers shot the show on Universal Studios backlots and soundstages.

Cheers uses the same paradigm, featuring exterior shots of the Bull & Finch Pub and other areas of Boston; Burrows et al. relied on the Bull & Finch interior as its template for the show's set on Paramount's Stage 25. A handful of scenes in later years were filmed outside the Bull & Finch. These exterior images always feature a Cheers sign.

Sam's ex-jock status gives *Cheers* an underlying foundation of sports fodder for dialogue, story lines, and characters, especially regarding Red Sox history in the show's first two seasons. Incorporating Sam's former occupation as a relief pitcher for the Red Sox and Bostonians' legendary passion for sports required more than having posters of icons like Larry Bird on the walls of the bar.

Consequently, *Cheers* lets the audience know that sports will be a basis from the start. When Ernie "Coach" Pantusso—Malone's former pitching coach in Double-A ball with Pawtucket and the Red Sox—makes his first appearance in the pilot episode, he laments the Patriots' latest draft pick. Beer-guzzling accountant and Cheers regular Norm Peterson remarks in the same episode that Sam "used to be one of the best pitchers in baseball."[4]

But in 1990 Norm offers a different take. When longtime Cheers waitress Carla Tortelli LeBec mentions that the Red Sox often called on the reliever and his "slider of death" in pressure situations, Norm responds that he usually gave up a three-run homer. Sam's Red Sox teammates nicknamed the pitch.[5]

Indeed, Sam's mound performance was uneven. In 1989 the Joint Chiefs of Staff chairman, Admiral William James Crowe Jr., visits Cheers and recognizes the ex-pitcher, saying, "Nobody gives up towering home runs like Sam Malone. I wish our missiles flew as high and as far."[6]

In 1992 Sam tries a comeback with the Red Sox's farm team in New Britain, Connecticut. After a good outing, he reveals, "I don't think I like baseball anymore." While his younger teammates revel in a victory and want to celebrate, Sam realizes that baseball's postgame shenanigans no longer hold appeal.[7]

Appropriately for a show set in a Boston sports bar, a first-season episode depicts the legendary cultural divide between the Yankees and the Red Sox. There's a friction between them that makes the conflict between the Hatfields and the McCoys look like a Harvard-Yale debate.

An obnoxious Yankees fan named Eddie—prone to gloating at the Beacon Street watering hole after the Bronx Bombers beat the Red Sox—provokes ire with snide comments about Boston's local nine. To Boston fans—and perhaps the national TV audience—Eddie represents the loud-mouth New Yorker stereotype whose rhetoric, tone, and sarcasm ignite animosity. He is the garish personification of Saul Steinberg's famed 1976 drawing *View of the World from 9th Avenue* visualizing New York City as the center of the world with the rest of its geography fading into the background.[8]

Although Eddie remarks that Sam had a "darn good hard slider," his respect does not, in any way, absolve his nastiness. It simply shows that Eddie is an astute though acidic fan. Carla assaults the New Yorker, who threatens to sue Sam unless he fires her.

After seeing a therapist, Carla learns to control her temper. When Eddie returns to Cheers, he trashes her with personal insults and knocks Boston legends Ted Williams ("overrated") and Bobby Orr ("wimp"). He further tests her by insulting her beloved Bruins ("ugly, stupid sissies"). Carla remains calm; Eddie drops his demand. But there's a consequence. One of the patrons reveals that he's a Bruin and extends an offer to Eddie: "Let me walk you to your car. I want to show you some of those sissy things I got suspended for."[9]

Eddie could have been a Packers fan in Chicago, an Ohio State fan in Ann Arbor, a Dodgers fan in San Francisco, or a Canadiens fan in Toronto. But those rivalries, while stormy, do not have a continued enmity marked by moments of one team's dominance and the other team's championship drought unquenched for several decades. By the time that *Cheers* debuted in 1982, New York's AL squad had notched twenty-two World Series titles. The Red Sox had been in the World Series twice since Harry Frazee sold Babe Ruth to the Yankees after the 1919 season; they lost both times.

Eddie's jibes underscore Boston's moments of misery that occurred because of the Yankees. In addition to the Ruth sale, Red Sox fans endure the knowledge that it was a Red Sox pitcher who gave up Roger Maris's record-setting sixty-first home run in 1961.

A home run over Fenway Park's thirty-seven-foot, two-inch-high Green Monster in the 1978 American League East one-game playoff earned the Yankees' starting shortstop a new middle nickname—Bucky "Fucking" Dent.

Cheers does not mention these hallmarks of the rivalry, but baseball fans are aware of the antipathy. For Red Sox fans, Eddie's character immediately represents pain that is palpable from internalizing disappointments balanced to some degree by successes, including Carl Yastrzemski's Triple Crown season in 1967, Ted Williams being the last batter to break .400 in the Major Leagues (in 1941), and Fred Lynn winning 1975 AL Rookie of the Year honors.

Another first-season episode elevates a cultural topic seen sporadically up to then on prime-time television—homosexuality. Billy Crystal played a gay character on ABC's 1977–81 soap-opera satire *Soap*. Marty Morrison was a recurring character on ABC's *Barney Miller*, appearing in 8 of 170 episodes of the sitcom about the fictional Twelfth Precinct in Greenwich Village, airing from 1975 to 1982; a pilot episode aired in August 1974. But the *Cheers* episode "The Boys in the Bar" is an incredibly poignant groundbreaker for its handling of the topic in a show where the lead male character has enough testosterone for an army battalion.

Sam's Major League status and bedroom exploits give the bar a masculine aura, leading Norm and his drinking compadre Cliff Clavin, the trivia-laden postal worker, plus other regulars to deify their bartender. But one of Sam's back-in-the-day pals threatens this standard; during a press conference at Cheers to celebrate his autobiography *Catcher's Mask*, former Red Sox catcher and Sam's running buddy Tom Kenderson reveals that he's gay.[10]

Even though Tom had sent a copy for his old friend to read before the media got to Cheers, Sam neglected to look at it. Tom's revelation, which Sam learns at the press conference, is not a betrayal as much as a surprise. He is stunned that his former battery mate hid this secret the entire time they played, drank, and chased women together.

It would be facile and perhaps expected for the rest of the story to be Sam coming to terms with Tom's disclosure according to the five stages of mourning: denial because of their history with women; anger because he feels confused about potentially losing a friend; bargaining because he wants to keep Tom's friendship without jeopardizing his own status as a ladies' man in the bar; depression because he can't believe what anyone says about anything; and acceptance because the friendship is invaluable.

It would likely include a mention that most of Tom's friends have abandoned him because they feel betrayed. Ashamed, perhaps.

Cheers does not follow that paradigm. Not exactly. Diane Chambers—a waitress and Sam's future on-again, off-again paramour, played by Shelley Long—convinces her boss that Tom is vulnerable and needs his amity. Sam accepts the truth. In what might be the best example of "less is more" dialogue on television, Diane's succinct approval says volumes when the ex-pitcher offers his pal a drink on the house: "Way to go, Mayday."

Instead of going the traditional sitcom route with funny but saccharine dialogue, the script by Ken Levine and David Isaacs uses Tom's coming out as a device to kick off a thoughtful story line about homophobia and Sam's reaction to his customers' biases.

Norm emphasizes that Vito's Pub became a gay bar suddenly, and he warns that the same thing could happen to Cheers because of the press conference. When Sam throws his arm around his former catcher at the event both before knowing what is in the book and after the revelation, it sends a message that he accepts his former teammate's sexuality. In the patrons' eyes, this is the beginning of the end of their beloved hangout; when the barflies think that two male customers appear to be gay, they begin an exodus.

Though Sam considers kicking those targets out of the bar, his integrity wins. After one of them praises the courage in hosting the press conference, the Cheers proprietor gives them beers on the house. His line is drawn to his regulars: "It's not gonna turn into the kind of bar that I have to throw people out of."

But the underlying story line goes further toward tolerance. Diane has installed two gay men undercover at the bar; Norm claims that he can spot them. When Diane reveals that the two previous customers were not gay—one of them hit on her—she asks the real gay men to drop their act. They both kiss Norm on the cheek, leading the rotund beer guzzler to say that one of them kisses better than his wife.

"The Boys in the Bar" is a terrific example of using Sam's baseball career as story material. It also was timely, airing three months after former Major Leaguer Glenn Burke divulged his homosexuality in the October 1982 issue of *Inside Sports*; Burke's MLB career had ended in 1979. Billy Bean played in the Majors from 1987 to 1995; his disclosure happened in 1999.

Cheers also tackled Sam's alcoholism, a topic just beginning to get mainstream attention and empathy after former First Lady Betty Ford revealed her addictions to liquor and medication in 1978. Her courage gave a public face to the issue; no longer was it a scourge to be an addict. She was not the only celebrity to expose her addiction, but she was the most prominent at the time.

Although it's an interesting basis to have a recovering alcoholic owning a bar, *Cheers* goes further in the first-season episode "Endless Slumper."[11] Here, we see an addict on the verge of succumbing in a rare dramatic moment for the show.

Sam carries a talisman inspiring him to refrain from drinking, no matter how great the temptation—a beer bottle cap from the last alcohol he ever drank. But in an act of generosity, he gives it to former Tigers ace and currently struggling Red Sox hurler Rick Walker as a good luck charm. Rick's fortunes change in the next couple of weeks. Sam's worsen. A series of events, including the inability to perform his bar slide—sending a mug of beer at a 90-degree angle to a waiting patron at the end of the bar—lead Sam to believe that he's jinxed without the bottle cap.

Alone with Diane when he closes the bar for the night, Sam calls Rick in the locker room after an extra-innings contest to get his lucky charm returned. But Boston's newest hero tells the barkeep that he lost it in Kansas City.

Sam pours a bottle, readies a return to drinking, and stands on the precipice of a tailspin. But he does the bar slide successfully and, to Diane's relief, keeps the cap as a new lucky charm.

In addition to the dramatic moment—when the camera is focused on the mug of beer that Sam just poured, the studio is as silent as a graveyard—"Endless Slumper" shows the camaraderie that ballplayers share. Even though Sam never played with Rick, they share a Red Sox lineage. Wearing the same logo years apart gives them a bond that rarely happens, if at all, with occupations outside sports.

Dialogue, too, affirms the importance of the Red Sox for *Cheers*. In the 1985 episode "The Heart Is a Lonely Snipehunter," Carla and Coach quiz each other on Red Sox trivia; their conversation showcases the depths of passion, knowledge, and pride involving the team.[12] With Sam's celebrity comes an image of a place where conversations about the Red Sox are commonplace, so the Carla-Coach trivia dialogue, while extraneous to the plot, is certainly believable.

When Carla asks about a .300 hitter's nickname, Coach responds, "Jimmie Foxx" before she can complete the question. The nickname would have been "Double X" or "The Beast." Foxx played six full seasons with the Red Sox and part of a seventh season.[13]

By invoking Foxx, the writers emphasize the contributions that the Red Sox icon made to baseball. It surely gave the Fenway Faithful a jolt to hear the name of this Hall of Famer who might not have been familiar to younger viewers despite his achievements. During his Beantown tenure from 1936 to 1942, Foxx was an All-Star for six seasons, won one of his three MVP Awards, led the Majors in slugging percentage twice, and led the AL in batting average once. The Red Sox never finished higher than second place in this period; they reached it three times.

Using Foxx's name in a prime-time television show emphasized the Hall of Fame slugger's triumphs. Joe DiMaggio, whose career overlapped Foxx's between 1936 to 1942 and 1944 to 1945, gets instant recognition. The "Yankee Clipper" holds the Major League record for a hitting streak—fifty-six consecutive games in 1941—and leveraged his fame for television advertisements: Mr. Coffee (nationwide) and Bowery Savings Bank (New York City metropolitan area).

But Double X had a stronger career than the Yankee Clipper. Both won the MVP three times and finished their careers with a .325 average. Foxx led the Majors in slugging percentage five times, on-base percentage twice, RBIs three times, and home runs four times. DiMaggio led in RBIs twice, batting average once, slugging percentage once, and never in on-base percentage.

During DiMaggio's 1936–51 Major League career, he won nine World

Series titles with the New York Yankees. Those victories plus the media access that comes with playing in New York increased his visibility; Les Brown's hit song "Joltin' Joe DiMaggio" integrated the fifty-six-game hitting streak into the lyrics. Had Foxx played with the Yankees instead of the Athletics and the Red Sox for most of his career, perhaps there would have been a song about him. "Crazy Like a Foxx" would be a probable title with lyrics such as: "Crazy like a Foxx, he's the slugger with the Boston Red Sox, Jimmie Jimmie he's so neat, they love him down on Beacon Street."

Red Sox trivia in this quiz scene from "Lonely Snipehunter" is even more potent when Don Buddin's name is mentioned before the question is completed. Buddin had a six-year career in the Majors, five of them with Boston. With Buddin having been a lifetime .241 hitter and error-prone shortstop, the finished question might have been: "What Red Sox shortstop led the AL in errors in 1958 and 1959?"

Here, Buddin's name probably had baseball fans scurrying to their reference books for more information. It shows a willingness on the part of the show's writers and producers not to rely just on Red Sox icons like Jimmie Foxx, Babe Ruth, Ted Williams, Carlton Fisk, and Carl Yastrzemski for dialogue. This attention to the lesser-known players continues when Carla answers "Lou Clinton" after Coach says, "The only man to pinch-hit . . ." She even knows the next answer will be "Frank Malzone."

Clinton, a right fielder, played four seasons and part of 1964 for the Red Sox. Malzone, a six-time All-Star, played for the Red Sox from 1955 to 1965 and finished his career with the Angels in 1966. These are names that die-hard Red Sox fans will know. It's one thing to ask the identity of the 1975 runner-up to Fred Lynn for AL Rookie of the Year (Jim Rice), the two .300 hitters on the Cinderella team of 1967 (George Scott, Carl Yastrzemski), or the number of home runs that Ted Williams hit during the year he batted .406 (thirty-seven). It's another to choose lesser-known players familiar mostly to New Englanders.

In the opening to the episode "Don Juan Is Hell," Norm quizzes Carla from a sports trivia book: 1955 AL MVP (Yogi Berra), height of Fenway Park's Green Monster (thirty-seven feet), Ike Delock's lifetime ERA (4.03).[14] Delock pitched for the Red Sox from 1952 to 1963. His best years were 1955–59, with a win-loss record of 56-36. Delock started five games and pitched in two others for Baltimore in 1963 before leaving baseball with a lifetime record of 84-75 (Boston, 83-72; Baltimore, 1-3).

Red Sox history gives *Cheers* a level of verisimilitude rarely seen in prime time. *Murphy Brown* is another good example. Airing from 1988 to 1998 on CBS—with a thirteen-episode reboot in 2018—this show starred Candice Bergen as the award-winning title character. Set at *FYI*, a fictional CBS prime-time newsmagazine show produced in Washington DC, *Murphy Brown* often featured names of political insiders during the show's run.

In fact, when the title character has a son with her ex-husband out of wedlock and raises him alone, Vice President Dan Quayle condemned it as "just another lifestyle choice." In an outstanding exemplar of art imitating life, *Murphy Brown* treats the Quayle criticism as a real happening in its fictional universe; Murphy responds to the vice president by saying that there is no such thing as a standard family.[15]

Celebrity cameos enhance the authenticity of *Cheers*, too. Dick Cavett recognizes Sam and encourages him to write an autobiography about his baseball career.[16] When Sam dates a Boston city councilwoman, presidential contender Gary Hart stops by the bar to thank him for his help with the sports questions during a game of Trivial Pursuit.[17] *Cheers* boasts another politico when Cambridge native and Speaker of the House Tip O'Neill guest stars as himself.[18]

In 1988 *Spenser: For Hire* star Robert Urich visits Cheers to see his pal—bartender Woody Boyd.[19] In the *Cheers* universe, Woody has a role as an extra in an episode of the Boston-set private-detective show, which aired on ABC from 1985 to 1988.

Wade Boggs has a cameo in a 1988 episode. But Cheers regulars believe the contemporary Red Sox icon is an impostor sent by Gary's Olde Towne Tavern, part of a running gag of pranks, insults, and competitions between the bars.[20] At the time the episode aired, Boggs was one of baseball's biggest stars. He led the Major Leagues in walks twice and batting average three times between 1983 and 1988. Patience at the plate gave the third baseman MLB on-base percentage leader honors in 1983 and for five consecutive seasons from 1985 to 1989.

In 1987 *Washington Post* scribe Thomas Boswell lauded Boggs's journey from a batter with a "compact, almost defensive swing" to "The Man Who Really Might Hit .400."[21] Boggs finished 1987 with a .363 average. But if the magical .400 barrier were to be broken for the first time since Ted Williams's fantastic hitting display in 1941, it would have been appropriate—and still is—that a Red Sox slugger be the one to do it.

Celtics power forward Kevin McHale appears in two episodes.[22] Carla marries a Bruins goalie played by Jay Thomas, reinforcing the show's bedrock of sports.[23]

NBC brass stood on the verge of shouting "last call" for *Cheers* after a few months during the inaugural season. Airing back-to-back with *Taxi*—which ABC canceled after four years before NBC picked it up for one season—both shows suffered in the ratings. "With them may go hopes for the future of intelligent, sophisticated comedy and diversity in prime time, where the pressures for survival inevitably result in sameness," wrote noted television critic Howard Rosenberg in December 1982.[24]

Indeed, *Cheers* has intellectual weight; Sam's contrast with Diane fuels the comedy. They are opposites. Art museums versus comic book stores. Champagne versus beer. The Three Tenors versus the Three Stooges. Burrows said, "I feel like we're struggling Impressionist painters who were not popular in their time. You do your best work, work your guts out. Your friends call you and tell you how much they love the show. Then, Glen, Les and I look at each other every week and say, 'Why aren't more people watching?' How do you get them to watch? Sex? Violence? We talk about it all the time."[25]

Shelley Long left *Cheers* after five seasons and returned for the ninety-minute series finale in 1993; Kirstie Alley replaced her as the show's female lead. NBC aired *Cheers* for another six seasons.

Though *Cheers* became a hit for NBC, its early survival mirrors baseball's sabermetrics. *Cheers* did not rise above the No. 60 spot in the Nielsen ratings during its rookie season; an episode in November ranked last.[26] Brandon Tartikoff, NBC's president of entertainment and a zealous baseball fan, studied the prime-time Nielsen ratings like general managers analyze statistics and kept *Cheers* in the lineup. In his 1992 autobiography, Tartikoff uses the show's Thursday night brethren at *Hill*

Street Blues as an example: "What this research said was that *Hill Street* was getting a higher rating in homes that had pay cable than in homes that didn't. That meant that the people who had the most options, the people who could choose from what was then about a twenty-channel cable universe, were seeking out our show to watch."[27]

Cable TV was not ubiquitous in the early 1980s. Households with cable TV meant higher disposable income, which are the households targeted by advertisers.

NBC renewed *Cheers* in March 1983.[28]

Cheers to *Cheers* for emphasizing Boston's sports legacy in stories, dialogue, and set dressing. This is critical to the show's success. Decades after they've ended, discussions of sitcom stalwarts *Mary Tyler Moore* and *Happy Days* may trigger memories of scenes, characters, and dialogue. But fans might have trouble remembering the settings of Minneapolis and Milwaukee because those cities were not integral to the stories. Mary Richards and the Cunninghams could have lived in any midwestern metropolis and the shows would not have lost their appeal.

Cheers signaled a change for quality programming led by NBC in the Reagan era. A year before the show's debut, *Hill Street Blues* premiered. *Family Ties* and *St. Elsewhere*, the same year. *Night Court, L.A. Law, Hunter, The Golden Girls, The Cosby Show,* and *Miami Vice* later contributed to NBC's dominance and excellence. *Cheers* also had the intangible asset of taking place in an identifiable setting. Most television viewers in the 1980s might not have been surgical patients, trial lawyers, or undercover detectives driving a Ferrari around South Beach. But it's a good bet that viewers at least eighteen years old had been in a bar at least once.

If it were a Boston establishment, then two words likely accompanied the conversation: Go Sox.

A Little Roller up along First

Game Six, *Curb Your Enthusiasm*, and
the Dignity of Bill Buckner

Forget the so-called curse of Babe Ruth.

Ignore the blamers, too.

It wasn't Bill Buckner's fault that the Boston Red Sox lost the 1986 World Series to the New York Mets. Full stop.

Buckner's error that secured a win for the Mets in Game Six obscures a lengthy, productive career for the California native, a journeyman ballplayer who finished with a .289 batting average and 2,715 hits. In 1974 he played on the NL pennant–winning Dodgers and tied for the third-highest batting average in the senior circuit. In 1980 he led the National League with a .324 average for the Cubs.

Perhaps they're not Cooperstown-worthy numbers. But Buckner was solid, playing nearly every game of the 1986 season. Through 153 games, he batted .267 and knocked in 102 runs. His strikeouts to plate appearances ratio was 3.6 percent, bettering Yankees first baseman Don Mattingly, who led the American League in 1986 in plate appearances, slugging percentage, and hits. Mattingly's ratio of strikeouts to plate appearances was 4.7 percent.

In Game Six of the World Series, Boston went up 1–0 in the top of the first inning. Wade Boggs led off with a single, followed by Marty Barrett and Buckner flying out to Lenny Dykstra in center field. Bobby Ojeda walked Jim Rice and gave up an RBI double to Dwight Evans, which scored Boggs.

Shea Stadium's visitors notched another run an inning later. Spike Owen banged a one-out single; Roger Clemens struck out trying to bunt. Then Boggs singled to move Owen to third base, and Barrett sent him home with another single.

Clemens kept the Mets in goose eggs through the fourth inning, but a terrific series of at bats gave the NL champs a pair of runs in the bottom of the fifth. Darryl Strawberry began with a walk, a stolen base, and a run scored on Ray Knight's single. Evans's error on Mookie Wilson's single put Knight at third base. Knight scored when Danny Heep, pinch-hitting for Rafael Santana, grounded into a double play.

The teams stayed tied at 2–2 until Boston notched a run in the top of the seventh. Barrett drew a walk to lead off, then got to second on Buckner's grounder to second baseman Wally Backman. Knight's error gave Rice first base as Barrett reached third. Evans grounded to Backman; Barrett scored.

The home team tied in the bottom of the eighth. Lee Mazzilli singled off Calvin Schiraldi and went to second on Dykstra's sacrifice bunt attempt, which was a fielder's choice resulting in a safe arrival at first base. Backman's similar attempt resulted in an out, but the runners advanced.

Schiraldi walked Keith Hernandez intentionally to load the bases for a double play opportunity, then Gary Carter's sacrifice fly scored Mazzilli to even the tally at 3–3.

In the top of the tenth, it looked like Boston's championship drought since 1918 would be finished. Dave Henderson led off with a homer. Ojeda followed by striking out Owen and Schiraldi. Then Boggs doubled and scored on Barrett's single.

With the score 5–3 and Boston having already notched three victories, a World Series championship was in the air as the Mets went to bat in the bottom of the tenth. Schiraldi retired Backman and Hernandez on fly balls to the outfield, readying Red Sox devotees to raise glasses of beer, liquor, or wine; give high fives; and sing "We Are the Champions" with the Boston accent replacing "Are" with "Ah."

The disappointments of 1946, 1967, and 1975—when the Red Sox lost each World Series in seven games—would be assuaged. Or so everyone believed, including at least one member of the Mets. "I thought we were done and I went up into the clubhouse because I didn't want to see Boston having fun on our field," said Hernandez in a 2020 interview. "And I'm very territorial that way."[1]

But the next three Mets singled off Schiraldi: Carter, Kevin Mitchell, and Knight. Knight's single scored Carter and advanced Mitchell to third base. Red Sox skipper John McNamara brought in Bob Stanley, who gave the Mets the tying run when he threw a wild pitch. Mitchell scored; Knight went to second.

"Playing extra deep because I didn't want the ball to get through the infield," explained Buckner about his defensive position with Mookie Wilson at bat.[2] Wilson hit a ground ball that went through Buckner's legs. The call by NBC's Vin Scully is etched into the joyous memories of Mets fans and the sorrowful ones of their Red Sox counterparts: "A little roller up along first. Behind the bag! It goes through Buckner! Here comes Knight and the Mets win it!"[3]

Buckner foreshadowed the moment in an October 6 interview before playing the California Angels in the American League Championship Series: "The dreams are that you're gonna have a great series and win and the nightmares are that you're gonna let the winning run score on a ground ball through your legs. Those things happen, you know. And I think a lot of it is just fate."[4]

But Buckner does not bear sole responsibility for the loss in Game Six.

A former Met, Schiraldi came to the Red Sox with Wes Gardner, John Christensen, and La Schelle Tarver in an off-season trade for Bobby Ojeda, John Mitchell, and Chris Bayer. McNamara could have replaced him after he gave up the first single to Mitchell; Schiraldi getting tagged for three base hits in a row put the Red Sox in terrific jeopardy.

There's also the wild pitch by Stanley that allowed Mitchell to score. Plus, Mookie Wilson's speed might have gotten him safely to first base even if Buckner fielded the ball.

Buckner played far behind the bag, so it is doubtful whether he would have either beaten Wilson to it if he fielded the ball or if a toss to Stanley would have sufficed, assuming the pitcher got there in time.

Wilson labeled the chances of beating Buckner as 50-50.[5] "He was the right guy up because Buckner was a Cub, he knew all about Mookie and I know he knew Mookie was busting it," explained Hernandez. "Buckner would have been able to take his time and backhand it, or even be a little more careful. I think with Mookie running, he flinched and he knew he had to rush the bag and he had the bad ankles. It was very opportune to have Mookie up in that situation. A lot of things went our way in that game."[6]

But there's a more basic question for consideration: should the thirty-six-year-old Buckner have even been in the game? McNamara put a potentially hobbled player in the game instead of Dave Stapleton.

The day before, at least three prominent sportswriters had called attention to Buckner's plight. An article by Leigh Montville in the *Boston Globe* explained the veteran's injuries and their toll. Where some might call him dedicated, Buckner labeled himself "stubborn."[7]

Prominent baseball author and *Washington Post* writer Thomas Boswell observed, "He has had nine cortisone shots this season. The X-rays of one ankle show bone virtually against bone."[8] Hal Bock of the Associated Press addressed the "aching ankles and sore Achilles' tendon," which were evident from Buckner's running form: "not very swiftly and not very steadily, limping along like a man with eggs in his shoes trying not to break the shells."[9]

Fans noticed it, too. They made their concern known to him. After the game, Buckner responded, "I had more people bad mouth me last night than [I] had all season. I was busting my butt with two bad legs and they're telling me to take myself out of the lineup."[10]

But even the most ardent Red Sox fan might not have been fully aware of the depths of the physical stress. "He said he ices—let's see—both feet, one knee, plus the backs of his quadriceps and hamstrings before and after every game," wrote Montville. "He said he was icing an aching shoulder earlier in the year. He said he tapes everywhere. He looks like the Invisible Man, out for a walk, the way he has so much tape after most games."[11]

Buckner played in every game of the ALCS and World Series, but his offensive output was below his standard. He batted .214 and scored three runs against the Angels. Facing New York's formidable pitching, his average dipped to .188.

For the superstitious who believe in jinxes and karma, consideration can be given to Oil Can Boyd hugging McNamara prematurely with one out still to go and the Shea Stadium scoreboard displaying a congratulatory message for the Red Sox. On the tangible side, the Red Sox left fourteen runners on base.

Since that late October night in 1986, Buckner's error has set off a torrent of expletives, insults, and ill wishes directed toward the veteran first baseman and usually reserved for those who commit mortal sins against loved ones. Verbal outpourings were immediate. Red Sox fans took it personally.

But the Red Sox still had Game Seven. After their getting a 3–0 lead in the top of the second, the emotional impact of the previous night's debacle began to fade. They kept the lead through the fifth inning; New York clawed back in the bottom of the sixth to tie the game and scored three more times in the bottom of the seventh. A three-run cushion put Mets fans at ease for a bit until Boston closed the gap with a pair of runs in the top of the eighth for a 6–5 score. The Mets responded with two insurance runs in the bottom half of the inning.

Final score: 8–5.

Larry David saw opportunities for laughter in Buckner's legacy where others saw openings for derision.

David cocreated NBC's 1990s juggernaut sitcom *Seinfeld* with Jerry Seinfeld and then created *Curb Your Enthusiasm*, which first aired on HBO in 1999 as a special. Celebrities populate this fictional take on David's life. One story arc features Mel Brooks casting David to appear on Broadway in *The Producers*. Ted Danson has a recurring role as himself. Others include Michael J. Fox, Mila Kunis, Rosie O'Donnell, Richard Lewis, and Jon Hamm. The *Seinfeld* cast appears in a story line revolving around a *Seinfeld* reunion episode.

But unlike the trademark sardonicism that marks this based-on-real-life, long-running, single-camera comedy series—and, to a degree, *Seinfeld*—the 2011 *Curb* episode "Mister Softee" has a rare sentimentality.

David is spending time in New York after his divorce. During a championship softball game in Central Park, he gets distracted at first base by the music from a Mister Softee truck because of a traumatic event in his childhood. A Mister Softee driver had caught his daughter playing strip poker with David, who was naked, and chased him onto the street where people ridiculed him.

The memory causes David to miss a crucial ground ball and lose the game.

He later goes to a baseball memorabilia show at the Loews Regency Hotel to get an autographed baseball from Mookie Wilson. It's a request from Susie Green for her husband's birthday gift; Jeff Green is David's best friend, manager, and sometimes coconspirator in covering up embarrassing moments. Wilson is his favorite player.

When David spots Buckner at a table next to Wilson's, he tells the ex-ballplayer about what happened and befriends him. Buckner graciously offers to get Wilson's autograph so David does not have to wait on line. Immediately after leaving the memorabilia show, David sees what Buckner endures, even twenty-five years after the error!

Heckled outside, Buckner ignores it with grace. Then, a gentleman approaches the duo and asks if either man is Jewish. His family needs a tenth man to complete a minyan. David, a Jew, explains to his new pal that when a Jewish person dies, custom requires a group of ten Jewish men to gather and say the Kaddish, a prayer for the dead. It takes place at a shiva call, a Jewish custom in which family and friends visit the mourners' home to offer condolences. Shiva is the period of mourning after a Jewish person dies, typically lasting a week.

David is Jewish, but Buckner is not. The gentleman offers free lunch to both; Jewish delicatessen food is a shiva staple. When they get upstairs, a mourner demands that Buckner leave the apartment. Immediately. He's a Red Sox fan who has not let the Game Six incident diminish in importance.

David parallels the Game Six gaffe when they go to deliver the Wilson-autographed ball to the Greens' apartment. He plays keep-away by tossing the ball to Buckner, who fails to catch it. And so, Jeff's spherical birthday gift with the moniker of his favorite player inscribed upon it goes out the window and onto the street. Susie, in her usual angry manner, chides Buckner, who claims it was "a horseshit throw." David contends that it was "a good throw."

At the end of the episode, an apartment building fire forces a woman to toss her baby toward the tarp that the firemen are holding. The baby bounces off it and Buckner, using his baseball skills, eyes the baby's arc and races to catch it before it hits the ground. He makes a diving catch, igniting applause from the crowd that had gathered. The firemen hoist Buckner on their shoulders; he receives and gives high fives to his admirers. It's quite a moment.

In a 2017 interview on *The Rich Eisen Show*, David admitted that Buckner—whom he labels "one of the great guys that I've ever met"—was a more difficult guest star to get for *Curb Your Enthusiasm* than Salman Rushdie. "I was very nervous about that call because I was so desperate to do that show," revealed David. "I love that episode."

But there was a sweetener.

"He didn't want to do it at first. I really had to stay on the phone with him and he had to think about it and then I had to send it to him to read. And then, his daughter was an actress. And I said, 'Well, we can put your daughter on the show, too.' His daughter's a good actress. She was in Los Angeles. And I think when I offered that . . ."

"The quid pro quo," said Eisen.

"The quid pro quo," confirmed David.[12]

To integrate a redemption story around Buckner and make him a sympathetic figure, David uses the highest of high-stakes possibilities for lifting him past the error that Red Sox fans have ranked on par with iconic Boston crimes like the Great Brinks Robbery, Charles Ponzi's financial schemes, and the unsolved art theft from the Isabella Stewart Gardner Museum.

Buckner's appearance as himself is logical within the story line that David constructed.

David and Seinfeld had utilized athletes throughout the nine-year run of *Seinfeld*. Paul O'Neill, Danny Tartabull, Derek Jeter, and Bernie Williams appear as themselves during episodes featuring George Costanza in his job as assistant to the traveling secretary of the New York Yankees.

Plus, *Seinfeld* featured an abundance of dialogue referencing sports figures, including Patrick Ewing, Michael Jordan, Joe DiMaggio, and Jay Buhner. In one episode, Kramer recounts a fracas between campers and the old-time Yankees—notably Moose Skowron and Mickey Mantle—at a Yankees fantasy camp that began when he hit Joe Pepitone with a pitch.

Scenes took place in the seats at Giants Stadium and Madison Square Garden. But they were actually shot on soundstages.

On *Curb Your Enthusiasm*, David has also incorporated sports. Shaquille O'Neal and Muggsy Bogues have had cameos. Scenes have been shot at Dodger Stadium. David's Pepitone jersey is mentioned in an episode revolving around David and his gorgeous, flirtatious dry cleaner, played by Gina Gershon.

The Buckner appearance and these examples fit nicely into the larger context of athletes portraying themselves, a device of verisimilitude that has been a touchstone of Hollywood storytelling ever since the silent film era, when Babe Ruth appeared in *Speedy* with Harold Lloyd.

Comedian and actor Robert Wuhl created and starred in HBO's *Arliss*, which ran from 1996 to 2002, focusing on the travails and triumphs of a sports agent. The theme song was The Four Tops's "I Can't Help Myself" for the first season and Dusty Springfield's "I Only Want to Be with You" for the remaining five seasons, all set against a montage of Wuhl in character interacting with athletes. The roster of cameos from the sports world includes Dan Marino, Dave Winfield, Jerry Jones, Tony Siragusa, and Bob Costas. Almost always, the main guest star plays a fictional character. In one episode, Ed Asner portrays a baseball announcer showing signs of Alzheimer's.

The Brady Bunch aired on ABC from 1969 to 1974. In the second-season premiere, Dodgers legend Don Drysdale appears as a client of patriarch Mike Brady, an architect. Mike often works out of the Brady abode at 4222 Clinton Way in an unnamed part of the Greater Los Angeles area, which gives a platform for the ex-pitcher, who had retired in 1969, to meet in Mike's home office and go over the plans for his new house. His visit offers an opening for the Brady boys—Greg, Peter, and Bobby—to meet one of their sports idols.

Greg, a Pony League pitcher, idolizes Drysdale, setting up the episode's story of Greg having visions of baseball splendor only to have them trampled when he gets butchered during a game.

Although the Bradys' location is never explained on the show, it's apparent that they live in LA. In addition to Drysdale, Dodgers first baseman Wes Parker and Rams defensive end Deacon Jones appear in other episodes. Lakers icon Jerry West is referenced in one scene. Another piece of evidence is the three-episode story set in Hawaii to kick off the fourth season. The hot spots for surfing in America are predominantly in Hawaii and Southern California. Greg looks forward to bringing his surfing skills to the fiftieth state but wipes out in a nearly fatal accident.

When FOX got the NFC package in 1994, it hired former Raiders defensive end Howie Long as a panelist on the pregame show *NFL on FOX*. The network—which had only existed since 1986—quickly used prime time as a billboard to promote its new acquisition. Long had a cameo as himself on the 1994–95 season premiere of *Beverly Hills 90210*.

Two-time Super Bowl MVP Terry Bradshaw guest-starred as himself on a 1995 episode of *Married with Children*, a blockbuster sitcom for FOX. In the story, the former Pittsburgh Steelers quarterback is an alumnus of Al Bundy's alma mater, Polk High School, albeit for two months. When Al learns that the bank employing his nemesis and neighbor, Marcy D'Arcy, will sponsor a new scoreboard, he thinks that it will be named after him because he scored four touchdowns in one game. Despite his brief Polk High tenure, Bradshaw is the more famous name that Marcy wants.

Evening Shade, a CBS sitcom from 1990 to 1994, starred Burt Reynolds as Wood Newton, a former Pittsburgh Steelers quarterback and high school football coach in Evening Shade, Arkansas. It's explained that he had a rivalry with Bradshaw, who played for the Steelers from 1970 to 1983. Bradshaw plays himself in an episode.

ABC sportscaster Howard Cosell appears as himself twice on the television version of *The Odd Couple* that aired from 1970 to 1975.[13] Deacon Jones, Bob Hope, and Bubba Smith have cameos as themselves in other episodes, while Garo Yepremian and Alex Karras have roles as fictional football players. Cosell's inclusions in the show about divorced roommates—*New York Herald* sportswriter Oscar Madison and photographer Felix Unger—are perfect examples of verisimilitude. It made sense that Oscar would know the bombastic announcer and share a print-versus-television friction with him.

Bobby Riggs guest-stars on an episode centering on his friendship and wagering with Oscar, whose gambling was a hallmark throughout the show. Billie Jean King made a cameo—the Battle of the Sexes opponents played Ping Pong.

But rarely does a show incorporate a real-life event, either in dialogue or story, to the extent that David did with Buckner in *Curb Your Enthusiasm*. Buckner had broken into the Majors at the age of nineteen, playing one game with the Dodgers in 1969. He stayed in Los Angeles until 1977, when he began his stint with the Cubs. That ended in a May 1984 trade with the Red Sox. He got released on July 23, 1987, and joined the California Angels less than a week later.

Buckner's stay with the Angels ended with his release on May 9, 1988. Again he found work quickly. The Kansas City Royals signed him four days later; Buckner played in seventy-nine games and hit .216 in 1989. Although he became a free agent after the season, he returned to Kansas City but joined the Red Sox during spring training.

On May 30, 1990, Buckner played in his last game in the Major Leagues. He went one-for-four in a 4–3 loss to the Texas Rangers; Boston released him on June 5.

Buckner returned to Fenway Park in 2008, a few months after the Red Sox captured their second World Series title in the twenty-first century. He threw out the first pitch to inaugurate the first of eighty-one regular-season games in the Boston ballyard. It was a cleansing, of sorts. Bostonians might have felt that the wounds of '86 had been bandaged and bound by the World Series titles in 2004 and 2007.

But Buckner felt betrayed by the aftermath of his error and the World Series loss. "I really had to forgive, not the fans of Boston, per se, but I would have to say in my heart I had to forgive the media," revealed the usually stoic Buckner. "For what they put me and my family through. So, you know, I've done that and I'm over that."[14]

Dwight Evans, his battery mate on this auspicious occasion, praised the man who suffered grand but misplaced ignominy. "No one played harder than Bill. No one prepared themselves as well as Bill Buckner did, and no one wanted to win as much as Bill Buckner."[15]

In some quarters of Red Sox Nation, ignoramuses had targeted the Buckner family with anger writ large. No one was exempt. Buckner's wife, Jody, disclosed a bone-chilling story about people talking to their four-year-old son at his preschool. "They said, 'Your daddy had to quit baseball because he missed the ball.'"[16]

The Buckners moved to a ranch outside Boise, Idaho, in 1993. Fans thirsty to commemorate Game Six could find Buckner and Wilson at appearances like the one depicted in *Curb Your Enthusiasm*. Though appearing at such events was lucrative, Buckner did not initially take to the idea. "It took a long time for me to kind of decide whether I want to do that or not," he revealed. "And then, the more I thought about it, I thought, well, taking a lot of heat over this. Might as well get something out of it. I had no idea that I'd put all my kids through college just by signing pictures."[17]

Buckner was also a hitting instructor with the Blue Jays, hitting coach with the White Sox, manager with the Brockton Rox in the Canadian American Association of Professional Baseball, and hitting coach with the Chicago Cubs.[18]

Suffering from Lewy body dementia, Buckner died on May 27, 2019, at the age of sixty-nine. Obituaries referenced the Game Six error in the first paragraph, causing him to be remembered primarily for an unfortunate mistake rather than a productive career.

But fans of David's work undoubtedly recalled the *Curb Your Enthusiasm* episode upon learning that Buckner had passed away. David gave him a touch of glory complemented by humor and grace. "It made me cry a little bit, when he caught the baby," said David in the Eisen interview.[19] Even though it's fiction, the redemptive story ought to be mentioned in tandem with the error. It ranks with other great combinations. The Kennedys and Hyannisport. Lobster and butter. Bill Buckner and *Curb Your Enthusiasm*.

"You know, there were a lot of players that were better than me," said Buckner in 2011. "A lot of people would have trouble remembering their names. But everybody still remembers me."[20]

Hopefully, the *Curb Your Enthusiasm* appearance inspires people to do so with admiration for his career, consistency, and character rather than disdain for his mishap in a moment.

PART 4

Heartbreaks and Happiness

10

Hope for Tomorrow

American Optimism, Cultural Revolutions, and Game Six of the 1975 World Series

New England's sports fans of a certain age recall 1975 with winces, not winks.

The pain is as real decades hence as it was when a disappointment set off an emotional squall, making them feel robbed of something precious, something substantial that didn't seem possible to belong to anyone but them.

Phil Esposito had been traded to the New York Rangers.

Esposito was hockey incarnate, signing with the Chicago Blackhawks at the age of eighteen in 1960 and playing in their minor league system until the middle of the 1963–64 season, when he first appeared in a Blackhawks uniform. In 1967 Chicago traded Esposito, Fred Stanfield, and Ken Hodge to the Boston Bruins for Jean Gilles Marotte, Pat Martin, and Jack Norris.

In six of his eight full seasons with Boston, Esposito led the NHL's East Division in goals scored. He topped his peers in points scored five times, assists three times, and game-winning goals three times.

Not since Harry Frazee sold Babe Ruth to the New York Yankees had Boston's sports fans felt such a void when the standout—an All-Star every year he played for the Bruins, including the season that he was traded—went to New York along with Carol Vadnais for Brad Park, Jean Ratelle, and Joe Zanussi. It happened on November 7, 1975. Like those who embraced his hard-nosed, competitive streak, Esposito could not make sense of the deal. "I'm crushed," said New York's newest acquisition. "I thought I had found a home in Boston."[1]

Further enhancing the shock was the blindsided way that he learned about the trade.

There was no discussion, no forewarning when Esposito got a phone call in his hotel room during a road trip to play the Vancouver Canucks. The two Stanley Cups during his time with the Bruins had seemingly been forgotten, like a fan's spilled beer at the Boston Garden when celebrating a goal. "I thought that [Bruins head coach] Harry Sinden would at least have the decency to tell me beforehand," revealed Esposito. "I think they could have told me another way."[2]

Leigh Montville described him based on the attitudes of those Bruins fans who never fully appreciated the star. "One difference already has surfaced here," wrote Montville. "The people—the same people who were cold toward Esposito and his records now seem worried. They see a big hole in the scoring totals. They see a lot of goals that aren't going to be scored. They see a lot of things that might not be done.

"That's the way it is with a garbageman. You never miss him until he's not around."[3]

Esposito's exit was the second part of a one-two punch for Boston's sports fans in 1975. The first was the World Series, an epic seven-game contest that the Red Sox lost to the Cincinnati Reds.

Often labeled as the best baseball game ever played, Game Six exemplifies baseball's unpredictability, excitement, and possibility. Cincinnati led three games to two. Carlton Fisk's game-winning home run in the bottom of the twelfth inning has become hallmark footage in TV documentaries, interviews, and news segments about the history of the Red Sox. And for good reason. It's the image of Fisk that endures from the NBC broadcast of his jumping that would make Jack LaLanne proud as he waves his arms to plead for the ball to stay on the right side of the left-field foul pole.

Since losing to the Cardinals in the 1967 World Series, the Red Sox had stagnated in the second division beginning with a drop to fourth place in 1968. The addition of four teams in 1969 created the American League East and West divisions. Boston placed either second or third in the AL East every season before 1975.

Fenway Park reverberated with cheers as the Red Sox began Game Six by vaulting to a three-run lead in the bottom of the first. With two outs,

Carl Yastrzemski and Carlton Fisk hit back-to-back singles followed by Fred Lynn's home run.

Reds manager Sparky Anderson pulled starting pitcher Gary Nolan—who went 15-9 in the regular season—in the top of the third after César Gerónimo struck out. Darrel Chaney pinch-hit, but the .219-hitting infielder banged a fly ball to Yaz in left field for the second out. A thorn in the side of Boston's pitching staff, Pete Rose, who played in all seven games and batted .370 in the World Series, kept Cincinnati alive with a single. But Ken Griffey's ground ball to Luis Tiant ended the visiting team's chances.

In the bottom of the third, southpaw Fred Norman became the second of nine Reds pitchers used in Game Six. Denny Doyle, who hit safely in all seven games of the World Series, smacked a one-out double. Yaz's pop fly to second baseman Joe Morgan was the second out. Norman avoided facing Fisk, a perennial slugger from the left side of home plate, by giving him an intentional walk. Lynn, a right-handed batter, drew a walk to load the bases. Anderson called on righty Jack Billingham to face Rico Petrocelli, also a right-handed batter; Petrocelli struck out.

Boston had another scoring chance with a lead-off, ground-rule double by Dwight Evans in the bottom of the fourth. Billingham walked Rick Burleson. Tiant's sacrifice bunt went over the head of a charging Tony Pérez; Cincinnati's first baseman recovered and tossed to Morgan, though the ploy advanced the Red Sox ninety feet closer to getting an insurance run or two. But Burleson and Evans stayed on second and third as Cecil Cooper grounded out to his first-base counterpart Pérez for an unassisted play, and Doyle's grounder to Morgan concluded the effort.

Cincinnati tied the game at 3-3 in the top of the fifth. Tiant—he of the corkscrew-like windup—walked Ed Armbrister, and Rose got his second hit of the night. With his teammates at the corners, Griffey bashed a triple to score them. Fenway Park was as silent as the Essex County morgue when Lynn crashed into the concrete wall at the 379-foot mark after trying to make a leaping catch. More than thirty-five thousand fans stood at attention, waiting for a sign of movement from the outfielder crumpled on the warning track.

Lynn stayed on the ground for about ninety seconds as teammates and coaches tended to him; then he got up and stretched. He stayed in the lineup for the remainder of the game. "It's hard to watch," said the 1975 American League Rookie of the Year as the footage played in a 2011 interview for MLB Network's *MLB's 20 Greatest Games*, which ranked Game Six at No. 1. "In fact, I didn't watch it for many many years. Everybody thought I was knocked out at this point. In reality, what happened is you'll see me come to the wall right here and I turn at the last second and I hit it with my backside.

"And when I went down, I had absolutely no feeling from the waist down. So, I thought I had either cracked my back, broken my back. I didn't know what was going on. I had no feeling. So, I just lay motionless. I was very alert. I knew what was going on. I listened to my teammates around me and when the trainer came out, I was fully conscious. But I took quite a whack. There's no question. There was no padding in those days. It was concrete."[4]

Lynn had once made a racing catch on a Griffey fly ball to deep center in Game Four at Riverfront Stadium, but the wall there was about twenty feet farther.

After the scare about Lynn's well-being moderated, Joe Morgan made the second out with a pop-up to third baseman Petrocelli. Johnny Bench, who had struck out twice earlier in the game, singled home Griffey for the third run with a bash off the Green Monster; Tiant struck out Pérez to cap the Big Red Machine's rally.

Two innings later, the Reds added a two-run cushion. It began with Griffey and Morgan standing on second and first after successive singles. They remained when Bench flied out to Yaz, but Griffey moved to third on Pérez's flyout to Evans in right field. George Foster's double scored both runners to make the score 5–3.

Gerónimo's lead-off home run gave the Reds an insurance run in the top of the eighth; Roger Moret replaced Tiant on the mound.

Red Sox fans were forlorn, but not for long. The bottom of the eighth has a sequence that Boston fans cherish as deeply as Norm Peterson does his corner bar stool and a draft beer on *Cheers*.

Pedro Borbón, the fifth Reds pitcher of the game, gave up an infield single to Lynn—the ball hit Borbón's right foot—and walked Petrocelli. Rawly Eastwick—the National League's leading fireman with twenty-two saves in 1975, his first full year in the Majors—replaced his bullpen mate, struck out Evans, and retired Burleson on a line drive to Griffey in left. All seemed calmer for the Reds. That changed with one swing.

Red Sox skipper Darrell Johnson, who showed about as much emotion as Joe Friday when asking a witness to just state the facts, sent in Bernie Carbo to pinch-hit for Moret. Carbo, who batted .257 with 15 home runs across 107 games in 1975, worked Eastwick to a 2-2 count. "Then we made a fat pitch right down the middle and he (Carbo) unloaded on it," said Bench, the Reds' star catcher.[5]

Boston was poised to break the 6-6 tie an inning later when Doyle led off with a walk and Yastrzemski moved him to third with a single. Anderson called upon Will McEnaney, a sophomore Major Leaguer with seventy games and fifteen saves that season. McEnaney walked Fisk intentionally, causing the Ohio Valley's baseball fans to imagine the next batter grounding into a bases-loaded double play, including cutting Doyle off at the plate. Maybe even a triple play.

But the opposition was formidable.

McEnaney faced rookie sensation Lynn boasting a slugging percentage that led both leagues, in addition to the second-highest batting average in the American League. New Englanders smiled in anticipation. It lasted about as long as it takes a Boston College senior to chug a beer. Foster snared Lynn's fly ball and heaved it to Bench, who tagged out Doyle; Rose fielded Petrocelli's ground ball for the third out.

Pat Darcy, a rookie who started twenty-two games and went 11-5 during the season, took over pitching for the visitors in the bottom of the tenth and retired the Red Sox three up, three down. In the top of the eleventh, Boston's devotees stood on the verge of more disappointment, lending further credence to the curse of Babe Ruth. They suffered in Suffolk. They brooded in Brookline. They deliberated in Dorchester.

Red Sox reliever Dick Drago began the inning by hitting Rose with a pitch. Griffey, a .305 hitter in '75, bunted to move Rose over to second. Fisk fielded it and fired to shortstop Burleson to nail Rose at second; Griffey got to first base safely.

In right field, Evans calculated defensive strategies against Morgan, the NL MVP and MLB leader in slugging percentage. He knew that if Morgan smacked a base hit in the gap between center and right, he'd need to cut it off and throw to the relay man, who would turn and throw to Fisk and prevent Griffey from scoring. But a hard-hit baseball directly in Evans's path might allow the outfielder to get Griffey at third base.

Morgan smacked a ball toward the right-field stands, separated from the warning track by a stomach-high wall. It looked for sure like the Reds would go ahead 8–6. Evans tracked the ball as best he could under the Fenway Park lights, but he lost it. "He hits it over my head so I turn towards the line because the ball normally turns towards the line, too," explained the right fielder. "Well, this particular ball didn't turn. This ball stayed straight. And you ask any player, when you lose a ball, that's a scary situation. And so, no one was more surprised than me. And I jumped and my glove went behind my head and the ball landed in my glove."[6]

An off-target throw headed toward the first-base coaching box. Yastrzemski fielded it on one hop and tossed to the quick-thinking Burleson, who had hustled from his shortstop position to take the throw and double up Griffey, who had already turned second base when Evans caught the ball.

There had been other fantastic plays in the field during previous Fall Classics.

In the 1947 Yankees-Dodgers World Series, the first of many matchups between the two Goliaths in the years after World War II, Al Gionfriddo's catch in left field caused the usually reserved Joe DiMaggio to kick the dirt.

Sandy Amorós sprinted like he had a rocket strapped to his back in Game Seven of the 1955 World Series and caught Yogi Berra's fly ball—sure to fall in fair territory—for a double. He made a bull's-eye throw to Dodgers shortstop Pee Wee Reese, who whirled and hurled to Gil Hodges to double off Gil McDougald at first base. Amorós's play gave Johnny Podres some breathing room as he tossed a 2–0, complete-game victory for the Dodgers' defeat of the Yankees and their only World Series title in Brooklyn.

Willie Mays's over-the-shoulder catch of a Vic Wertz fly ball—with his back facing home plate—in the 1954 Giants-Indians World Series underscores the legend of the Say Hey Kid.

Yankees icon Mickey Mantle preserved Don Larsen's perfect game in 1956 with a running catch of a ball hit squarely by Hodges to the imaginary plane between center field and right field. Dodgers outfielder Duke Snider also had a great defensive play with a diving catch of Berra's "hard, low line drive into left center field." But Snider's diving snare has been overshadowed because of the prominence of Larsen's feat and Mantle's protection of it.[7]

Ron Swoboda's diving catch of a Brooks Robinson fly ball in the 1969 Mets-Orioles World Series prompted the Mets outfielder to title his memoir *Here's the Catch.*

Those were feats of defensive excellence combining physical prowess with split-second timing. But a World Series didn't hang in the balance. At least not definitively.

Amorós's catch happened in the sixth inning with the Dodgers leading 2–0 and two Yankees on base—Billy Martin at second and McDougald at first. Even if the ball dropped fair and Martin scored, McDougald would probably have stopped at second base. Even if the Yankees tied, there were at least three more innings for the Dodgers to score runs.

The Red Sox didn't have that luxury. Evans's extra-innings grab was a crucial point in the game, causing the fans to temporarily stop worrying about Cincinnati's offense and focus on the Boston batsmen. The top of the order headed to the plate with the hopes of the Fenway Faithful upon them. Alas, they went three up, three down.

New Englanders' hearts beat faster again in the top of the twelfth, when Pérez and Foster hit back-to-back singles off reliever Rick Wise with one out. Wise then retired Dave Concepción on a fly ball to Evans and struck out Gerónimo looking.

Red Sox fans stifled yawns and steadied nerves as Fisk—Boston's cleanup hitter with a .331 average across seventy-nine games during the season—stepped into the batter's box in the bottom of the twelfth. It was just a few minutes after 12:30 a.m. when the six-foot-two, 215-pound slugger faced right-hander Darcy, the eighth hurler for the NL champs that night. He had retired six consecutive Red Sox batters.

Bam!

Into the sky went the baseball, seeming almost as if it were suspended, then dallying before deciding whether to be called fair or foul. Although only a few seconds passed before the ball hit the left-field foul pole's mesh, it felt like an hour. Hope abounded. Fisk's leaps, combined with pushing his arms to the right as if he could communicate with the ball, reflected what every Red Sox fan was also doing either mentally or in mimicry.

Bars and taverns across Boston filled with the sounds of celebration as the patrons raised a glass of Narragansett or whatever they chose to imbibe and ordered another round for good measure. Businessmen who stayed up late to watch the game despite an early morning meeting felt justified and sated by their choice. Same for college students who had an 8:00 a.m. class.

Darcy explained, "I tried to overthrow the ball. The pitch was low, but Fisk went down and got it."[8]

Besides keeping the Red Sox afloat for a seventh game, which they lost 4-3, Fisk's home run has terrific cultural significance. TV audiences would never have seen Fisk behaving like a member of the ground crew at Logan International Airport had it not been for a tale that has grown from a footnote to folklore.

Harry Coyle, a TV producer with street cred dating back to DiMaggio's fly ball and aborted extra-base hit snared by Gionfriddo, went ahead with the plan of camera operator Lou Gerard. Instead of tracking a hit ball in flight, Gerard suggested focusing on Fisk from his vantage point in the Fenway Park scoreboard because of two distractions: "a rat on my leg that's as big as a cat" and "a piece of metal" obstructing him on the right.[9]

NBC did not invent the "reaction" shot. ABC's Monday Night Football had premiered in 1970 with groundbreaking techniques like broadcasting reactions after a play, score, or sequence as a regular part of game coverage. But the Fisk footage was a defining moment, especially for baseball.

It was a symbol of hope, too.

Optimism was scarce in 1975 given the state of the country's psyche, reeling from recent events, including America's involvement in the Vietnam War ending with no clear outcome and more than fifty thousand service members dead; Richard Nixon becoming the first American president to resign; several presidential aides going to prison because of the Watergate scandal; the Dow Jones Industrial Average beginning the year 26 percent lower than it began 1974; and inflation, hovering around the low double digits.

In New York City, the *Daily News* ran the infamous headline "Ford to City: Drop Dead," summarizing the federal government's refusal to help the Big Apple escape bankruptcy. Boston dealt with the controversial busing program that led to riots and violence. Hollywood reflected the aura of cynicism with an outstanding roster of films, including *The Taking of Pelham 1-2-3*, *Three Days of the Condor*, *Dog Day Afternoon*, *Prisoner of Second Avenue*, *Shampoo*, *Report to the Commissioner*, and *Rollerball*.

But optimism was not completely absent. Like Fisk's homer penetrating the postmidnight air on a vector toward the foul pole at Fenway Park, America found glimmers of hope and faith through the clouds of gloom and pessimism. There were cultural breakthroughs that gave Americans a smidgen of much-needed assurance as the dawn preceding the following year's Bicentennial began to break.

Bruce Springsteen and the E Street Band released *Born to Run*, elevating the New Jersey native to the apex of rock and roll. The Superdome in New Orleans debuted. ABC's *Good Morning America*, too. The Apollo-Soyuz mission joined astronauts and cosmonauts in space, giving hope to sustained peaceful relations between the United States and the Soviet Union in the name of science during the Cold War. NASA's Viking 1 and Viking 2 spacecrafts launched, each with an orbiter and lander heading for Mars. The landers touched down in 1976 and sent back thousands of images.

Four talent agents left the William Morris Agency to form their own shop—Creative Artists Agency. It was a bold move to some in show business, foolish to others. Abandoning the entertainment Goliath meant leaving behind the cachet that came with it. William Morris had represented superstars ever since its inception at the end of the nineteenth century. Frank Sinatra. Marilyn Monroe. Paul Newman. CAA built its own clientele, image, and strength.

One of CAA's most famous efforts was cofounder Michael Ovitz representing David Letterman when the star of NBC's *Late Night* wanted to leave after getting passed over to succeed Johnny Carson as host of *The Tonight Show* in 1992. It culminated in the Indiana-born comedian breaking ties with NBC to begin a new franchise called *Late Show with David Letterman* for CBS at 11:30 p.m. the following year.

Steven Spielberg, then in his midtwenties, created the summer blockbuster genre with his first major film; it launched him into the higher ranks of Hollywood directors. Based on the novel of the same name by Peter Benchley, *Jaws* discarded the novel's subplot of oceanographer and shark expert Matt Hooper having a sexual encounter with the wife of Amity police chief Martin Brody, instead concentrating on a classic three-act structure: shark scares beachgoers, Brody gets together a crew, the shark is killed.

Looking at any of these examples might prompt admiration, respect, envy, or a combination therein from competitors. The people who made them happen could be labeled as ambitious, starry-eyed, or visionary. But their successes stirred the same feeling of hope in their universes that happened throughout Red Sox Nation with Carbo's home run, Evans's catch, and Fisk's game-winning clout.

The 1975 Boston Red Sox also mirrored a cultural icon of the era who gained the affection of Americans. Both were scrappy. Both were determined. Both were valiant though unsuccessful underdogs in their pursuits to be atop their fields.

Rocky Balboa. The Italian Stallion.

The 1976 film *Rocky* charts a club fighter with great potential but no discipline getting a chance to fight the heavyweight champion of the world. Apollo Creed is Muhammad Ali by way of P. T. Barnum.

Taking place between Thanksgiving Week of 1975 and New Year's Day—described by Creed as "the country's biggest birthday" because of the Bicentennial—*Rocky* showcases an underdog who only wants to "go the distance" with Creed because no fighter has ever gone fifteen rounds with him. Creed selects Balboa because the initial contender suffered an injury during training that prevents him from going through with the title bout. Giving the obscure pug a chance will be a great promotional device and a surefire victory. Or so Creed thinks.

Balboa does not win but achieves his goal of standing toe to toe with the best fighter in the world for fifteen rounds.

Rich with location shots in Philadelphia, *Rocky* earned Stallone an Oscar for the screenplay, leading-man status in Hollywood, and plaudits from the critics. "'Rocky' is a movie that convincingly exudes a quality that has enjoyed a conspicuous absence from recent cinema, namely hope, optimism and a belief in the power of individual will and determination," wrote movie critic Desmond Ryan in the *Philadelphia Inquirer*.[10]

Red Sox fans know that power all too well. At 12:34 a.m. on October 23, 1975, they lived it.

11

Out of Sight, Baby

The Sixties and the Sox

1960.

The outlook wasn't brilliant for the Boston Red Sox that year.

Or the next one.

Or the next five thereafter.

For the first seven years of the 1960s—and the last two of the 1950s—the fan base endured sub-.500 records, a trend reversed in 1967, which began a string of fourteen winning seasons. An unquestionable factor in the disappointing records was the lack of minority talent on the rosters due to shortsightedness, bigotry, or both. Jackie Robinson had broken baseball's color line in the modern era with the Brooklyn Dodgers in 1947, but it took twelve more years for the Red Sox to follow suit and expand the possibilities for their roster. They were the last MLB team to integrate; Pumpsie Green played his first Major League game on July 21, 1959.

Culturally, America went through seismic shifts.

The formation of NATO, Disneyland's opening, Boeing's first jetliner, NBC's peacock logo, the first color TV broadcasts, IBM's hard disk drive, and the space age all began between the Robinson and Green debuts. The Supreme Court's decision in *Brown v. Board of Education of Topeka* struck down segregation in schools. There were forty-eight states in 1947. Alaska got added to the roster at the beginning of 1959, six months before Green's first game. Hawaii, a month after it.

Migration disrupted long-standing ties between teams and cities once thought unbreakable. Philadelphia lost the Athletics to Kansas City. The Giants left Upper Manhattan and settled in San Francisco; Brooklyn's love affair with the Dodgers ended when team owner Walter O'Malley moved the beloved squad to Los Angeles.

Boston bid farewell to the Braves, a city-team link dating back to 1871.

Against this backdrop of change, the Red Sox became New England's sole Major League outlet. But the national pastime had terrific company in the 1960s. Being a four-team city—Red Sox in summer, Patriots in fall, Bruins in winter, Celtics in spring—is a boon for the area's sports fans.

The Bruins went through a drought similar to what the Red Sox experienced in the 1960s, never tallying more than twenty-one wins in a seventy-game season from 1960 to 1967. In the 1967–68 campaign, they turned around with a 37-27-10 record and a playoff berth against the Montreal Canadiens. Montreal won the quarterfinals, but Boston rallied the following year and went to the semifinals, only to lose to Montreal again. In the 1969–70 season, the Bruins were the Stanley Cup champions.

Boston's basketball fans got more succor. Much more. From the 1956–57 to 1968–69 seasons, the Celtics went to the NBA finals thirteen straight times and lost only twice. The St. Louis Hawks won in 1957. Ten years later, the Philadelphia 76ers captured the title.

For professional sports in Boston, 1967 was a banner year indeed. Besides the Bruins skating on a path of prosperity and the Celtics beginning their rebound for another championship after losing to Philadelphia, the Red Sox topped the American League. It was not, by any means, easily achieved. Using the unofficial standard of whatever team is in first place on July 4 being likely to remain there, Boston's outlook wasn't terribly good.

July 4—Anaheim Stadium

As fireworks lit up New England's skies, the Red Sox were within striking distance of where they wanted to be. The Chicago White Sox led the American League, followed by the Minnesota Twins and Detroit Tigers at three games and three and a half games behind, respectively. Boston trailed in fourth place by four and a half games.

Earlier that day, the Red Sox had a nice rally against the Angels. With the Bosox trailing 4-1 going into the bottom of the ninth, Jerry Adair led off with a single and Reggie Smith doubled. Red Sox manager Dick Williams sent Ken Poulsen to pinch-hit for Sparky Lyle; Poulsen struck out. But Russ Gibson's grounder to Angels second baseman Bobby Knoop scored Adair and allowed Smith to move to third base. Mike Andrews singled him home to make the score 4-3. Unfortunately, Joe Foy's whiff ended the effort.

August 18—Fenway Park

Red Sox fans were in a stupor after Tony Conigliaro got knocked down by a Jack Hamilton pitch in the fourth inning of another home game against the Angels. The ball broke Conigliaro's cheekbone, causing the left eye to shut, with a black-and-blue mark around it in addition to "a severe nose hemorrhage and scalp cuts and swelling."[1]

Hamilton blamed Conigliaro's batting stance while pointing out it was the first time that he had struck a batter in the '67 season. "I was just trying to get the ball over," said the right-hander, who had come to the Angels in a June trade with the Mets for southpaw Nick Willhite. "Tony stands right on top of the plate." In contrast, Conigliaro recounted, "I had no chance of getting out of the way of the pitch."[2]

The score had been tied at 0-0 when Conigliaro got beaned, with two outs. José Tartabull ran for Conigliaro and scored on Rico Petrocelli's triple to center field, where José Cardenal nearly caught the ball but couldn't quite keep it in his glove. When he fired to cutoff man Jim Fregosi, it looked like Petrocelli would stay at third, but Fregosi's throw to Angels backstop Bob "Buck" Rodgers was off target, giving an error to the shortstop and allowing Petrocelli to score. He crossed the plate again in the bottom of the sixth on a single by Red Sox pitcher Gary Bell. Boston won 3-2.

August 19—Fenway Park

While Conigliaro recuperated in Cambridge's Sancta Maria Hospital, treated by a team led by Dr. Joseph Dorsey, his medical condition dominated the thoughts and prayers of Bostonians and their fellow New Englanders.

The Red Sox suited up for an afternoon game marked by a fluke play, a ninth-inning rally by the visitors, and Yaz's exemplary performance. It was a victory that almost became a loss. Leading the Angels 7-6 when the bottom of the seventh began, the home team soon expanded their shield with another three runs.

After Reggie Smith's ground ball to Knoop, Petrocelli singled and went to third base on Elston Howard's double. Minnie Rojas gave Mike

Andrews an intentional walk to set up a double play, Williams substituted Norm Siebern for John Wyatt, and the pinch hitter cleared the bases with a triple for a 10–6 score.

It was one of two triples in 1967 for Siebern, a recent import from San Francisco signed in mid-July on waivers and appearing in thirty-three games for the Red Sox in the Cinderella season.[3]

Angels left fielder Rick Reichardt had a terrific day, going two-for-four with three RBIs and a run scored. His solo homer in the top of the eighth made the score 10–7. The Red Sox tacked on two more runs in bottom of the eighth. Yaz led off with a double, his fourth hit in a four-for-five outing, followed by George Scott and Reggie Smith hitting back-to-back singles to load the bases. After Petrocelli got out, Howard's sacrifice fly scored Yaz and Scott.

When Yastrzemski collided with Rodgers at home plate, the Angels backstop lost the ball and his glove. Bill Kelso, a stalwart reliever, backed up his battery mate, retrieved the ball about twenty-five feet from home plate, and threw to Rodgers, who had only a golf glove for protection. Scott slid; a repeat happened with the ball.

With the scoreboard reading 12–7, a five-run lead seemed comfortable. It wasn't the case. The Angels notched four runs in the top of the ninth.

Knoop walked and scored when Yastrzemski made a rare fielding error on Johnny Werhas's single. Roger Repoz and Jimmie Hall each went yard with solo bashes. Jerry Stephenson, Boston's sixth hurler of the game, plunked Reichardt and gave up a single to Moose Skowron, poising the visitors for a victory with runners at the corners. Or at least a tie to send the game into extra innings. But Rodgers's grounder to second baseman Andrews secured the victory.

Boston Herald Traveler scribe Henry McKenna aptly described Boston's 12–11 win, which ended with seventeen hits for the Red Sox and twelve hits for the Angels, as "a real daffy afternoon of baseball."[4]

August 27—Comiskey Park

The Red Sox won the first game of a doubleheader at Comiskey Park 4–3; Yastrzemski clocked two home runs and notched two RBIs. But Chicago squeaked out a 1–0 victory in the second game, an eleven-inning battle.

It was not a glamorous event.

In the bottom of the eleventh, Bucky Brandon began by walking Duane Josephson. Ron Hansen's sacrifice bunt moved him to second; Brandon intentionally walked Smoky Burgess, whom White Sox skipper Eddie Stanky then replaced with pinch runner Joe Horlen. Josephson and Horlen advanced on a wild pitch.

Ken Boyer, pinch-hitting for Walt Williams, got to first base on a fielder's choice to Brandon, who made an unassisted play at home plate to get Josephson out. Brandon then loaded the bases with a walk to Don Buford and sent home the winning run with a walk to Rocky Colavito, pinch-hitting for Tommie Agee.

In an exclusive interview with the *Boston Record-American*, a recovering Conigliaro revealed, "It's tough just sitting here while the boys are knocking themselves out to bring us the pennant. I'm positive we're going to win."[5]

August 29—Yankee Stadium

The Red Sox were on enemy territory for a doubleheader.

Facing the Yankees, Jim Lonborg pitched a complete game with eleven strikeouts in a 2–1 victory at Yankee Stadium for the first game. Boston led 2–0 in the bottom of the seventh when Tom Tresh's solo blast gave the Yankees their first and only run. It was the eighteenth victory for Lonborg; he finished the season at 22-9.

The second game was a twenty-inning bout that ended in a heartbreaking loss for the Bosox. Yastrzemski had a zero-for-six day with three walks. Boston scored first and early. Smith doubled to begin the top of the second inning, then stole third base and scored on an error by Yankees catcher Bob Tillman.

Ken "Hawk" Harrelson followed with a home run in his Red Sox debut to make the score 2–0. Formerly of the Kansas City Athletics, Harrelson became available because of a misunderstanding. When A's owner Charlie Finley fired his manager, Alvin Dark, earlier in the month, Harrelson expressed his displeasure but denied labeling Finley "a menace." Although the White Sox reportedly dangled a $100,000 contract when Finley dubbed Harrelson a free agent, the money wasn't enough to lure one of the most colorful players in baseball.

Instead, he packed his bags for Boston and an $80,000 contract, attracted by the possibility of a pennant. Reportedly, seven teams vied for Harrelson.[6]

Dick Williams explained that Yastrzemski would not be moved from his patrol duties in left field; Harrelson became the fourth right fielder since Conigliaro went down. "The Red Sox will win the pennant," declared Harrelson. "It's not something I know, it's something I feel."[7]

The Yankees scored a run with Mike Hegan crossing the plate after banging a lead-off double in the bottom of the fourth. Tresh had grounded into a put-out at first; Hegan went to third base and scored on cleanup hitter Steve Whitaker's triple. New York evened the score at 2–2 in the bottom of the seventh. With one out, Bill Robinson and Tillman hit back-to-back singles. A sacrifice fly by Roy White, pinch-hitting for Rubén Amaro, scored Robinson.

Boston went up by a run in the top of the eleventh. Petrocelli smacked a two-out double and scored on Norm Siebern's pinch-hit single.

Whitaker's home run in the bottom of the eleventh evened the score at 3–3, where it stayed until the bottom of the twentieth, when the Yankees got their fourth and final tally. John Kennedy, who had replaced Amaro at shortstop in the top of the eighth, hit a one-out single. Brandon, the sixth Sox hurler in this epic clash, hit his counterpart, Jim Bouton. José Santiago took over; Horace Clarke got his fourth hit of the night and the game-winning RBI.

August 30—Yankee Stadium

The Red Sox and Yankees matched up again the next afternoon in another extra-innings game. Scoreless through four innings, Boston tagged Al Downing for three consecutive base hits and broke the 0–0 standoff in the top of the fifth. Smith began with a one-out double; Petrocelli's single moved him to third base and George Thomas's single scored him.

In the bottom of the sixth, Hegan's ground ball to Red Sox first base-man George Scott was a put-out, but it scored Kennedy from third base to make the tally 1–1. The teams stayed deadlocked until the top of the eleventh, when Yastrzemski's solo blast gave Boston the winning run. It was cathartic. Yaz's performance against the Yankees had been as lackluster as a jalopy racing at the Indianapolis 500. He went zero-for-sixteen until his home run.

Williams had benched his star to give him a rest but sent him to replace Thomas in the top of the eighth.

September 18—Tiger Stadium

Boston's 6–5 victory against Detroit came after a seesaw-like battle.

Pounding Motown ace Denny McLain for three runs in the top of the first gave the visitors a nice lead, which they relinquished an inning later when the Tigers got a troika of scores.

Smith's sacrifice fly scored Andrews in the top of the third. Norm Cash's home run in the bottom of the sixth tied the game at 4–4.

Al Kaline singled to lead off the bottom of the eighth, went to second on Willie Horton's sacrifice bunt, and scored on Jim Northrup's double. In the top of the ninth, Yaz tied the score at 5–5 with his fortieth home run of the season. Dalton Jones followed suit with a solo homer in the top of the tenth, securing the win.

Yaz put his round-tripper—part of a three-for-four, one-walk, two-RBI day—in context afterward: "They're all big. But if we'd lost this game we really would have been in trouble as far as winning the pennant is concerned. But nobody quit tonight and that's the way it's been all year. Everybody's battling."[8]

September 19—Tiger Stadium

Russ Gibson knocked an RBI single in the top of the first, but the Tigers went ahead 2–1 in the bottom of the sixth on Northrup's two-run blast. Boston scored three times in the top of the ninth for another heart-pounding win.

Adair led off with a single, then left the game for pinch runner Tartabull. Yastrzemski walked; Tartabull went to second base on Scott's single. Tigers manager Mayo Smith pulled fireballer Mickey Lolich, who had struck out thirteen, for Earl Wilson, who had pitched a no-hitter for the Red Sox in 1962.

Reggie Smith's sacrifice bunt moved the runners to second and third. Wilson intentionally walked Jones to load the bases. Williams chose

Siebern to pinch-hit for Petrocelli, which resulted in another intentional walk that leveled the score at 2–2. Yaz crossed the plate on Wilson's wild pitch, and Gibson's sacrifice fly scored Scott for the third run of the inning.

Larry Claflin began his recount in the *Boston Record-American* by pointing to the supernatural: "The Red Sox must be destined by the Gods of Fate to win the American League Pennant after what happened last night."[9]

It certainly seemed that way.

September 20—Municipal Stadium

Another ninth-inning win for the Bosox.

With the score tied 4–4 against the Cleveland Indians, Yastrzemski hit a two-out single and advanced to second on George Culver's wild pitch. Culver walked Scott and gave up a right-field single to Reggie Smith, which sent Yaz home for the winning run. It was a bona fide performance for the man who wore No. 8 for the Red Sox. He went four-for-five, scored twice, and notched an RBI.

Henry McKenna acknowledged the excitement of the pennant race as well as the toll on fans: "It's all wonderful, this daffy AL race, but you can't imagine what it's doing to the blood pressure. How's yours?"[10]

September 22—Memorial Stadium

The Orioles blanked the Red Sox in the first game of a doubleheader 10–0.

Baltimore right-hander Jim Hardin threw a complete game, struck out seven, and allowed five hits. Boston returned with a 10–3 victory in the second game; Santiago struck out eight. Williams maintained a philosophical approach, emphasizing that he wanted the Red Sox to be viable pennant winners until the two-game series with the Twins at the end of the season: "Then we can either win or lose it. It'll be up to us and if we can't do it then at least we'll have the satisfaction of going almost all the way."[11]

September 30—Fenway Park

The Red Sox were in second place, a game behind the Minnesota Twins, when the teams faced off at Fenway Park on September 30. The Twins scored in the top of the first and held a 1–0 lead until the bottom of the fifth, when the Red Sox scored twice. Rich Reese evened the score at 2–2 for the Minnesota men, knocking a pinch-hit RBI single in the top of the sixth to tie the score. But Scott's lead-off homer in the bottom of the inning put the home team up by a run.

Boston scored three runs in the bottom of the seventh on Yaz's round-tripper for a 6–2 score. Minnesota came back with a pair of runs on Harmon Killebrew's two-run blast in the top of the ninth, but that was it for the visitors.

Yastrzemski noted the loyalty that is a trademark of Red Sox fandom: "The fans, they really own it for us. If they got down on us and started booing after we went behind, 1–0 in the first, I think our guys would have tightened up. But the crowd stayed with us, and that really gave us a lift."[12]

October 1—Fenway Park

"Today the pennant. Tomorrow the world."

That was the caption in a full-page newspaper ad for Gillette honoring the Bosox for beating the Twins 5–3 on October 1 to capture the American League pennant.[13]

TWA offered, "TWA congratulates the Red Sox on winning the American League pennant. (We knew it all the time.)"[14]

A Filene's ad was a cartoon montage of Red Sox Nation, including a depiction of Yastrzemski, mustard, popcorn, a Red Sox cap, the emblem of two red socks, three four-leaf clovers, a baseball in a glove, a trophy, a bat, a receptacle for Jimmy Fund donations, and fans in the bleachers with a sign that said "Go Go Red Sox."[15]

Lechmere, a retailer with two outlets that later grew to twenty in New England with seven others in New York and the Southeast, advertised Zenith color televisions with this message: "Thanks Champs (each and every one of you) for bringing the American League pennant back to Boston after 21 years . . . now go get 'em in the World Series. P.S. thanks ANGELS wherever you are!"[16]

Indeed, Lonborg's twenty-second victory would have meant bupkis if the Angels hadn't been spoilers. Boston and Minnesota were tied at 91–70 with one game remaining; Detroit played California in back-to-back, season-ending doubleheaders on September 30 and October 1. They split the first, giving the Tigers a 90-70 record and an opportunity to tie either Boston or Minnesota and force a playoff if they swept the next twin bill.

Lolich struck out eleven in the first game and got decent run support for a 5-0 shutout. But the Angels rebounded for an 8-6 victory in the second game, clearing the Red Sox for sole possession of first place with a victory over the Twins. Using late 1960s slang, Red Sox relief pitcher John Wyatt exclaimed, "How do I feel? Out of sight, baby. Right out of sight."[17]

Conigliaro, who had been released from the hospital, stood more as an observer than a participant in the Red Sox clubhouse celebration. It was an emotional moment. While his teammates rejoiced, Conigliaro lamented. Through tears, he said, "I just don't feel a part of this." Team owner Tom Yawkey offered solace by underlining that Conigliaro's efforts were crucial in the team's journey. "And if you'd been in there all the way, we'd have won it easier," said Yawkey.[18]

Yastrzemski went four-for-four with two RBIs and won the Triple Crown. Larry Claflin compared his presence to Jimmie Foxx, recalling the potential when Yaz debuted in 1959 but underscoring the distinct specialness of the '67 season: "But, not even his devoted but stern father could have believed Carl would become what he became this year of Yastrzemski."[19]

The slugger earned his praise, leading the AL in runs scored, hits, and batting average while topping the majors in RBIs, on-base percentage, and slugging percentage. He tied with Harmon Killebrew as the home run leader in the Major Leagues.

Ballplayers' talent is a given factor in the calculus of success. Effort is a variable. Veteran sportswriter Jimmy Cannon highlighted rookie skipper Williams as the X factor for the Bosox. "The difference is this is a team with a renovated character," wrote Cannon. "They have the style of champions. Men play baseball with their bodies. But it is what is up in their minds that got them down to here. They could always do the big things, but Williams forced them to perform the small ones."[20]

Sandy Koufax, winner of the 1965 World Series MVP, spread his plaudits across the team. He called Lonborg "tremendous" and Santiago and

Bell "clutch performers." While stating that "he never saw a player more spectacular both at bat and afield in the stretch run of a hectic pennant race than Carl Yastrzemski," he also described Adair as "invaluable." Rookies, too, got the spotlight from the legendary southpaw: "They both kept getting better and better as the pressure kept getting heavier and heavier."[21]

Jimmy "The Greek" Snyder, the gold standard of Las Vegas oddsmakers, gave the Cardinals 3-2 odds to win the World Series against the Red Sox.[22]

World Series—Game One, Fenway Park

Bob Gibson struck out ten in the first game of the World Series, giving the Cardinals a 2-1 win. He declared his power early with five strikeouts of the first eight Boston batters. His counterpart, Santiago, was responsible for the Red Sox's only run with a solo homer in the bottom of the third. Adair, Yastrzemski, Harrelson, and Petrocelli were hitless. Regardless, Yastrzemski affirmed his pre–World Series prediction that Boston would bring home a title in six games.[23]

World Series—Game Two, Fenway Park

Boston won the second game 5-0.

Jim Lonborg was a master of the pitching craft. Working on a no-hitter, he gave up a two-out double to Julián Javier in the eighth inning. The only other tarnish was a walk. Lonborg credited teammate Dennis Bennett, who had pitched in the National League, with giving him insight regarding the Cardinals lineup, notably the need to pitch Lou Brock on the inside, which resulted in three ground balls to second baseman Adair and an easy lineout to Petrocelli. "Before dinner Wednesday night, we sat down and went over each Cardinal batter," Lonborg wrote. "And when I finished talking to him, I felt so confident I didn't see any way I could lose."[24]

Boston's quintet of scores came on nine hits. Yastrzemski's lead-off homer in the fourth and three-run blast in the seventh accounted for four of the runs; Petrocelli hit a bases-loaded sacrifice fly with one out in the sixth to score Scott.

World Series—Game Three, Busch Stadium

Dalton Jones's RBI single in the sixth inning gave Boston the first of a pair of runs in a 5–2 loss to St. Louis.

Reggie Smith's two-for-four day included a lead-off home run in the seventh inning. But the Cardinals outpaced them. Brock went two-for-four and scored twice. Roger Maris had the same batting output with an RBI and a run scored. Mike Shannon had a two-for-three performance highlighted by his two-run homer in the second inning.

The game was marred by Nelson Briles hitting Carl Yastrzemski on the left leg in the first inning. Briles protested that he didn't deliberately try to hit the slugger. "I just wanted to challenge him and I got the pitch a little too far inside," said the righty who led the National League in winning percentage.[25] In his series of first-person articles for the *Boston Globe*, Yastrzemski disagreed and shrugged it off: "But he didn't throw at my head, so I wasn't irritated."[26]

World Series—Game Four, Busch Stadium

Gibson blanked the visitors 6–0 in Game Four with a Herculean effort of 130 pitches.

St. Louis compiled four runs in the bottom of the first inning, prompting Cardinals manager Red Schoendienst to praise both the opposition and his star pitcher. "We feel that as long as we can jump in front of a team, particularly one like the Red Sox, we'll be in good shape," he said. "We want to force a team to catch us and with a pitcher like Gibson, you don't play too much catch-up baseball."[27]

Indeed. The Cardinals went through their batting order as they notched the quartet of runs and knocked Santiago out of the game. Gibson also had some generous words for Boston. Attributing his success partly to their lack of familiarity with him, the fireballer said, "I don't think I'd do as well if I faced them on a regular basis."[28]

The other two runs for the sons of St. Louis happened in the bottom of the third. Williams had Stephenson replace Bell on the mound. It was fruitless. Orlando Cepeda hit a lead-off double, got to third base on a wild pitch, and scored when Tim McCarver hit a sacrifice fly that Smith snared in center field. Mike Shannon walked, then scored on Javier's double.

World Series—Game Five, Busch Stadium

Nursing a cold, Lonborg remained focused on winning. But he didn't need the strategy imparted by Sandy Koufax, which worked in Game One—visualize pitching to the Cardinals lineup during the warm-up session—for a 3–1 victory in Game Five. "I was getting to know the hitters better in my own mind," said Lonborg.[29]

During the warm-ups, Lonborg was wild. So, he focused "more on getting my arm loose than trying to hit the spots." He also praised the Boston defense.[30]

Lonborg's masterful three-hitter kept the Red Sox breathing with a one-run padding; Harrelson singled home Joe Foy in the top of the third. Elston Howard knocked a two-RBI single toward Maris—his former Yankees teammate—in right field with the bases loaded to score Scott and Smith in the top of the ninth. But it's likely that only Scott would have scored if Maris's throw hadn't been high.[31]

It looked like Lonborg was headed toward a shutout until Maris went yard with two outs in the bottom of the ninth to make the score 3–1. Foy protected the area around third base, fielding difficult ground balls, by Dal Maxvill in the bottom of the fifth and Cepeda in the bottom of the ninth, that were sure to be doubles, at least.

Anticipating the proper location to snare the ball, Foy proved to be a valuable defensive asset. "Cepeda hit it good but I had moved over closer to the line when Lonborg worked the count to 2 and 2 on him," explained Foy. "After Maris hit the homer, I knew Lonborg would be throwing him fast balls because he wouldn't want to walk him and bring the tying run to the plate. That's what happened. He hit the fast ball and hit it good. But I was right where I wanted to be."[32]

Yastrzemski credited Foy for his defensive greatness—including playing in on Brock in case the St. Louis speedster decided to bunt—as well as being a trigger on offense, noting the third baseman's three strikeouts but highlighting his single and run scored for Boston's first tally.[33]

Frustrated, Curt Flood, who went zero-for-four in Game Five and zero-for-three with a walk in Game Two, wanted "another crack at this Lonborg."[34]

He and his fellow Redbirds would get one.

World Series—Game Six, Fenway Park

The Cardinals went through eight pitchers in their 8–4 loss in Game Six, which tied the Series at three games apiece.

Rico Petrocelli was the man of the moment, bashing two home runs off righty Dick Hughes; both were solo dingers. The first one happened in the second inning with two outs. In the bottom of the fourth, Hughes suffered solo homers by Yastrzemski, Smith, and Petrocelli. The Red Sox shortstop credited a star alumnus with giving him a crucial observation. "I had been fouling off pitches and Bobby Doerr told me I was undercutting the ball," said Petrocelli. "After I hit that second one I got chills running around the bases."[35]

Boston's other four runs came in a seventh-inning barrage that sent the home team batting around the order with symmetry; Howard began and ended with a groundout to Mike Shannon at third base.

Game Seven would match the team's two aces—Lonborg and Gibson. But Gibson's presence had no impact on George Scott, who declared that the Cardinals hurler would leave the game in the fifth inning.[36]

It didn't quite go as planned.

World Series—Game Seven, Fenway Park

There was no joy on Jersey Street.

There was no revelry in Revere.

There was no cheering in Charlestown.

There was no boisterousness on Boylston Street.

Dorchester was dormant. Merrimac, miserable. They were wistful in Winthrop, hapless in Haverhill, and low in Lynn.

The Cinderella season did not end like a fairy tale for Boston. St. Louis won the seventh game 7–2 on another Gibson masterpiece—a three-hit, ten-strikeout performance. Lou Brock broke a World Series record with seven stolen bases and most runs scored. He also had the most consecutive base hits in a game. Gibson had won his three contests, tying another World Series record. Cardinals pitcher Hughes also tied a record—most home runs allowed in a game.

A recap of interesting snippets titled "Series Sidelights" in the *Boston Globe* recounted a nod to a popular culture icon of the late 1960s. St. Louis mayor Alfonso J. Cervantes sent a telegram to his counterpart, Boston mayor John Collins, with the trademark phrase of Maxwell Smart, main character of the espionage-themed sitcom *Get Smart*: "Sorry about that, Chief."[37]

The Cardinals leaped to a 2-0 lead in the top of the third and scored twice more in the top of the fifth. Boston's first run came in the bottom of the fifth when Scott tripled and scored on Javier's error. Javier got redemption when he sent St. Louis up 7-1 in the top of the sixth with a three-run homer.

Petrocelli led off the bottom of the eighth with a double and moved to third base when Gibson tossed a wild pitch. Pinch-hitting for Howard, Jones drew a walk. Siebern pinch-hit for Santiago; Javier fielded his grounder and forced out Jones at second while Petrocelli scored Boston's second run.

Disappointment did not, in any way, lead to disrespect from the Boston fans at Fenway Park. "Never has a loser been given a louder salute," began John Gilooly's column in the *Record-American*.[38] *Globe* readers saw syndicated columnist Red Smith kick off his recount with an allusion to the Cinderella season nickname: "That glittering coach turned out to be just a pumpkin after all, but it was a grand ride while it lasted."[39] That same newspaper edition's front page also invoked Cinderella in the headline of the game account: "The Slipper Wouldn't Fit."

Red Sox fans honored their team's endurance and defiance of oddsmakers who had given the team as much a chance to win the AL flag in the beginning of the season as Jughead ordering a salad instead of a hamburger at Pop Tate's Chock'lit Shoppe. Boston had emerged as the victors in a four-way pennant race, bounced back from a 3-1 deficit against the mighty Cardinals, and forced a seventh game in the World Series. It was an effort that deserved respect.

But this loss wasn't the first letdown. Not by a long shot.

The teams had faced off in the 1946 World Series, which also ended in a seventh-game defeat of the Bosox. To find glory, you needed to go back a few decades. When Boston's AL squad was known as the Americans, they won the first World Series, in 1903. They captured four titles in the 1910s.

In '67, though, the team had an emotional component reflected in conversations and chronicles using the word "destiny" to describe the journey. It stemmed from the culture of community among fans of the Red Sox dating back to the days of Nuf Ced McGreevy and underlined by the 1967 effort.

Lonborg's loss led Yastrzemski to observe, "What you have in your heart, you can't always put into your arm."[40] Boston's newspapers concurred. The front-page banner headline on top of the recounts by W. J. McCarthy and Henry McKenna in the *Herald Traveler* gave solace to the players: "Sox Lose, but Still Our Champs." In the *Record-American*, the caption "Sox Lose Series, but We Love 'Em" was in the middle of a heart occupying the entire front page.

Advertisers honored the team, too. A State Street Bank and Trust Company advertisement declared, "A standing ovation to the 1967 Red Sox for a terrific year!"[41] Star Markets placed its logo along with those of other concerns in its portfolio—Turn-Style, Osco, Brigham's—with cartoon likenesses of generic players in Red Sox uniforms stacked on top of one another. The caption read, "Red Sox you're still the tallest team in the world!"[42]

The Cardinals' skipper was patronizing, if not demeaning, in a contrast to his comments after Game Four. "I think they were pretty lucky," stated Schoendienst.[43] His thesis was flimsy, given the evidence. Orlando Cepeda had led the National League in RBIs. He placed in the top ten in batting average, on-base percentage, slugging percentage, total bases, and hits. Against Boston's pitchers, he batted .103.

Curt Flood also placed in the NL's top ten for batting average and on-base percentage. He didn't even reach the Mendoza Line in the Fall Classic, compiling a .179 average.

Massachusetts governor John Volpe embraced intangible factors that fuel love, fortitude, and hopefulness among Red Sox fans: "We are tremendously grateful, in this age of computers, statistics and analysis, that our Red Sox have proved that baseball is truly a game of inches, intuition, and ability. The Red Sox, in our mind, are champions in the finest sense of the word."[44]

In 1968 the Red Sox finished in fourth place with an 86-76 record and closed out the sixties with a third-place finish in 1969. But the brightest spot in that last season of the decade was undoubtedly the return of Tony Conigliaro, who did not play in 1968. On Opening Day in 1969, Conigliaro went two-for-four: a fifth-inning single and a two-run homer off Orioles southpaw Pete Richert in the top of the tenth, which broke a 2–2 tie. Baltimore tied it at 4–4 on Frank Robinson's two-run homer.

Conigliaro scored the winning run in the top of the twelfth after drawing a lead-off walk, moving to second on George Scott's single, and then to third when Bill Landis walked Petrocelli. Jones's sacrifice fly sent Conigliaro across Memorial Stadium's home plate. It was a storybook moment, one of many signifying the endurance of the Boston ball club.

There were plenty of heroes in popular culture during the 1960s, of course. Captain James Tiberius Kirk led the USS *Enterprise* to explore strange new worlds in the twenty-third century in *Star Trek*. James Bond defeated villains and bedded gorgeous women with sexually suggestive names. Batman got a pop-art overhaul for television.

In Boston, none compared to Yastrzemski, Lonborg, Petrocelli, Scott, Smith, and their brethren for importance, heroism, or inspiration.

12

Worthy Rivals

The Red Sox and the Yankees

Rivalry is the heart of sports.

When Ohio State meets Michigan on the gridiron, the tension is so substantial, you need a steak knife from The Top in Columbus to cut through it. The UCLA-USC battles for college football's bragging rights in Southern California highlight the sun-soaked region's tremendous sports legacy. Larry Bird and Magic Johnson elevated the NBA's television exposure, fan base, and profit margins in the 1980s with the epic Celtics-Lakers championship clashes. The Giants-Dodgers conflict goes back to the teams' late nineteenth-century beginnings.

Count the clashes between the Red Sox and the Yankees among these epic oppositions.

The First Meeting

Their history together began with a win for Boston on May 7, 1903, when the teams were known as the Highlanders and the Americans. At Huntington Avenue Grounds, New York won 6-2. Boston pitcher Bill Dinneen limited the visiting team to six hits; the Americans had thirteen.[1] A familiar figure to Bostonians started for the Highlanders, then in their debut season. Herman Long began his Major League career with the Kansas City Cowboys of the American Association in 1889, then joined the Boston Braves for the 1890 season and stayed there until 1902—he was part of a nineteen-player bounty fortifying the junior circuit and resulting from American League president Ban Johnson thieving from National League teams.

Boston finished the 1903 season atop the American League with a cushion of fourteen and a half games separating the squad from the second-place Philadelphia Athletics. Facing the Pittsburgh Pirates in the first World Series, then a best-of-nine competition, Boston captured the championship in eight games.

New York ended 1903 with a respectable, if not overwhelming, 72-62 record in fourth place.

What a difference a year makes.

The First Pennant Race

On October 11, 1904, the two teams met in New York's American League Park for a season-ending doubleheader that decided the AL title. Boston took the crown in the first game.

It was not a contest for the faint of heart.

A crowd estimated at thirty thousand watched the ninth-inning dramatics hinging on two New York errors, which led to Boston breaking a 2–2 tie for the winning run. Rarely has a New Englander been speechless in victory, but that's what occurred throughout the throngs of fans visiting Gotham for this crucial game. "The big delegation which came on from Boston to whoop it up for the champions in the decisive games of the season couldn't shout," reported the *Evening World*, one of several New York newspapers in the early twentieth century. "They were too overcome. They simply fell on one another's necks and gurgled out their happiness."[2]

New York registered their tallies in the bottom of the fifth inning. A trio of batsmen got singles—battery mates Jack Chesbro and Red Kleinow, followed by Patsy Dougherty; two walks forced home the pair of runs.

Boston tied it in the top of the seventh. Highlanders shortstop Kid Elberfeld fielded George LaChance's grounder in the top of the ninth, but LaChance beat the throw. After two ground balls by Dinneen and Kip Selbach, LaChance was on third base. On a 2-1 count to Freddy Parent, Chesbro's next pitch cleared Kleinow's head and went to the backstop, giving LaChance a scoring opportunity.

Dinneen struck out John Ganzel but walked Wid Conroy, a result disputed by the *Boston Globe*, which stated that the hurler "really had him out on strikes." Still, Dinneen remained silent. "It was a raw piece of work by Sheridan [the umpire], but not a word spoke Sir William."[3]

Kleinow stepped to the plate, having gotten two hits earlier. But Dinneen retired him on a pop fly to second baseman Hobe Ferris. Then, Highlanders manager Clark Griffith sent Jim Deacon McGuire to pinch-hit for pitcher Jack Chesbro, whose forty-one wins that season set a Major League record in the modern (post-1900) era. McGuire got a walk. With runners on first and second, Dougherty got his chance to be a hero; Dinneen struck him out on a 2-2 count.

The *Globe* acknowledged the friction between the teams and praised the Boston skipper: "It was Boston's third straight victory over its worthy rivals. Every game was played for all it was worth, and was won on the merits of baseball. It was a signal victory for clean, honest ball playing; it was the triumph of nerve and skill combined, and a glorious realization of Jimmie Collins' wisdom in selecting his team and managing the club to his own liking."[4] Yankees manager Griffith got praise, too.

Fifteen years later, a deal cemented the teams' rivalry and, according to some quarters, began a curse that prevented the Red Sox from getting a World Series title for one hundred years after capturing the 1904 AL flag.

The Babe Leaves Boston

Three months after the Cincinnati Reds won the 1919 World Series, which was later determined to have been fixed by eight White Sox players even though a Chicago jury acquitted them of any wrongdoing, Boston lost its brightest star to New York when Red Sox owner Harry Frazee sold Babe Ruth to the New York Yankees.

It was just another baseball deal in the way that the Louisiana Purchase was just another land acquisition. Reports varied on the dollar amount, but it was largely believed to be in the $100,000–$125,000 range.

Ruth had joined the Red Sox in 1914 and led them to three World Series titles during his six years in Boston. Later known as a tremendous offensive threat, the left-handed Baltimore native began as a pitcher: an 89-46 record, including an AL-leading 1.75 ERA in 1916 and a record twenty-nine and two-thirds consecutive scoreless innings in the World Series. Whitey Ford broke that record in 1961.

Clocking eleven home runs in 1918, Ruth led the Majors and stood ahead of his peers again the following year by nearly tripling that number with twenty-nine round-trippers in addition to being No. 1 in slugging percentage, runs scored, and total bases while placing eighth in batting average.

Homers notwithstanding, the Red Sox ended 1919 in sixth place.

Losing Ruth was a terrific blow with the emotional wallop of a Jack Dempsey left hook, though Ed Cunningham of the *Boston Herald* counseled, "Boston fans undoubtedly will be up in arms but they should reserve judgment until they see how it works out."[5]

Cunningham and his fellow scribblers covered this story as if New England had been invaded by enemy forces. In a sense, that's exactly what happened. But there's another side to the lore that has put Frazee on par with Benedict Arnold for generations of Red Sox fans who have believed that the owner sold Ruth solely for greenbacks to finance his theater interests. It had been argued by the front office that Ruth's behavior and the Red Sox essentially being a "one-man club" led to "dissension." The *Boston Advertiser* mentioned this but noted that its investigation found the declaration to be unsubstantiated.[6]

Other newspapers affirmed it.

The *Evening Transcript* declared, "Red Sox players doubtless will be pleased with the disposal of the incorrigible slugger, and team play should be more in evidence."[7] Volatility prompted the *Boston Traveler* to observe, "Ruth had many faults. In many respects he was as hard a man to handle as some of the temperamental stars of a dozen and 20 years ago."[8]

Indeed, the coverage in the Boston press underscored the slugger's attitude, particularly the lack of attention to being a team player in favor of solo glory by bashing the ball over the fence. Although they acknowledged that Ruth's contributions sometimes led to victories, a sad void remained.[9] "One-man clubs seldom win pennants," reminded Eddie Hurley in his "Looking 'Em Over" column for the *Boston Evening Record*. Ty Cobb and the Detroit Tigers, Walter Johnson and the Washington Senators, George Sisler and the St. Louis Browns, and Tris Speaker and the Cleveland Indians were the supporting examples.

This analysis did not account for Cobb's early years, when the Tigers won the AL flag three years in a row. Nor did it highlight that Ruth was part of three World Series championship teams with the Red Sox.

There was also a morale factor to consider. Hurley highlighted that press attention to Ruth's exploits caused the unhappiness of some Red Sox players and their threats not to play in 1920. "In spite of the fact that the Red Sox heads denied rumors of internal dissension in the club, it is nevertheless a fact that the Red Sox were not a happy family," he wrote.[10]

Ruth, however, liked it in Boston. He did not want to venture elsewhere, though he believed that his salary demand of $20,000 a year would ignite a sale and classified the Yankees as "the most probable purchasers."[11] For the money that Frazee got from the Yankees, he could bolster Boston's lineup. Theoretically, anyway. The Red Sox's owner needed to mollify stunned fans with a less expensive but solid replacement, perhaps not a batter approaching Ruth's power but one who could surpass him on defense. *Boston Post* sportswriter Paul H. Shannon described Ruth as having "played very satisfactorily at Fenway Park," but that level of play did not earn him a residency in the upper echelons of previous Red Sox left fielders.[12]

From Frazee's standpoint, Ruth created more problems than he solved. And it wasn't merely a personality conflict. In a lengthy statement accompanying the announcement, Frazee honored Ruth for his accomplishments on the field and his allure for fans but also laid out the reasons for the sale with the aplomb of an appellate lawyer.

In part, Frazee's statement read as follows:

"Ruth had become simply impossible and the Boston club could no longer put up with his eccentricities. While Ruth without question is the greatest hitter that the game has ever seen, he is likewise one of the most selfish and inconsiderate men that ever wore a baseball uniform and the baseball public, according to press reports from all over the country, are beginning to wake up to the fact.

"Some people may say perhaps that the Boston club sold Babe Ruth simply because of the tremendous sum of money handed over by the New York club, but let them listen to a few facts and perhaps they will change their mind. Ruth is a wonderful box office attraction and he drew many thousands of people to see the Sox play all over the circuit. Had he been possessed of the right disposition, had he been willing to take orders and work for the good of the club like the other men on the team

I would never have dared let him go, for he has youth and strength, baseball intelligence and was a popular idol. But lately this idol has been shattered in the public estimation because of the way in which he has refused to respect his contract and his given word. But I shall enlighten the public some more.

"Twice within the past two seasons Babe has jumped the club and revolted. He refused to obey orders of the manager and he finally became so arrogant that discipline in his case was ruined.

"He would not pitch, but insisted upon playing in the outfield. He had no regard for the feelings of anyone but himself. He was a bad influence upon other and still younger players on the team.

"He left us in the lurch many times and just because of his abnormal swatting powers and the fact that he had been given such tremendous advertising by the newspapers he obeyed none but his own sweet will. At the end you could not talk to him."[13]

Ruth played with the Yankees from 1920 to 1934 and ended his career with the Boston Braves in 1935. His prosperous tenure in New York furthered the Yankees–Red Sox rift. Bostonians learned with great anguish about Ruth's home run exploits reaching new heights, thanks in large part to the end of the dead-ball era; a livelier ball combined with powerful swings gave the legendary ballplayer fifty-four home runs in his first year with the Yankees.

Ruth led the Majors in round-trippers nine of his fifteen years with New York, including the iconic year of 1927 when he hit sixty, a single-season record that stood until Roger Maris hit sixty-one in 1961. Coincidence or curse, Maris's sixty-first homer happened during a game against the Red Sox. Moreover, Ruth's slugging percentage topped the Majors eight times and the American League thirteen times.

Far from a one-man operation, the Yankees were stocked with blue-chip players. Lou Gehrig led the Majors in RBIs four times; Tony Lazzeri hit .300 or better in five of his first seven seasons; Earle Combs finished his career with a .325 lifetime average; and Waite Hoyt compiled a 157-98 record with the Yankees.

Earning seven World Series berths, the Yankees won four titles with Ruth.

Between 1920 and 1934, the Red Sox had nine last-place finishes.

Boston got to the World Series in 1946, 1975, and 1986. Each went seven games. Each resulted in the National League team winning. Was there a curse? Were the Red Sox doomed because the ghost of Babe Ruth exerted force from the great beyond, denying them a championship? It depends on whom you ask.

But the Yankees–Red Sox rivalry that began in the 1904 American League pennant race and escalated with the Ruth sale reached a new level of intensity in 1978.

The Boston Massacre and Bucky F***ing Dent

Mention the name "Bucky Dent" to a Red Sox fan and the reaction will be about as welcoming as the one that independence-seeking colonists gave to British loyalists at the Constitutional Convention in Philadelphia. "Bucky Dent bastard," said Lenny Clarke, a comedian and Cambridge native in explaining how the moniker can be transformed into a curse word.[14]

Dent's three-run clout off Mike Torrez shot the Yankees ahead of the Red Sox 3–2 in the top of the seventh inning of the 1978 American League East playoff. Having gone yard four times in the 1978 regular season, Dent prompted an observation from Yankees broadcaster Bill White shared by everyone at Fenway Park along with those watching the game on TV or listening on the radio: "Well, the last guy on the ball club you'd expect to hit a home run just hit one into the screen."[15]

Ignominy ignited.

A solid shortstop who placed second in AL Rookie of the Year voting in 1974, Dent came to the Yankees from the White Sox at the beginning of the 1977 season. His home run in the AL East playoff is a highlight of the Yankees–Red Sox enmity. During a panel covering the teams' rivalry at The Connecticut Forum in 2005, Red Sox catcher Carlton Fisk confirmed, "It may be the only time in Bucky's career that he heard this: 'There's a long fly ball deep deep deep to left!' He never hit a ball deep to left."

"I tell you what. It was a great sound, too," responded Dent to some laughs.[16]

Thurman Munson—who had struck out in his three previous at bats—

doubled home Mickey Rivers to give the Yankees a two-run shield. Reggie Jackson's solo home run led off the top of the eighth for a 5–2 lead, but the Red Sox revived New England's hopes by tallying a pair of runs on four consecutive hits in the bottom of the inning. Jerry Remy led off with a double and scored on Yastrzemski's single; Yaz went to second when Fisk singled, then crossed the plate on Fred Lynn's base hit.

It looked like Boston might have cause to celebrate when Rick Burleson drew a one-out walk and Remy got a base hit in the bottom of the ninth.

Jim Rice stepped into the batter's box with the confidence of Red Sox fans resting upon his bat. And with good reason. Rice, the 1978 American League Most Valuable Player, had played in every game that season, leading the Majors in hits, triples, home runs, RBIs, and slugging percentage. He was one-for-three with an RBI single when he bashed a ball that right fielder Lou Piniella caught in the Boston sunshine; Burleson tagged up and ran to third base.

Yastrzemski, who had hit a solo homer for the first Red Sox run, prepared with stretches and practice swings as Yankees manager Bob Lemon consulted with the battery of Munson and relief pitcher Goose Gossage. On an 0-1 count, Yaz popped up to third baseman Graig Nettles, who moved about a dozen steps into foul territory to catch the ball and end the 1978 season for the lancers of Lansdowne Street. Final score: 5-4.

Boston had begun 1978 with dominance, compiling a 52-24 record by July 1 for a winning percentage near .700. A seven-game cushion separated the Fenway fellas from the Milwaukee Brewers, in second place with forty-five wins and thirty-one losses. New York trailed by nine games at 43-33; Baltimore's 42-35 record caused a ten-and-a-half-game gap.

By July 19 the Yankees had dropped to fourth place and fourteen games behind Boston.

For Red Sox fans, the Yankees' AL East playoff victory had a special tinge of bitterness, like ordering a vanilla ice cream sundae with raspberry sauce, crushed graham crackers, and rainbow jimmies at The Four Seas in Centerville only to blindly take a spoonful and realize somebody replaced the toppings with hot pepper, shiitake mushrooms, and Brazilian steak seasoning.

The Yankees were the cousin showing up at family gatherings now and then, always with a yarn about his latest seven-figure business deal, luxury car, or home remodeling.

They were the rich kid in high school talking about her family's dilemma in deciding whether to take a cruise vacation in the Gulf of Mexico, a ski vacation in Jackson Hole, or a sightseeing vacation in Hawaii.

They were Wall Street, not Main Street. Grey Poupon, not Gulden's. Fitzgerald, not Hemingway. Omega Theta Pi, not Delta Tau Chi.

But facts are facts. The Yankees carried twenty-one World Series titles in thirty-one appearances on their portfolio. Boston hadn't won a World Series since 1918.

The Red Sox had been shaky in the second half of the '78 season, beginning a ten-game home stand on August 25 by winning the first six games and then dropping three of the next four. They lost the first two games in a three-game series against the Orioles at Memorial Stadium. Luis Tiant and Dennis Martinez each threw masterful two-hitters in the third game; Yastrzemski's two-run homer broke a scoreless tie in the seventh inning and secured a 2-0 victory.

Then the Red Sox returned to Fenway Park and faced the Yankees in what became labeled the Boston Massacre. On the morning of September 7, the Yankees were in second place, having chipped away at Boston's lead. Four games separated the rivals in the standings.

New York pounded twenty-one hits against Torrez—who had already won fifteen games—and relievers Andy Hassler, Dick Drago, and Bill Campbell for a 15-3 victory. The game's first four innings yielded a dozen runs. "It wasn't a contest, it was a mugging," wrote Ray Fitzgerald in the *Globe*.[17]

The drubbing was the twenty-third win in the last thirty games for the Yankees.

Boston had an equally disastrous result in the second game—a 13-2 Yankees victory with seventeen hits for the visitors. Right-hander Jim Beattie kept the home team in goose eggs until the bottom of the ninth; Fisk and Jack Brohamer each had an RBI single. In addition to Beattie's pitching and the Yankees' offense, the Red Sox flubbed in the field. Often.

The scorekeepers tallied seven errors. "I can't believe we could have hitting, pitching and defense all go like this at once," lamented Fisk.[18] Neither could New England's baseball fans.

Ron Guidry—who went 25-3, led MLB in ERA and winning percentage, and won the Cy Young Award in 1978—tossed a two-hit, 7-0 shutout in the third game; Rice and Burleson notched the hits for Boston. For the first three innings, all seemed placid for Boston as Dennis Eckersley restricted the Yankees lineup to two men on base—Munson got hit by a pitch in the top of the first and Nettles singled an inning later.

The fourth inning began positively enough for Boston. Munson singled, but he got nailed at first base in a double play—Reggie Jackson flied out to Yastrzemski, who fired the ball to second baseman Frank Duffy, who threw to George Scott to get the stocky Yankees catcher out.

Then the Yankees began a rally that accounted for all seven runs. Red Sox skipper Don Zimmer kept Eckersley in the game until the sixth Yankee crossed the plate. Tom Burgmeier took over and faced a precarious situation with Munson on second base and Willie Randolph on third base; a passed ball credited to Fisk gave Randolph the chance to score the seventh run.

Burgmeier walked Jackson and, to the relief of the hometown crowd, retired Chris Chambliss on a fly ball to Lynn in center field.

The final game of the quartet commenced with New York scoring three times in the top of the first. Bobby Sprowl, a rookie southpaw for the Red Sox with only one Major League game on his résumé, walked Rivers—who stole second base—and then walked Randolph. Munson's ground ball to Burleson began a double play while Rivers went to third base.

Sprowl loaded the bases with Reggie Jackson's single, which scored Rivers, and walks to the next two batters, Piniella and Chambliss.

Zimmer pulled the novice for Bob Stanley. It didn't matter. Nettles banged a two-RBI single to put the Yankees up 3-0. They tacked on another two runs in the top of the second. Piniella's sacrifice fly in the top of the fourth scored Randolph for the sixth run, causing Zimmer to bring in Hassler.

Boston got two runs in the bottom of the fourth. With Lynn and Yastrzemski on base from walks, Fisk smashed a double to score Lynn. Garry

Hancock's sacrifice fly brought Yaz home. In the bottom of the sixth, Lynn's solo round-tripper made the score 6–3.

The Yankees got their final run in the top of the seventh, and the Red Sox responded in kind when Brohamer pinch-hit for Remy and hit a double to score Scott, who had gotten a walk, from first base.

Ed Figueroa had scattered five hits in the 7–4 victory against Boston— his sixteenth win on his way to a 20-9 finish. New York counted eighteen hits for the afternoon.

The latter-day Boston Massacre brought the Yankees even with their New England rivals in the AL East standings. In a touch of foreshadowing, Dent was exemplary at the plate. He batted in seven runs during the series; Boston scored a total of eight runs. At Yankee Stadium a week later, the Bronx Bombers took two of three games from the Red Sox.

With one game left in the season, the Yankees topped the AL East. Boston had a seven-game winning streak but trailed the Bronx Bombers by one game. Luis Tiant shut out the Blue Jays for Boston's ninety-ninth win; New York lost to Cleveland 9–2, leading to the showdown at Fenway Park.

After the one-game playoff, the Yankees beat the Kansas City Royals for the AL championship. They dropped the first two games to the Los Angeles Dodgers in the World Series, then won four straight to capture the title for the second year in a row. Batting .417 and knocking in seven runs earned Dent the World Series MVP Award.

The Yankees had continued their seemingly destined mission of being jagged thorns in the sides of the Red Sox. There didn't seem to be an end to this trend. No reverse to the curse.

That changed in 2004.

"Red Sox Fans Have Longed to Hear It!"

On July 23, 2004, *The Bourne Supremacy* opened in theaters. Bostonians celebrated because it marked another success for Cambridge native Matt Damon in the role of Jason Bourne, a former CIA assassin suffering from severe amnesia regarding his identity. The second installment of the Bourne film series eventually grossed nearly $300 million worldwide. A day after its release, Boston's baseball fans rejoiced again when the

PART 4

Red Sox mounted an epic comeback against the Yankees at Fenway Park. The rivalry got violent early.

The Yankees were up 2-0 in the top of the third when Bernie Williams led off with a double. Derek Jeter's single sent him to third base; Gary Sheffield's double-play ground ball to second baseman Mark Bellhorn gave Williams an opening to score the third run for New York.

Then, Bronson Arroyo plunked Alex "A-Rod" Rodriguez on his left elbow, prompting a florid exchange between the Yankees' newly acquired slugger and Red Sox backstop Jason Varitek; FOX cameras showed A-Rod repeatedly shouting, "Fuck you!" to Varitek, who tried to prevent him from charging the mound. "I was just trying to protect Bronson," explained Varitek. "For protecting a teammate, I'll take whatever comes."

Breaking down the expletive-filled banter, he said, "I told him in choice words to go to first base. Then things got out of hand. You lose your emotions sometimes. He lost his emotions, I lost mine."[19]

Punches were thrown. Faster than a lit match can ignite gasoline-soaked rags, a bench-clearing clash commenced. It ended with ejections of Rodriguez and Varitek. The Red Sox also lost the services of Gabe Kapler, and the Yankees were absent Kenny Lofton for their roles in the brawl.

It took nearly nine minutes until the game resumed and Arroyo threw his next pitch.

Boston scored two runs in the bottom of the third and another two runs an inning later to go ahead 4-3.

More drama happened in the bottom of the fifth. Johnny Damon led off with a single. After Doug Mirabelli—Varitek's replacement—whiffed, David Ortiz hit a blooper into shallow right field with a full count. Yankees second baseman Enrique Wilson tried to make an over-the-shoulder catch, but it fell out of his glove and bounced on the outfield turf; Sheffield gloved it and fired to Jeter to nail Damon. Red Sox skipper Terry Francona got tossed during his argument with second-base umpire Mike Winters on the close call.

A six-run sixth inning gave New York a comfortable padding with a 9-4 score. It didn't last long; Boston crossed the plate four times in its half of the inning to make the score 9-8. Rubén Sierra's lead-off homer in the top of the seventh put New York in double digits, but Bill Mueller homered in storybook fashion in the bottom of the ninth with Nomar Garciaparra and Kevin Millar aboard for an 11-10 victory.

In the postseason, the rivals met again after Boston earned a wild card berth and vanquished AL West champion Anaheim in three games as New York, the AL East champion, took Minnesota in four games.

Down 3-0 in a best-of-seven playoff to determine the American League title, the Red Sox mounted a comeback worthy of Hollywood. "It felt like that part in *A Christmas Story* where Ralphie finally snaps and beats up Scut Farkus," said Red Sox fan Jerry Thornton in the 2004 HBO Sports documentary *Reverse of the Curse of the Bambino*.[20]

Indeed. It was Marshal Will Kane killing Frank Miller's gang in *High Noon*. It was Tess McGill getting promoted at the end of *Working Girl*. It was Frank Galvin winning a multimillion-dollar medical malpractice lawsuit against a Catholic hospital and the Archdiocese of Boston represented by a powerful Boston law firm in *The Verdict*. But any movie analogy, however apt, didn't have a story line backed by one hundred years of drama.

The Yankees had won the first two games of the playoff at Yankee Stadium, 10-7 and 3-1; Game Three at Fenway Park was a 19-8 rout. A pall encircled Boston, leaving Red Sox fans at the familiar crossroads of despair and hopelessness. The Yankees had bested their rivals in the playoffs the year before, though they lost to the Florida Marlins in the World Series. The 2004 postseason looked like a repeat of 2003—New York going to the World Series and Boston mourning another defeat at the hands of their rivals.

But the Red Sox weren't flatlining yet.

The next two games, both extra-inning affairs, ended with David "Big Papi" Ortiz fortifying his status as a Red Sox icon. His two-run homer in the bottom of the twelfth inning gave Boston a 6-4 victory in Game Four, followed by an RBI single to break a 4-4 tie in the bottom of the fourteenth inning of Game Five.

Going back to enemy territory, the Red Sox severed the curse of Babe Ruth for superstitious folks with 4-2 and 10-3 victories at Yankee Stadium to win the American League pennant.

Facing the St. Louis Cardinals, their nemeses from the 1946 and 1967 World Series, the Red Sox captured the label that had eluded them since 1918. With two outs in the bottom of the ninth in Game Four, Red Sox pitcher Keith Foulke fielded a ground ball by Cardinals shortstop Édgar Rentería—who wore No. 3 on his uniform, Babe Ruth's number—and tossed it to first baseman Doug Mientkiewicz to conclude a four-game sweep.

FOX announcer Joe Buck verbalized decades of frustration being pushed aside as he declared, "Red Sox fans have longed to hear it! The Boston Red Sox are world champions."[21]

Boston also celebrated World Series titles in 2007, 2013, and 2018. Somewhere, Nuf Ced McGreevy is smiling.

1. From 1901 to 1911, Huntington Avenue Grounds was the home field for Boston's American League ball club, originally known as the Americans. Fenway Park debuted in 1912. Boston Public Library, Michael T. "Nuf Ced" McGreevy Collection.

2. (*opposite top*) The Boston fans known as the "Royal Rooters" cheer on the Boston players at Huntington Avenue Grounds during the 1903 World Series. Boston Public Library, Michael T. "Nuf Ced" McGreevy Collection.

3. (*opposite bottom*) The Boston Americans mark their 1903 World Series victory over the Pittsburgh Pirates by raising the championship flag on Opening Day in 1904. Player-manager Jimmie Collins has the honors. Boston Public Library, Michael T. "Nuf Ced" McGreevy Collection.

4. (*above*) John I. Taylor bought the Americans in 1904 from Henry Killilea, who bought the team from Charles Somers. Taylor sold half his interest in 1911 and soon sold the remainder. Boston Public Library, Michael T. "Nuf Ced" McGreevy Collection.

5. Michael McGreevy was a fixture for the Red Sox fan base dating back to the team's origins in 1901. He called his saloon Third Base, a reference to being the last stop before going home. It was located at 940 Columbus Avenue in Roxbury. Boston lore says that McGreevy's nickname "Nuf Ced"—a shortened version of "Enough Said"—came from his declaration that stopped arguments in his bar. Boston Public Library, Michael T. "Nuf Ced" McGreevy Collection.

6. After Michael "Nuf Ced" McGreevy died in 1943, *Boston Daily Record* sportswriter Dave Egan suggested that he belonged in the Baseball Hall of Fame. "It was he, most of all, who by his enthusiasm popularized baseball and helped make it the national sport," wrote Egan. Boston Public Library, Michael T. "Nuf Ced" McGreevy Collection.

7. Cy Young pitched a perfect game for Boston in 1904. Four years later, the team honored him with Cy Young Day at Huntington Avenue Grounds. Fans contributed money to buy a "loving cup" sponsored by the *Boston Post*. Boston Public Library, Michael T. "Nuf Ced" McGreevy Collection.

8. Babe Ruth was an outstanding pitcher for the Red Sox before owner Harry Frazee sold him to the New York Yankees. In 1916 he led the American League in ERA, games started, and shutouts. The following year, he finished the season atop the AL in complete games. His record of twenty-nine and two-thirds consecutive scoreless innings in World Series games stood until Whitey Ford broke it in 1961. National Baseball Hall of Fame and Museum.

9. Harry Frazee, shown here in 1916, prompted decades of disappointment and despair for Red Sox fans after he sold Babe Ruth to the New York Yankees. But some members of the Boston press initially supported Frazee's deal. "Red Sox players doubtless will be pleased with the disposal of the incorrigible slugger, and team play should be more in evidence," declared the *Boston Evening Transcript*. Library of Congress, George Grantham Bain Collection.

10. Ted Williams crosses home plate and shakes hands with Red Sox
second baseman Bobby Doerr. The Baseball Hall of Fame inducted
Williams in 1966. Doerr's induction came twenty years later.
Williams used his induction speech to advocate for the inclusion
of Negro Leaguers like Satchel Paige and Josh Gibson.
Boston Public Library, Leslie Jones Collection.

11. Jimmie Foxx and Bobby Doerr look at Fenway Park's field in this photo from 1937. The following year "Double X" led the Major Leagues in RBIS, walks, and total bases in addition to topping the American League in batting average, on-base percentage, and slugging percentage. His tremendous output garnered him the MVP Award. The Hall of Fame inducted Foxx in 1951. Boston Public Library, Leslie Jones Collection.

12. Narragansett Beer began sponsoring Boston Braves radio broadcasts in 1944. Two years later, Narragansett brought the Red Sox into its portfolio. The Braves left Boston for Milwaukee in 1953, and Narragansett's relationship with the Red Sox continued until 1975, when the beer company's new owners ended it. © Richard Merrill. Boston Public Library, Richard Merrill Collection. https://creativecommons.org/licenses/by-nc-nd/4.0.

13. Jimmy Piersall, shown here in 1952, chronicled his mental breakdown in his autobiography *Fear Strikes Out*. It became the source for a movie of the same name starring Anthony Perkins as Piersall. Boston Public Library, Leslie Jones Collection.

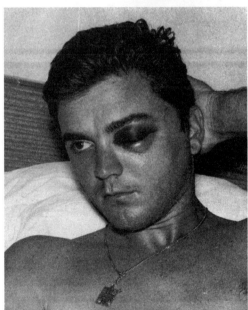

14. Tony Conigliaro after getting beaned by Jack Hamilton during an Angels–Red Sox game at Fenway Park on August 18, 1967. It sidelined Conigliaro for the remainder of the team's Cinderella season. AP Photo.

15. (*opposite top*) Carlton Fisk uses body language to will his twelfth-inning smash over the Green Monster. The ball hit the foul pole and secured a victory for the Red Sox over the Reds in Game Six of the 1975 World Series. The game is often cited as the best baseball game ever by the sport's journalists and scholars. AP Photo / Harry Cabluck.

16. (*opposite bottom*) The year 1978 was a rollercoaster one for the Red Sox. In mid-July they were in first place with a fourteen-game lead over the fourth-place Yankees. By late September the rivals were battling for the AL East pennant. Carl Yastrzemski beats Bob Bailor's throw in this 11–0 victory against the Blue Jays on September 29. Three days later, the Yankees won the pennant in a one-game playoff against the Red Sox. AP Photo / Tannen Maury.

17. (*above*) The Citgo sign outside Fenway Park is a Kenmore Square landmark. Despite the link to the Red Sox, it's been a source of controversy. During the energy crisis of the late 1970s, Massachusetts governor Edward King called for it to be turned off, if only as a symbolic gesture. It was relit in 1983. AP Photo / Charles Krupa.

18. The Boston Marathon bombing by the Tsarnaev brothers on April 15, 2013, shook the world. Three people died and more than 260 were injured. David Ortiz rallies the Fenway Park crowd during a pregame event on April 20. The previous night, Dzhokar Tsarnaev had surrendered after several hours hiding in a boat in a driveway. He had accidentally run over his brother, Tamerlan, with a stolen SUV and killed him during a shootout with Watertown police officers a few nights earlier. Kyodo via AP Images.

PART 5

Icons

13

A Man Called Yastrzemski

Replacing a legend is an unenviable task measured by an impossible standard.

Carl Yastrzemski faced this challenge in 1961 when the Red Sox tapped the twenty-one-year-old to take over patrolling duties in left field from Ted Williams, who ended his career with a dramatic flourish by cracking a home run in his last at bat in 1960. Williams's final total for round-trippers was 521—including an inside-the-park home run that clinched the 1946 AL pennant—but the tally might have been at least 600 if he hadn't served in the military for three seasons as a Marine pilot during World War II and missed most of 1952 and 1953 during the Korean War.[1]

A mainstay of the Red Sox lineup since 1939, except for his years of military service, Williams had a staggering array of statistics and achievements, including six-time American League batting champion; two-time MLB batting champion; five-time MLB leader in runs scored; seven-time MLB leader in walks; two-time AL MVP; eighteen-time All-Star, with a career batting average of .344; and MLB leader in career on-base percentage.

Williams was the last Major Leaguer to break .400. Strength, reliability, and skills were substantial; replacing him with a comparable player seemed like a futile goal.

Yastrzemski had bona fides coming into 1961 spring training, causing fantastic anticipation. Playing for the 1959 Raleigh Capitals in the Carolina League, Yaz topped the CL with a .377 average. He placed second in slugging percentage, third in RBIs, first in doubles, fourth in runs scored, and eighth in walks.

Player of the Year and Rookie of the Year honors followed. A second baseman before eventually transitioning to the outfield, Yaz got seventeen of nineteen votes for first place for Player of the Year. For Rookie of the Year, it was a unanimous first-place vote.

In 1960 the Red Sox advanced him from Class B to the Triple-A Minneapolis Millers, where his .339 average gave him third place behind Ozzie Virgil and Bobo Osborne; Yastrzemski led American Association batters with 193 hits.

During 1961 spring training, *Boston Globe* sportswriter Bob Holbrook acknowledged the weight upon the Bridgehampton, Long Island, native set to follow one of the game's most revered players. "Yaz, of course, is a special subject in the Red Sox camp," affirmed Holbrook. "He's Ted Williams' most likely successor in left field. This fact is sufficient to put the pressure on any ball player.

"Great things are expected of Carl. Rival players, and fans, will be eyeing him closely."[2]

Additionally, Yastrzemski replaced a personal hero. "Ted always was the big man to Carl," revealed Carl Yastrzemski Sr. "And Stan Musial, too. He admired them both greatly."[3] Before a preseason game in 1961, idol and novice talked about hitting. Williams's conversation with Yaz, certainly not the only time they exchanged ideas, resulted in Yastrzemski pounding the Los Angeles Angels, an expansion team, for four hits in Boston's 10–5 victory. "Ted was suggesting that I shorten my stride and just flick my wrists," said the rookie. "He said I have the ability to do it, just as he did. It worked out pretty good today."[4]

Pretty good? That's like saying the Union Oyster House has a touch of Boston history. Then again, the description was pure Yaz. He let his performance be his mouthpiece, such was the working-class comportment of this son of a potato farmer.

Yastrzemski played in 148 games and batted .266 in his rookie season. It was a solid start with signs of improvement on the horizon. In mid-September former Red Sox second baseman and nine-time All-Star Bobby Doerr said, "I caught a glimpse of Carl on television a couple of weeks back and I said to myself now he's got it. . . . He's got that snap he showed me before. He isn't lunging at the ball as he used to. Before that he wasn't doing it and he wasn't hitting like I know he can hit. He does some unorthodox things at the plate, but that's his natural way of hitting and I'm certainly glad he's back in the groove."[5]

In his twenty-three-year career, which he spent in a Boston uniform,

Yaz was an All-Star seventeen times. Like his predecessor, he frustrated American League pitchers: three-time batting champion, five-time on-base percentage leader, three-time leader in runs scored, three-time slugging percentage leader, and Triple Crown winner in 1967. Three times he led the Majors in on-base percentage.

Yastrzemski's defense led to a Gold Glove seven times. He retired in 1983 with a .285 batting average, 3,419 hits, and 452 home runs. In his last game, a 3-1 victory over the Cleveland Indians at Fenway Park on October 2, 1983, Yaz went one-for-three and drew a walk. A group of fans held a white banner with words painted in red: Thanks for the Memories Yaz. It was heartfelt. No. 8 provided more moments of greatness and joy for New England's baseball fans than there are steps on the Freedom Trail.

Most prominent was his leadership of the Red Sox on their drive to the World Series in 1967, dubbed their "Cinderella season." But the Cardinals beat the Red Sox in seven games, as did the Cincinnati Reds in 1975. Exemplary in the postseason, Yastrzemski batted .400 against the Cardinals and .310 against the Reds.

In a 1967 preseason game against the Red Sox's future World Series opponents that season, Yaz was a template of excellence at bat and in the field. Six RBIs, three runs scored, two home runs, and "three outstanding catches, including the game saver in the ninth inning," helped the Red Sox edge the Cardinals 10-9. Again Red Sox legends Williams and Doerr had counseled the star player. "I've been having a little trouble with my hitting lately," said Yaz. "Ted Williams gave me a tip that's been working pretty good. He told me to keep my right hip closer to the plate. Somehow, I got away from this idea in the last few days. Then Bobby Doerr called it to my attention."[6]

In the Yankees' 1967 home opener against the Red Sox, Yastrzemski protected the viability of a no-hitter for Boston rookie hurler Bill Rohr—pitching his first Major League game—when he made a spectacular snare of Tom Tresh's line drive to begin the bottom of the ninth.[7]

Rohr retired Joe Pepitone on a fly ball to right fielder Tony Conigliaro. Elston Howard broke the chance at a no-hitter with a single on a 3-2 count. Charley Smith flied out to Conigliaro to end the game, a 3-0 victory for Boston.

On May 31 Yastrzemski crashed two solo home runs in a 3–2 victory against the White Sox. In August, Twins third base coach Billy Martin hailed the left fielder's prowess on defense: "The way he's been playing this season, Yastrzemski is the greatest leftfielder I've ever seen," said the future manager of the Twins, Yankees, Rangers, and A's, appraising the young player. "Nobody in my years in baseball could make the plays out there that 'Yaz' does. He has a wider range in every direction than any other leftfielder I can remember. He never drops a ball he gets his glove on. He charges ground balls like an infielder and rarely misses one. And while he isn't the batter Williams was, he is that good right now [and] he might finish the season wearing the MVP."[8]

Martin was an astute forecaster. Yaz won the American League MVP after an outstanding season in which he led the AL in runs scored, hits, and batting average. He topped the Majors in home runs, RBIS, on-base percentage, and slugging percentage.

A few days after the Red Sox clinched the pennant, Yastrzemski got high praise from Williams and Musial. "I'm talking all-around baseball performance, running the bases, catching flies, throwing out baserunners and hitting," said Williams. "Yaz is the greatest baseball player I've seen—doing everything—for a single season."[9]

In an interview that Yastrzemski conducted for the *Boston Globe*, part of a series of articles that he wrote, he talked about baseball with Musial, who compared him to Williams and another slugger: "You remind me of Roger Maris when he was in his prime. You take a good, hard level swing and you're built about the same. You hit them like Ted. While we're talking about hitting, I'd like to compliment you on the year that you had. You had a phenomenal year and you've been a great asset to baseball."[10]

Yaz got his three thousandth hit when he smacked a ground ball past New York Yankees second baseman Willie Randolph in a September 12, 1979, game at Fenway Park. Boston beat the rivals 9–2. Two members of Congress from Massachusetts, Silvio Conte and Joe Moakley, honored this momentous occasion along with Yastrzemski's body of work on the floor of the U.S. House of Representatives.[11]

Senator Ted Kennedy mirrored these declarations in the U.S. Senate and noted the three-day wait between hits 2,999 and 3,000: "Mr. President, if historians of the future look back and wonder why the United States of America seemed to pause in the past few days, they may well find the pause was not over inflation, or energy, or Soviet combat troops in Cuba, or politics, but over an eighth inning single in Fenway Park in Boston by Carl Yastrzemski."[12]

Regarding the drought before reaching the three-thousand-hit mark, Yastrzemski reasoned, "The only explanation I can think of is the way the fans reacted the last three days, I wanted to get the hit for the fans in the stands that day. I was chasing pitches, going after pitchers' pitches. I was anxious."[13]

Yastrzemski became part of an even more exclusive club—only Hank Aaron, Stan Musial, and Willie Mays had gotten three thousand hits and four hundred home runs. Yaz was the first American Leaguer to do it. Earlier that season, he tagged number four hundred off Oakland A's right-hander Mike Morgan in a 7-3 victory, also a home game. His trademark modesty emerged again. "I haven't had the greatest ability in the world," said Yaz. "I'm not a big, strong guy. I've made nine million adjustments, nine million changes. I've worked hard over the wintertime, I've paid the price, and God gave me a tremendous incentive and body to excel and that desire inside of me that passes the point."[14]

But if one were to select a feat best representing the prominence of Carl Michael Yastrzemski Jr., his batting performance over two games on May 19-20, 1976, would be a formidable contender. Both games were on the road.

Against the Detroit Tigers, the thirty-six-year-old Yastrzemski went four-for-four, notched four RBIs, scored four runs, and walked once in Boston's 9-2 thrashing. The Tigers went up 2-0 in the bottom of the first. Ron LeFlore cracked a lead-off triple against Red Sox starter Fergie Jenkins—in the first of a two-year stint with the Boston ball club—and scored on Alex Johnson's sacrifice fly to right fielder Dwight Evans. Willie Horton followed with a solo bash.

Yastrzemski drew a walk with two outs in the top of the first, but Rico Petrocelli's grounder to Tigers shortstop Tom Veryzer forced him out at second. Boston closed the gap to one run in the top of the third when Rick Miller singled home Rick Burleson.

An inning later, Boston went ahead 3–2; Yaz bashed a two-run homer after Carlton Fisk hit a lead-off single and Jim Rice struck out looking.

The Red Sox made the score 7–2 in the top of the fifth. Evans led off with a single and Fred Lynn got to first base on an error by Tigers starting pitcher Dave Roberts. Fisk lined out to LeFlore in center field, then Rice cleared the bases with a three-run blast. Tigers skipper Ralph Houk called for Steve Grilli to replace Roberts. The reliever's efforts were for naught; Yaz went yard for the second time that night.

Beginning the seventh, Yaz singled and scampered 270 feet to score on an error. The plan was a simple hit-and-run, but it went in a different direction thanks to the veteran's base-running experience. Petrocelli had gone out of the game with an injured left foot. Steve Dillard pinch-hit and smacked a ground ball to Tigers third baseman Aurelio Rodríguez, whom Yaz had observed as focusing on Dillard rather than him. "But I saw him pretty far away from the bag, so I thought I had a real good chance," said Yastrzemski of Rodríguez.[15]

Consequently, he had passed second base as the ball was on its way to first baseman Jason Thompson, who fired back to Rodríguez for a potential second out. But he threw wide of his fellow infielder, making Yaz's slide into third unnecessary and allowing a score for Boston's eighth run.

In the top of the ninth, Yastrzemski hit his third home run—each had been off a different pitcher—a massive shot that sent the spheroid with red stitching into the upper deck of Tiger Stadium.

Rather than blare his own exploits, Yaz simply said, "I was pretty lucky tonight."[16] Well, luck is what happens when preparation meets opportunity. And so it was on this mid-May evening. Yaz attributed the success to changing how he positioned his arms during his at bats. "They were up high again, like they used to be when I was hitting home runs a lot," explained the recently slumping Yastrzemski, who had entered the game with a sub-.200 average. "I made up my mind tonight I was going to do it, and I did. I had been holding them low for a long time. Last year, when I was hitting well, that's the way I held them. You'd think as you get older, you could drop them and still improve. It hasn't been that way with me."[17]

The following night at Yankee Stadium, Yastrzemski went three-for-five with two home runs, four RBIs, and two runs scored in Boston's 8–2 victory against the Bronx Bombers. He got his base hit in the top of the second, a one-out single.

New York broke a scoreless tie in the bottom of the fourth. Thurman Munson and Chris Chambliss hit back-to-back singles, then Lou Piniella got on base because of an error by shortstop Rick Burleson. Munson scored.

An epic clash ignited in the top of the sixth. With two outs, Piniella and Graig Nettles singled. Otto Vélez followed suit with another base hit; Piniella tried to score from second and crashed into Fisk, who held on to the ball. Yaz darted to home plate to separate the two combatants but got rewarded with a leg injury moments later when the fray expanded.[18] "Until the fight, we were too complacent," Yastrzemski later recounted. "That seemed to shake us up."[19]

Red Sox hurler Bill "Spaceman" Lee scuffled with Mickey Rivers and Nettles in the dugout-clearing brawl; Nettles and Lee got tossed for fighting. Lee suffered a shoulder injury.[20]

Yankees right-hander Ed Figueroa kept Boston scoreless through the sixth inning. In the top of the seventh, the Red Sox made the score 2-1. Evans drew a lead-off walk, then got forced at second on Petrocelli's ground ball to Sandy Alomar, playing third base. Burleson redeemed himself with a home run. The Yankees evened the score in the bottom half of the inning on Rivers's RBI single, which scored Alomar from second base.

Yastrzemski's two-run blast gave the Red Sox a 4-2 lead in the top of the eighth. An inning later, they added four runs. Denny Doyle led off with a single, followed by Lynn's triple; Fisk singled and Yaz put the ball in the stands for the second time.

As he approached retirement from baseball in 1983, the ballplayer who exhibited a workman-like aura got honors reserved for the most elite athletes—a U.S. Senate resolution. Ted Kennedy introduced it, highlighted Yastrzemski's career, and declared, "Yaz will always be remembered as a winner."[21]

Upon his election to the Baseball Hall of Fame in 1989 along with Reds catcher Johnny Bench, Yaz underscored his appreciation for the beginning of his career when he succeeded a Boston legend: "Taking over Ted Williams' spot was the toughest thing I had to do—it almost broke me—really. The first three months of the season I really didn't know if I could play in the big leagues or not."[22]

Yastrzemski acknowledged Williams's generosity in his speech on Carl Yastrzemski Day—also in 1989—when the Red Sox retired his number. Slumping at the beginning of his rookie season, Yastrzemski had asked for insight from his predecessor: "He flew into Boston, worked with me for three days, helped me mentally, gave me confidence that I could play in the big leagues. I hit .300 for the rest of the season. I'd like to thank Ted Williams."[23]

Following a legend is a touchstone in American culture. Sometimes it's smooth. Other times, not so much.

The 1980–81 season of *Saturday Night Live* began with an expository sketch featuring the new cast explaining to host Elliott Gould how they compare to the legendary "Not Ready for Prime Time Players"—John Belushi, Dan Aykroyd, Jane Curtin, Gilda Radner, Garrett Morris, Laraine Newman, Chevy Chase, and Bill Murray. After five years, the original cast had left along with executive producer and creator Lorne Michaels. Of the newcomers, only Joe Piscopo and Eddie Murphy made the cut for the next season.

When Johnny Carson stepped down as host of *The Tonight Show* in 1992 after thirty years, Jay Leno, despite a solid five-year run as Carson's permanent guest host, had a rough start replacing the "King of Late Night." Conan O'Brien had a similar challenge. Primarily a writer whose main accomplishments were being a writer for *Saturday Night Live* and *The Simpsons*, O'Brien took over the *Late Night* franchise in 1993, when David Letterman left NBC to establish an 11:30 p.m. show at CBS.

Phil Bengtson followed Vince Lombardi's shoe prints to the sidelines as head coach of the Green Bay Packers in 1968. Lombardi had quit the helm after racking up championships like Kennedys won elections. Five in all. Bengtson's record in his three years leading the Packers was 20-21-1. Lombardi's was 89-29-4 across nine seasons.

There's a scene in the 2001 HBO TV movie *61** where Mickey Mantle—a contemporary of both Williams and Yastrzemski—recalls his plight as a rookie to Roger Maris, played by Thomas Jane and Barry Pepper, respectively: "You know, when I first come up, I was under so much pressure from Casey and everybody telling me I was going to be the next Joe DiMaggio. They gave me No. 6, right. Ruth was 3, Gehrig's 4, DiMaggio's 5, and me, No. 6. I hated that. Being in line with the other guys.

"And the press, man, they was all over me. Calling me a hillbilly. I mean, I was, you know. I get to New York, I got a seven-dollar suitcase and an eight-dollar suit. My whole town's got two thousand people in it. Yankee Stadium's got forty times that. Eighteen years old and everybody's expecting me to hit a home run every time I get up to the plate. It was killing me. I couldn't hit the ball."

When Mantle didn't perform as expected, Yankees skipper Casey Stengel sent him to the Minors. Upon his return, he got No. 7 for his uniform. "I was glad about it. I hated that No. 6."

Bobby Murcer, an Oklahoman like Mantle, was described as a worthy successor to the Commerce Comet in center field. Even though his numbers weren't stratospheric, it's fair to say that Murcer was a beloved Yankee, both as a player and a broadcaster. His best season was 1971, when he led the Majors in on-base percentage and tied for fourth place in RBIS.

Steve Young replaced four-time Super Bowl champion and three-time Super Bowl MVP Joe Montana as the San Francisco 49ers' quarterback. Montana, a Notre Dame alumnus who was on the team when Rudy Ruettiger had his moment of fame, became an NFL standout: passing percentage leader five times, passing touchdown leader twice, and Most Valuable Player twice.

The 49ers won another title with Young, who also earned MVP honors in Super Bowl XXIX for his stellar performance—throwing a record six touchdown passes and completing twenty-four of thirty-six pass attempts for 325 yards in the 49–26 victory over the San Diego Chargers. Young was the NFL passing touchdowns leader four times; he won the MVP twice.

Sidney Crosby earned deep respect from opponents and a place in the hearts of Pittsburgh Penguins fans who had espoused Mario Lemieux as the gold standard of hockey players in Steel City.

President John F. Kennedy shared his rookie year in the White House with Yastrzemski's in the Major Leagues. The youngest president ever elected (at forty-three) and the first born in the twentieth century, Kennedy replaced Dwight Eisenhower—an iconic leader who had risen from lieutenant colonel to five-star general commanding the Allied forces in the European theater during World War II before guiding the country through a peace-and-prosperity era as a two-term president in the 1950s.

Replacing a legend who's revered, celebrated, and, to a certain extent, viewed as sacrosanct is a burden requiring sacrifice, skill, and endurance. When Yastrzemski had triple bypass heart surgery in 2008 at the age of sixty-nine, Jerry Remy, who played for the Sox from 1978 to 1984 and later became a broadcaster for the team, extolled his former teammate: "I don't think he became the most talented of the Hall of Famers, but no one outworked him. Up until the day he retired, he wanted to be the best.... He spent hours and hours and hours hitting."[24]

Such was the journey of a man called Yastrzemski. Star. Icon. Legend.

14

Tom Seaver's Last Hurrah

In the 1980s, nostalgia's currency was as secure as Fort Knox. It might have begun with Tom Seaver.

During the 1981 players strike, *Sports Illustrated* put the fireballer on the cover of the July 27 issue with this caption: "Hey, baseball fans, need a quick fix? Want a little instant nostalgia? We bring you Tom Seaver . . . still terrific after all these years."

The 1983 film *The Big Chill* and its Motown-laden soundtrack targeted the nostalgia of baby boomers. CBS's *Hometown* had a similar setup, focusing on people in their thirties balancing the adult responsibilities of the present with the youthful idealism of their past. It lasted two months on the network's prime-time lineup in 1985.

ABC leveraged its broadcasts of the 1984 Summer Olympics for commercials promoting *Call to Glory*, which premiered that fall. Set in the early 1960s, it starred Craig T. Nelson as U.S. Air Force pilot Raynor Sarnac guiding his family through emerging tensions, including the civil rights movement and the Vietnam War. ABC canceled *Call to Glory* in its first season, airing twenty episodes and then burning off two others in June 1985.[1]

Back to the Future soaked 1985 moviegoers in 1955 iconography. A year later, Hollywood manifested its love affair with nostalgia in four movies. *Peggy Sue Got Married* transported the title character from her twenty-five-year high school reunion back to 1960 and her senior year of high school. Matthew Broderick lip-synced the version of "Twist and Shout" by The Beatles in *Ferris Bueller's Day Off*; Rodney Dangerfield gave his interpretation of the song—first recorded by The Top Notes in 1961—in *Back to School*.

Stand by Me—based on Stephen King's 1982 novella *The Body* and directed by Rob Reiner—takes place in 1959, but it is recognizable in any era for its realistic depiction of friendship among four twelve-year-old boys.

Songs that had been popular in the 1960s got a resurgence with covered versions in the 1980s. David Bowie and Mick Jagger recorded "Dancing in the Street," a signature song from Martha and the Vandellas. Phil Collins selected "You Can't Hurry Love," one of the most popular songs from the portfolio of Diana Ross and the Supremes. Tiffany's "I Think We're Alone Now" became a No. 1 hit. Its predecessor, sung by Tommy James and the Shondells, got to No. 4 in 1967. John Cougar Mellencamp acknowledges the past icons of music with his homage "R.O.C.K. in the U.S.A." Billy Joel's songs "Tell Her About It" and "The Longest Time" have an aura reminiscent of the late 1950s and early 1960s.

John Fogerty's 1985 hit "Centerfield" reflects a fantasy of playing in the Major Leagues. The music video opens with baseball cards and features archival film footage of baseball greats.[2]

Seaver closed out his career with the Red Sox in 1986. It was obvious that the right-hander was going to retire soon. If not after that season, then certainly in a year or two. Nostalgia kicked in and fans recalled an outstanding career: five-time National League leader in strikeouts, three-time Cy Young Award winner, two-time MLB ERA leader, two-time MLB shutouts leader, twelve-time All-Star.

In 1967 the New York Mets rookie placed tenth in the number of wins for the Major Leagues. It was an eight-way tie, actually. Seaver's sixteen wins matched the totals for Jim Kaat, Gary Peters, Joe Sparma, Mike Cuellar, Dick Hughes, Milt Pappas, and Bob Veale. He won Rookie of the Year. Two years later, he led the Mets to a World Series title in 1969. They went seven games against the Oakland A's in 1973, but the AL squad beat the fellas from Queens for the second of three consecutive World Series championships.

When the Mets traded Seaver to the Reds in what became known as the Midnight Massacre on June 15, 1977, it devastated Mets fans. Imported from Cincinnati were Doug Flynn, Pat Zachry, Steve Henderson, and Dan Norman. Gone was the fireballer known as "The Franchise" for his importance to the Mets. It just didn't seem right that Seaver wore a uniform other than one with blue and orange. Mickey Mantle was a lifelong Yankee. Sandy Koufax always wore Dodger blue. Ernie Banks symbolized the Cubs for his nineteen-year career. Al Kaline's unbroken link with Detroit equaled the Fox Theatre, Belle Isle Park, and the automobile industry in the annals of Motor City.

Seaver would fit among those one-team icons. Or so it seemed.

In a Reds uniform, Seaver notched his only no-hitter and led the Majors in victories for the strike-shortened 1981 season. Christmas came nine days early for Mets fans in 1982, when the Reds traded Seaver back on December 16 for Charlie Puleo, Lloyd McClendon, and Jason Felice. Seaver admitted, "When I left here, I never thought I'd be back."[3]

Mets fans got an emotional boost from seeing Tom Terrific squaring off against his familiar Opening Day counterpart, Steve Carlton of the Philadelphia Phillies, in 1983. It was Seaver's fourteenth Opening Day start. But the moment didn't just affect the 46,687 fans attending this homecoming. "I knew it would be emotional, but I didn't think it would be that emotional," confessed Seaver. "I had to block out a lot of it because I was pitching, but if I wasn't, I would have cried. I know my mother lost it."[4]

Seaver pitched six innings, walked one batter, and added five strikeouts to his burgeoning total. He left with the game scoreless; New York hit three straight singles to load the bases in the seventh. Mike Howard followed with a fourth, which scored Dave Kingman. Brian Giles's sacrifice fly allowed George Foster to score. Relief pitcher Doug Sisk got credited with the 2–0 victory, but the day belonged to Seaver.

His one-year stay with the Mets yielded a 9-14 record. Combined with his '82 output, the right-hander was 14-27 for the past two seasons.

Seaver went to the Chicago White Sox on January 20, 1984, because the Mets didn't protect him in the player compensation draft; Chicago wanted the veteran pitcher because it lost Dennis Lamp, a free agent. The Mets' failure to protect Seaver was a result of misjudgment, not disregard for what he meant to the team's legacy or his valuable knowledge of National League hitters. Mets general manager Frank Cashen confessed, "I didn't feel the White Sox would be interested in starting pitching. I made a mistake. I'm not here to say I didn't."[5]

On August 4, 1985, the forty-year-old Seaver took the mound and pitched a complete game for a 3-1 victory. His three hundredth. Seaver became the seventeenth hurler to reach the triple-century club, but where he did it was somewhat ironic—Yankee Stadium.

Even the most diehard of Yankees fans knew what Seaver meant to the city of New York when he pitched for the Mets, indicated by the crowd of more than fifty-four thousand giving him a lengthy standing ovation. When Don Baylor pinch-hit for Bob Meacham in the bottom of the ninth and cracked a fly ball to left field, Reid Nichols waited patiently under the Bronx sky to catch the ball for the twenty-seventh out and elevate Seaver into a category that included Christy Mathewson, Warren Spahn, Lefty Grove, and Grover Cleveland Alexander.

The White Sox relinquished Seaver for Red Sox outfielder Steve Lyons on June 29, 1986. New England's sports fans had started the year on a positive note—the Patriots were ascending to the playoffs and the Celtics were in the middle of a stellar season that finished with a 67-15 record. Alas, the Bears overwhelmed the Patriots' defense with a 46-10 thrashing in the Super Bowl. But the Celtics won the NBA title in five games against an outstanding Houston Rockets team.

Baseball fortunes looked immense, too.

The Red Sox led the American League, with eight games separating them from the second-place Yankees when Seaver arrived, so the value of a veteran pitcher with a 2-6 record almost midway through the season was questionable. But the *Boston Globe* pointed out that the pennant-winning seasons of 1967 and 1975 also had midseason trades, which magnified the team's strength. Notably, right-hander Gary Bell added a 12-8 record to the Cinderella season, and Elston Howard, acquired in an early August trade with Yankees, contributed an outstanding knowledge of AL hitters. The *Globe* noted that "while Howard hit only .147 in 42 games, he provided the Sox with a veteran catcher, something they needed with their relatively inexperienced pitching staff."[6]

In 1975 new arrival and solid defensive second baseman Denny Doyle wowed the AL with a twenty-two-game hitting streak. He played in eighty-nine games and hit .310, which made him a key component of the '75 squad.

Seaver had value even if he could not go nine with the fearsomeness that he once possessed. You can't put a price on experience. Seaver's 306-198 career record and career 2.84 ERA reflected the excellence that long ago secured his credentials for Cooperstown. No longer the hurler whose delivery concluded with an awesome stretch causing his right knee to touch the dirt, the forty-one-year-old reminded fans, peers, and the press that wisdom honed over two decades can compensate for the erosion of youthful stamina.

Roger Clemens had a 14-0 record when Seaver came to Fenway Park. It didn't seem like he needed any tutelage. But the great ones are always looking for an edge.

Seaver instructed the twenty-three-year-old hurler (about to turn twenty-four at the beginning of August) regarding the importance of a pitcher protecting his individuality. "Tom had the gift of keeping things really simple when it came to pitching," revealed Clemens in 2020. "I still remember him telling me, 'Don't let anybody mess with your mechanics. The way they are, they'll carry you a long way.' I remember telling him about three or four of my hot spots, and the knowledge he gave me back was invaluable. It had nothing to do with analytics, nothing crazy like that, it was real simple stuff—but stuff you need to have to pitch in the major leagues."[7]

In his first outing with the Red Sox, Seaver pitched seven innings in a 9–7 victory against the Blue Jays at Fenway Park on July 1. He gave up nine hits and four runs—all earned—while striking out two and allowing two walks.

Boston's offense provided sufficient support, allowing Seaver to leave the game with a five-run cushion and the score 9–4. But his last sequence was not an easygoing endeavor. After retiring the first two Blue Jays, Seaver plunked Jesse Barfield on the left arm; Cliff Johnson's single put runners on first and second. Seaver had thrown 126 pitches, the last resulting in Kevin Romine catching Willie Upshaw's fly ball to the deep part of Fenway Park's center field.[8]

Red Sox skipper John McNamara, whose 1979–82 tenure helming the Reds coincided with four of Seaver's five years there, commended his new hurler but acknowledged the impact of time. "He may not be the same as he was," allowed McNamara. "But he's a surgeon at his craft. He kept us in the game. That's what exactly we were looking for."[9]

Steve Crawford allowed a pair of runs in relief. Joe Sambito got the save, relieving Crawford with two outs in the bottom of the eighth. Toronto scored its seventh and final run when George Bell singled home Tony Fernández.

Seaver started against the Seattle Mariners five days later, again lasting seven innings. The Red Sox's offense had another decent showing, giving the righty a 4–1 lead when he departed the Fenway Park mound for the afternoon. Seattle mounted a comeback, tallying a pair of runs on a two-run homer by third baseman Jim Presley.

But Baylor singled with one out in the bottom of the eighth. Dwight Evans struck out, followed by Romine—who had replaced Tony Armas in center field in the top of the eighth—drawing a walk and Marc Sullivan's three-run blast to make the score 7–3 and give No. 41 his second straight win as a Boston pitcher.

On August 18, 1986, Seaver pitched a 3–1 victory—the 311th and final time that he added an entry in the "W" column. It was a classic Seaver outing: eight and two-thirds innings, seven strikeouts, four walks, and three hits anchoring the victory for the Red Sox over the Minnesota Twins.

For the 20,492 people in the stands at the Hubert H. Humphrey Metrodome, it was a privilege to watch the aging but still effective hurler work. But the stadium's temporary dwellers could not have known that it would be Seaver's last victory. He started five days later in Cleveland and lasted five and a third innings; Boston lost 5–4, but Seaver did not get credited with the "L." Six days hence, he faced the Indians again at Fenway Park and left the game after four and a third innings with a 5–2 deficit. Cleveland later tacked on two more runs and the Red Sox scored once, giving the 7–3 loss to Seaver.

In his first two starts in September, he looked like the Seaver of old, at least in endurance, when he held the mound for eight innings on September 3 against the Rangers and again on September 8 against the Orioles. Each game was a no-decision.

Seaver lost the last two games of his career; he went four innings at Yankee Stadium and lasted the same amount in Toronto. His record with Boston: 5-7.

The pitching lineup was already sound when Seaver donned a Red Sox uniform for the first time. Clemens finished 1986 at 24-4, leading the Majors in wins and winning percentage (.857); among AL pitchers, he had the second-highest strikeout total behind Mark Langston of the Mariners and the lowest ERA. Dennis "Oil Can" Boyd had a 16-10 record; Bruce Hurst won thirteen and lost eight.

It had not been an easy climb to the AL pennant, though. Boston won the AL East in the 155th game of the 162-game season. The AL Championship Series against the Angels went the full seven games; Boston was down three games to two but rebounded to win Game Six 10-4 and Game Seven 8-1.

For those wanting to see the veteran right-hander get tapped for another shot at postseason glory, they found disappointment. Before the playoffs against the California Angels, Seaver disclosed, "I do know that with my [right] knee the way it is right now, it's impossible for me to pitch in the championship series."[10] A World Series opportunity for him remained if the Red Sox won AL flag. Win, they did. Pitch, he didn't.

The Mets had a smoother journey to the NL pennant, clinching it on September 16. They won the NL Championship Series in six games against the Astros, concluded by an epic sixteen-inning affair at the Astrodome. With the score tied 4-4, the Mets crossed the plate three times in the top of the sixteenth and kept the Astros from scoring in the bottom half of the inning.

Two days before the 1986 World Series began, McNamara announced Seaver's unavailability because of the ongoing knee problems. Associated Press reported the diagnosis: Seaver suffered "a sprained ligament on the outside of his right knee" during the Blue Jays game on September 19.[11] Seaver's presence at the World Series, even though it wasn't in a Mets uniform, represented the power of nostalgia that marked his career. It's great fodder for one of three great "What if" questions involving sports in Boston.

What if the rumored trade of Joe DiMaggio for Ted Williams had happened? Statisticians can speculate and Yankees fans can salivate over how many home runs the Splendid Splinter would have hit with a short right-field fence 314 feet from Yankee Stadium's home plate.

What if Len Bias hadn't died of a cocaine overdose two days after getting drafted by the Boston Celtics? The epic Celtics-Lakers match-ups might have resulted in more championship banners at Boston Garden with the University of Maryland alumnus in the lineup.

What if Tom Seaver had stayed healthy enough to pitch in spots during the rest of 1986? One can fantasize about John McNamara calling on Seaver to face his former team, silence their bats, and add a second World Series title to his already outstanding list of achievements.

How might Vin Scully have set the tone during the warm-up pitches?

"Everywhere you turn at Shea Stadium, there are people wearing Mets paraphernalia. They wear their blue hats with the familiar, intertwined N-Y in orange. The color scheme is an homage to the National League teams that once occupied Gotham: blue for Dodgers, orange for Giants. You can easily spot many of them wearing Mets jerseys with Tom Seaver's name and his number. No. 41.

"There stands Seaver on the patch of Shea Stadium dirt that was his workplace so many years ago. He came to the Mets in 1967, winning Rookie of the Year honors with a 16-13 record, 170 strikeouts, 18 complete games, and a 2.76 ERA. Consistency is his trademark. The man known as Tom Terrific brought joy to Mets fans as he frustrated National League lineups time and time again. Three Cy Young Awards, a World Series title in 1969, and another NL pennant in 1973 testify to his excellence.

"But on June 15, 1977, Seaver left New York, a result of acrimony with Mets general manager Donald Grant and unkind remarks about Seaver's wife by *Daily News* columnist Dick Young. With the Reds, he got his only no-hitter. With the White Sox, he tallied his three hundredth victory.

"And now, the forty-one-year-old veteran dons a Red Sox uniform for what will most likely be his final appearance as a Major League pitcher. Seaver has an encyclopedic knowledge about pitching strategies and tactics that he will tap into as he faces off against his old team in front of a Shea Stadium crowd.

"Even if their beloved Mets lose to the legend tonight, you have to wonder if the fans will be glad, albeit quietly, for their former leader."

The Mets won the World Series in seven games.

Al Nipper was Seaver's teammate on the '86 Red Sox. He recalls:

"Tom was my idol growing up. When I was in college at Truman State in Missouri, I absolutely loved him. As a kid, I would take the Redbird Express, a double-decker red bus, from the Village Square shopping center by my house in Hazelwood and go to the Cardinals games with friends or by myself. I always went to watch him pitch. In 1984 I'm pitching against him in a nationally televised game against the White Sox at Fenway Park. We won. He went seven, I went nine and a third. The next day, he's walking toward the corner of our dugout, and he's coming in my direction. I was nervous and excited. He comes right up to me and held out his right hand and said, 'Mr. Nipper, you threw one whale of a game last night.'

"I told him that he's my idol. He told me, 'Next week, you're coming to Comiskey. We'll meet on the mound at 1:00 p.m. and we'll talk.'"[12]

After the World Series, Seaver had surgery to get rid of the torn cartilage in his knee. The Red Sox released him in mid-November; Seaver was a free agent. The Yankees were a potential landing site because Seaver's status meant that George Steinbrenner would have to open his checkbook without giving up players in a trade. Plus, the marquee value of Seaver in New York was a bedrock fact, like heavy traffic on the Long Island Expressway during the late afternoon on a Friday in July and August.

Before Seaver's release, Yankees manager Lou Piniella had offered praise: "He's a bulldog who gives you 100 per cent and, if healthy, could help us, I'm sure."[13] A month later, the Yankees affirmed that they would not pursue Seaver.[14]

The Mets made an offer and signed Seaver in early June. Nostalgia was evident, though not overriding, according to Mets general manager Frank Cashen: "Believe me, this was not a deal made out of marketability or sentimentality—although parenthetically, let me add that I have always believed Tom Seaver deserved to end his career here. It was made out of a firm conviction Tom can help us in late June, July, August, September and hopefully in October."[15]

Seaver's stay with the Mets organization lasted two weeks. An exhibition against the Tidewater Tides—the Mets' Triple-A team—was disastrous. Tidewater hammered him for five hits and seven runs in the first two innings, then racked up three more hits in the third inning; Seaver threw fifty-eight pitches and notched two strikeouts and a walk.[16]

A five-inning simulation in Montreal during a road trip yielded eighty-eight pitches, which Seaver acknowledged as an improvement of stamina, if not skill.[17] Another simulation yielded four innings and introspection from the Mets icon: "The doubts that I've had all along are still quite evident in my mind."[18]

The price tag for his 1987 services would have been $750,000. "But this was a 'good faith' contract and when I realized I couldn't do it, I decided not to go any further," said the forty-two-year-old pitcher. "I set high goals for myself and it would have been unfair to me and to everyone in that clubhouse to create a logjam."[19]

A year later, the Mets retired No. 41 during Tom Seaver Day.

During his speech, Seaver told the Shea Stadium crowd, "I came to a decision a long time ago that if my number was ever retired, there would be one way that I wanted to say thank you to everybody. Everybody that's here on the field. Everybody that's in the stands. Everybody that's home watching on television. If you just allow me one moment, I'm going to say thank you in my own very special way. And if you know me, how much I love pitching, you'll know what it means to me."[20]

Seaver trotted to the pitching mound, saluted Gil Hodges's No. 14, bowed to the crowd several times and then to his former teammates who had voyaged to Queens, Jerry Grote and Jerry Koosman among them. It was a tangible reminder of the Mets' glory days. Nostalgia permeated the crowd on that late July day in 1988 as it did four years later in Cooperstown, when the Baseball Hall of Fame formally inducted Seaver. He got a 98.84 percent vote for the Baseball Hall of Fame, a record for the highest percentage until Ken Griffey Jr. got 99.32 percent in 2016.

Twenty years after Tom Seaver Day, the country suffered financial whiplash during the worst stock market crash since the Great Depression. On September 28, 2008, Seaver took the mound again and offered a sorely needed emotional salve for New Yorkers. After the last game at Shea Stadium—a Mets-Marlins contest—Seaver tossed a ball to Mike Piazza from the pitching mound. It bounced once. But that did not tarnish in any way the moment's joyful poignancy.

Citi Field debuted in 2009. It has used the address 41 Seaver Way since 2019. A year later, Seaver passed away at age seventy-five from complications involving Lewy body dementia and COVID-19. Before the Mets' home opener in 2022, a long overdue event took place—the unveiling of a Tom Seaver statue in front of the ballpark.

Although his time with the Mets amounted to a little more than half his career, Tom Seaver has an unbreakable bond with the city of New York. But the one year that he spent with the Red Sox prompts examination of his place in baseball as a cultural figure because of the nostalgia that was a bedrock of the 1980s. NBC broadcast the World Series in 1986. An appearance by Seaver in the playoffs against the Angels and subsequent World Series against the Mets would have fit nicely into the cultural paradigm highlighted by the network's back-to-the-past aura in its prime-time lineup.

Matlock premiered, giving Andy Griffith his second blockbuster show. Set in Atlanta, *Matlock* had a format similar to the one used by *Perry Mason*—Ben Matlock, a folksy, clever defense attorney, uncovers the real criminal at the end of the episode, usually during a trial. NBC leveraged Griffith's popularity and nostalgia, evidenced the previous spring in the TV movie *Return to Mayberry*, a reunion of *The Andy Griffith Show*.[21] Its high Nielsen ratings indicated Griffith's tremendous appeal, sourced in the aura of nostalgia.[22]

Crime Story was an ambitious one-hour drama tracking a group of cops targeting a mobster and his brethren from the early 1960s to the early 1980s. The first season was set in Chicago, with indicators that never let the viewer forget the time frame. The cops' favorite hangout was the Orbit Room, a bar with a moniker reflecting the space age of the early 1960s.

In the second and final season, *Crime Story* moved the plot to Las Vegas, with the Chicago gangsters morphing into casino operators. The story line was in the mid-1960s when NBC canceled the show.

Rags to Riches was set in the same time frame. Its premise relied somewhat on *Annie* in its format and advertising—a Bel Air business mogul uses six orphan girls to close a business deal, but his fondness inspires him to adopt them.

Tom Seaver's last appearance at Shea Stadium was bittersweet for Mets fans attending the 1986 World Series. They looked in the visitors' dugout and saw an athlete not exactly decaying but certainly not the model of superiority he was in days of yore. Had the legend with 311 wins been sufficiently healthy to take one last shot at postseason laurels—whether as a starter or a reliever—pitching against the Mets at his former home would undoubtedly have been described as ironic, poetic, and operatic.

Nostalgic, even.

15

Location, Location, Location
The Tales and Travails of the Citgo Sign

The Citgo sign outside Fenway Park is a bedrock of Red Sox culture.

Sitting on top of a six-story building outside the left-field wall, the sign watches over the storied ballpark as its predecessor did when the company was called Cities Service. It's a different form of advertising. Visible from any vantage point in the ballpark, the Citgo sign links the oil-and-gas Goliath to the team without the financial burden of TV commercials, billboard space within the confines of Fenway Park, or the right to be the official gasoline station sponsor. TV viewers of Red Sox home games see it constantly.

Cities Service initially placed its sign in 1940. Changing the company name to Citgo and its logo to a stylized red triangle with dark blue lettering in 1965 called for a new sign. But not all New Englanders are fans; reactions are mixed. A 1974 letter to the editor of the *Boston Globe* expressed frustration at the "ugly Citgo sign" being lit during an energy crisis while citizens were urged to cut back on electricity use.[1]

In 1976 a New Bedford resident praised it: "Funny, but I and a lot of others think it's beautiful! It's colorful, imaginative, is helping promote the economy and is just one small part of our tremendously successful free-enterprise system."[2]

The *Globe* published four letters about the sign on October 12, 1976. One writer called it "Boston's very own 'North Star.'"[3] Another likened its iconography to the Woodstock album and to Rick urging Ilsa to go with Victor at the end of *Casablanca*, then saying to her, for the last time, "Here's looking at you, kid."[4] It was described as an "eyesore" by one New Englander and "loved and admired" by another.[5]

In 1977 its guidepost status caused *Globe* correspondent Christina Robb to issue a challenge in a detailed article about the lights around

Boston: "Could you find Kenmore Square without the CITGO sign, or McDonald's without the golden arch?"[6]

During the energy crisis of the late 1970s, Massachusetts governor Edward King called for the Citgo and White Fuel signs to be turned off. While not financially significant—the *Globe* cited a spokesperson from Boston Edison claiming that the cost to operate the Citgo sign was about "60 cents an hour"—going dark would ideally inspire people to reduce electricity use in their homes and offices. "The ban on outdoor advertising is more of a symbolic move," stated a spokesperson from the Massachusetts Energy Office. "People see lights out that used to be on, especially on two popular signs, and it brings home the fact that there is an energy problem."[7]

And so the lights went out for the famed sixty-foot-by-sixty-foot, neon-lit Kenmore Square marker.

It was symbolic in another sense. Two weeks earlier, President Jimmy Carter gave a televised speech highlighting the "malaise" felt throughout the country because of a sour economy. Having one of Boston's most notable icons no longer lighting up the skyline reflected, and perhaps added to, the immense dimming of optimism that Americans felt after the emotional pummeling from political assassinations, more than fifty thousand service members killed in the Vietnam War, the Watergate scandal that led to a presidential resignation and several prison terms for top White House aides, and now the second energy crisis of the 1970s.

But the Citgo sign endured in the hearts and minds of many Bostonians and their neighbors across New England.

"Citgo is bright lights and glamour," stated Pauline Chase Harrell, the Boston Landmarks Commission chair, in 1980. "It's always meant excitement and a ball game. I can't think of anything in Boston that's more a landmark in the sense of marking the land. I wish we could find a way to save it. If the Landmarks Commission received a petition from ten registered voters, we'd be happy to consider it."[8]

After forty years, the Citgo sign had achieved small landmark status, if not officially. But there had been some whiffs of jeopardy for the sign in the early 1980s. Citgo showed reluctance to reach into its oil-rich coffers for renovation; a company official said the price tag would be $40,000.[9]

There was noise about the sign getting formal recognition when the city's Landmarks Commission received a petition started by citizens wanting to give legal acknowledgment of its importance to Boston.[10] Detractors emerged again. A Cambridge resident complained, "To consider perpetuating this piece of private advertising at public expense is as much of an outrage as fiddling while Rome burns."[11]

As workers prepared to take the sign down under orders from Citgo, the Landmarks Commission stepped in with a cease-and-desist order.[12]

At a hearing on January 11, 1983, Citgo agreed to pay for the sign's renovation—now estimated at $300,000—but with a catch. Citgo did not want landmark recognition, which would compel the company to continue maintenance. In the corporate world, change is a constant. So, keeping the sign in tip-top shape could contravene future marketing strategies. One example would be a logo change. As Citgo's attorney pointed out, landmark status would give the sign a historical base and the company, in turn, might "be forced to maintain something that may not have anything to do with business."[13]

The hearing prompted another round of letters to the editor in the *Globe*. Again, opinions varied. A New Hampshire resident wrote that preservation of "this obsolete and extravagant piece of Americana" was "absurd."[14] One scribe suggested that the money be invested in Kenmore Square's economy and proposed that this "garish orgy of commercialism" be put in a museum.[15] Another letter writer proposed a museum as a new home for this piece of "pop art."[16]

The day of the Landmarks Commission vote, a *Globe* editorial asked that no permanency be granted regarding the sign's placement. It also suggested a museum solution.[17]

The eight-member commission voted against landmark status in a 7–1 tally.[18]

On August 10, 1983, the sign blazed forth once again after its four-year hiatus.[19] Six years later, it went out of commission when a windstorm broke "scores of its 5,000 neon tubes." Citgo had seen the light—or neon—so to speak. A company spokesperson stated, "We had no idea it would receive such a response. Now we know how much people in Boston love that sign."[20]

Venezuela's state-owned oil company, Petróleos de Venezuela, S.A. (PDVSA), bought 50 percent of Citgo in 1986 and the remaining 50 percent four years later. When President Hugo Chávez referred to President George W. Bush in 2006 as "the devil," it ignited a firestorm of responses, both in words and deeds. Boston city councilor Jerry McDermott called for the removal of the iconic, neon-lit feature. An editorial by the *Globe* opposed this response and praised Citgo's offering heating oil to low-income New Englanders: "Whoever owns the company, the sign is an integral part of Kenmore Square and the city."[21]

A *Globe* reader responded, "It is unfortunate to see how these marketing schemes are so successful that Bostonians, and newspaper editorial boards, would actually consider a giant company logo to be part of Boston's character, even more so than the American flag.

"Better to spend our efforts advocating the preservation of Outer Brewster Island, H. H. Richardson buildings, and other features that are truly valuable."[22]

In 2005 there were improvements costing $1.5 million. Five years later, the sign got another round of upgrades.[23]

Alison Frazee is the executive director of the Boston Preservation Alliance. She explains:

"The Citgo sign is a beloved feature of the Boston skyline. Most viewers don't associate it with the Citgo brand, it's more often and closely tied to the Boston Red Sox. From the inside of the ballpark fans can see the sign and encourage hitters to 'C-it-go' or hit the ball out of the park. In our campaign to protect the sign, the sign appeared everywhere—hats, shirts, wall art, pop art, menus, city logos and advertisements, brochures, and even quite a few tattoos. The Citgo sign represents Boston and is often used to make that association. Many former students told us they used the glow of the sign to find their way back to their dorms late at night.

"It's an orientation, [a] wayfinding tool for many finding the ballpark as well. It's also a special moment, as one emerges from the Green Line station in Kenmore Square, to see the enormous sign so close. Like a full moon rising over the horizon. It marks the last leg for Boston Marathon runners. It's an icon of the city.

"I don't think anyone from Boston would say its removal would have no impact. But I have heard people raise the desire to change the imagery on the sign to something less controversial. A sign in the same place, that's the same size and has similar movement, but with a neutral symbol of some kind, could be a compromise.

"We form relationships with our surroundings over time. We create associations, build memories, and rely on the constants in our built environment for wayfinding and sense of place. Whether it's a gas station ad, splashes of paint on a huge gas tank, ads painted on the side of a building, or even billboards, if it's there long enough it becomes part of our sense of place which can define our sense of place. This symbol means home to me and I belong here.

"To me, old buildings are storytellers. They are art made and transformed by the lives lived within them. I wanted to help save them. And as I've worked in this field for over a decade I have seen how important historic places are to structuring our identities, sense of self, and placing ourselves in our cultures and societies.

"We have embraced reusable bags, straws, cups, and bottles[,] but we throw away an entire building without thinking twice. The average single-family home in America, when demolished, creates about the same amount of waste as the average American. It's imperative that we reuse buildings for the health of the planet as well as the stability and sustainability of our neighborhoods. Our biggest job is to help decision-makers understand the value of existing and historic buildings to our neighborhoods, our cities, and our planet."[24]

The Citgo sign's importance in American culture is undeniable. The Red Sox connection has given it goodwill by being visually accessible, perhaps more than any other corporate logo in or around the ballpark. In the always competitive oil-and-gas fraternity, this has been an advantage against peers with bigger bank accounts and marketing budgets.

Bruce Wells, executive director of the Oil and Gas Historical Society, weighs in:

"Although now owned by a country with no formal diplomatic ties [to the United States], Citgo Petroleum Corporation has played a considerable role in U.S. oil and natural gas history. The red triangle logo evolved from the green-outlined one inside a trefoil. Cities Service was founded in 1910 by Henry Latham Doherty in Bartlesville, Oklahoma. (Phillips 66 also was founded in Bartlesville.) The future Citgo began as a public utility holding company that quickly expanded into oil exploration and production.

"Doherty's company fortunes rose in 1915, when a subsidiary, Wichita Natural Gas Company, discovered the 34-square-mile El Dorado oilfield in Kansas. In 1928, a Cities Service subsidiary, Empire Oil & Refining, discovered another giant Mid-Continent field at Oklahoma City. Meanwhile, another oil giant also founded in Bartlesville, Phillips Petroleum, created its own distinctive Phillips 66 logo.

"By 1932, with a move of headquarters to New York City (and a triangle in a trefoil logo), Doherty opened the amazing Art Deco inspired Cities Service Building in Lower Manhattan. Of course, Petróleos de Venezuela has owned Citgo for more than three decades now.

"I'm sure Red Sox fans nationwide would recognize the red triangle alone. Many other gasoline consumers too, thanks to the company's marketing budget, especially in the eastern part of the country with its many Citgo stations. TV coverage of home runs at Fenway Park have helped with national recognition.

"I think the name removal could happen someday soon. The best example of an established petroleum company's marketing symbol without the brand name is Shell Oil, subsidiary of Royal Dutch Shell. That iconic clamshell began in the early 1900s. The company dropped the name Shell beneath the modern red and yellow shell in 1999. Other famous oil logos like Chevron's could do it too.

"Citgo's iconic logo already is part of the petroleum industry and modern energy history. It will be preserved. This also applies to other oil company logos. For example, after BP acquired Amoco in the late 1990s, the BP green-and-yellow sunflower logo replaced all Amoco logos of a blue-and-red torch inside an oval logo. Amoco service station signs are popular with collectors and can be found in museums.

"The even more popular Mobil red Pegasus is displayed in many museums—and displayed above the historic Dallas building where it first rotated in 1934. Fenway Park's Cities Service red triangle deserves to be preserved, just like the company's 'Koolmotor' signs introduced a century earlier.

"Mobil's longtime Masterpiece Theatre sponsorship has made a difference in cultural education and set a good example like the founder of Standard Oil's Rockefeller Foundation. But the petroleum industry's most successful 'wildcatters' have a long history of philanthropy and paying for public works. The Citgo connection to Fenway works in its own way. Recently here in DC, I saw a Boston baseball fan wearing a white T-shirt with the red triangle and Fenway Park instead of the word Citgo. Another fine example of successful corporate brand marketing.

"Petroleum history is energy education, offering one of many ways to accelerate the world's energy transition. The now controversial use of fossil fuels, burning coal, oil and natural gas helped create the modern civilization of today (kerosene alone changed the world for the better by far). The economics, technologies, and earth sciences behind these still vital energy resources offer a context for understanding modern energy challenges.

"Informed policy decisions should come from knowing the history of petroleum exploration, production, refining, transportation, and the almost countless petroleum products—like asphalt, plastics, and petrochemical medicines. The nation's energy industry oil spills and environmental harm, which must and should be prevented, are the cost of social economic advancements since the first U.S. [commercial] oil well of 1859 in Pennsylvania—drilled to find oil for refining into kerosene for lamps."[25]

The Citgo sign was on the verge of having the protection of the Boston Landmarks Commission in 2018 with a unanimous, affirmative vote. Boston mayor Marty Walsh kiboshed it.

A landmark designation could have chilled development in Kenmore Square and the surrounding area. Instead, the mayor helped with negotiations between Citgo and the building's owner, Related Beal. It's a reprieve. For a while. "We are pleased to share that we have reached a long-term resolution that will preserve the Citgo sign and allow for it to remain in place in Kenmore Square for years to come, recognizing the significance that this sign has on our landscape in Boston, while balancing the opportunity for our horizons to continue evolving in future years," read the mayor's statement.[26]

Sometimes it takes a politician to be the mediator and protect all sides as much as possible. "Mayor Walsh was probably hoping that Citgo and Related Beal could negotiate a solution on their own," Frazee stated. "At the time, there were ongoing talks about a lease for the sign to remain in place. Walsh was considered to be a pro-developer mayor and he may have seen this Landmark designation as [limiting] development potential. A lease was not signed between the two parties until 2022."[27]

Related Beal bought the building from Boston University in 2016. Its development in the area includes a building obscuring part of the sign; it's still visible and prominent for pedestrians, but there's no clear view of it.[28]

The sign's impact is well remembered by Boston-area natives, transplants, visitors, and especially BU alumni decades after their first in-person encounter. Warren Thayer grew up about forty miles from Boston on a dairy farm in Salisbury, Massachusetts, where he pitched hay, milked cows, and performed various chores that might have been talked about or depicted on *Green Acres*, a popular sitcom airing on CBS at the time he matriculated at Boston University. A journalism major, Thayer, like thousands of other BU students, used the Citgo sign's massive presence to his advantage. Thayer remembers, "I fell in love with the sign in the fall of 1966 when I entered BU. In my earliest days on campus, it was my North Star and helped me find my way around. I was a rural farm kid and all things 'city' both enthralled and intimidated me.

"After a while, it was just somehow reassuring to see it there on my way back and forth to classes. I would be a tad upset when some of the bulbs blew out and weren't replaced quickly. Some of us loved it, some were indifferent, but I think about everyone liked it enough to want it to stay.

"And yes, I did share some joints with friends on the 9th floor of Myles Standish Hall, not often just to watch the sign, but it was always a nice view. When you got too stoned you sometimes forgot the sequence of the sign 'movements' and we'd joke about it. Rumor had it that Babe Ruth stayed at Myles sometimes while pitching for the Bosox.

"When I moved to an apartment on Beacon Street near the Mass Pike in my junior year, I could still see the sign out my window."[29]

Eddie Bruckner is a Boston-based visual artist whose portfolio includes depictions of the Citgo sign either alone or with Fenway Park. "I am drawn to the Citgo Sign for its ability to evoke a sense of nostalgia and pride among Bostonians, Red Sox fans, tourists, and the countless number of students who come to Boston for their college education," says Bruckner. "The Citgo Sign no longer represents a gas station and has now evolved into a cultural landmark and powerful unofficial symbol of Boston."[30]

Indeed, the Fenway Park experience without the Citgo sign is as unthinkable as Yaz in a Yankees uniform, as improbable as Alaskan crab being served at an MIT black-tie affair, and as unusual as Boston having a Republican mayor.

"We're lucky to still have it," says urban historian Arthur Krim. "It has become encased as a permanent icon of the city skyline even under changing conditions. Boston has accumulated these long-standing icons that have become embedded in the symbolism of the city. The Swan Boats have been operated by the Paget family since 1870. Harvard began in 1636."[31]

The Citgo sign is in good company. Those with a nostalgic bent refer to the Berkeley weather beacon as the John Hancock weather beacon, so named because the Berkeley Building at 200 Berkeley Street served as the John Hancock Life Insurance Company headquarters for thirty years, from 1947 to 1977. Bigelow Cleaners in Newton has a neon sign reflecting a retro style. The exterior of Symphony Hall brandishes a brightly lit "BSO" in red to reflect the Boston Symphony Orchestra.

In Alton, New Hampshire, a Little League ball field named Little Fenway pays homage to its namesake with a scaled-down version of the Boston ballpark, including a replica of the Citgo sign. But neither the Citgo name nor the logo may be eternal. Some companies forgo names for initials, as when Schlumberger became SLB. Standard Oil became Esso and then switched to Exxon during the Nixon administration. After British Petroleum merged with Amoco, the company became BP. Gone were Amoco's torch and BP's shield in favor of a green-and-yellow sunburst logo softening the image of Big Oil.

Bank mergers have consumed several companies serving New England with decades of goodwill. In turn, their names, logos, and trademarks were retired from use. What if the sign had belonged to Bank of Boston? Fleet Bank? Bank of New England? Shawmut Bank? It's difficult to imagine an argument advocating for these defunct signifiers in place of the new corporate name.

As long as Citgo retains its name and triangular logo, however, the sign's endorsers will speak of tradition as if removal is akin to selling corporate naming rights for Fenway Park, tearing down the Green Monster, or changing Boston's name to Massachusetts City.

They provide examples with the rapidity of an Oil Can Boyd fastball. It's argued that the Kenmore Square sign rivals London's Big Ben and other symbols in metropolitan importance. Long Island City has the Pepsi-Cola sign. Jersey City, the Colgate clock. Mobil's flying Pegasus lit in red once stood atop the Magnolia Hotel in Dallas, beginning in 1934. But six decades of weather forced it to be taken down; it stands outside the Omni Dallas hotel as a symbol of the city's roots in the oil industry while a replacement brightens the skyline.

At the top of the skyscraper above New York City's Grand Central Terminal, a corporate logo rests on the outside—first Pan Am's, then MetLife's. Removing it would leave New Yorkers walking or driving up Park Avenue in Midtown Manhattan feeling as empty as Kenmore Square travelers no longer seeing the famous marker.

Indeed, Citgo's recognition factor is strong in a competitive advertising culture booming with slogans and logos. We remember that Nationwide is on our side for insurance needs because of a rhyming slogan; Apple embraces our individualism because we think different; and our sinful secrets stay kept with the strength of a Fort Knox vault because what happens in Las Vegas stays in Las Vegas.

Animation is especially powerful in helping children identify products, sometimes even before they can read. "Snap! Crackle! Pop!" are the names of the characters for Rice Krispies and the cereal's sonic descriptors, while their elfin brethren at Keebler advocate a snack of cookies for the toddler set.

Logos are shorthand for communicating a product or service. We accept the Nike swoosh as an emblem of primacy in athletic footwear. Merrill Lynch's bull reflects optimism for investing with the financial behemoth. The golden arches of McDonald's equal Chicken McNuggets for tired parents looking to fast food as an efficient, if not wholly nutritious, option for their kids. A business executive's long, tired day might prompt a well-earned nightcap of Jack Daniels on the rocks inspired by the whiskey giant's slogan: "Make It Count."

Hollywood has tapped into the world of advertising as terrific fodder for storytelling. *Mr. Blandings Builds His Dream House. Will Success Spoil Rock Hunter? Bewitched. Bosom Buddies. Kramer vs. Kramer. thirtysomething. Mad Men.*

But Don Draper's keen sense of the emotional draw that advertising created for products in the 1960s and Miles Drentell's unyielding arrogance wrapped around inherent talent reflecting the yuppie-inspired, materialism-craving, red-power-tie sensibility of the late 1980s—and, to an extent, early 1990s—cannot compete with the factors of luck and location that Citgo has enjoyed since before America entered World War II, when one of the company's filling stations began operations behind the left-field wall at Fenway Park.

After emotion-filled diatribes about the necessity of continuity in an ever-changing world, New Englanders and Red Sox fans around the world can raise a mug of Narragansett and exclaim, "Vive the Citgo sign!"

16

Of Sluggers and Statues

Statues are as much a part of the ballpark experience as beer-hawking vendors, the national anthem, and the seventh-inning stretch.

Capturing moments reflecting the essences of iconic players and typically sculpted in bronze, they represent the highest standard of the baseball diamond, trigger memories of golden eras that warm our hearts during dreary seasons, and inspire silver-haired fans to pass on stories about the game's elite to younger ones as they walk into one of baseball's cathedrals.

Fenway Park, for instance.

Likenesses of Carl Yastrzemski, Ted Williams, Bobby Doerr, Johnny Pesky, and Dom DiMaggio stand in its environs to welcome passersby, whether friend or foe of the Red Sox, and remind them of past glory. Doerr notching more than one hundred RBIs six times, Pesky leading the American League in hits two consecutive years right after World War II, DiMaggio twice being the AL leader in runs scored, Yastrzemski winning a Triple Crown Award for his outstanding performance in 1967, and Williams winning two MVP Awards are a few memories that may be stirred.

There are three statues. Ted Williams and Carl Yastrzemski each have one, unveiled in 2004 and 2013, respectively. The other depicts four players: Williams, Doerr, Pesky, DiMaggio. Debuting in 2010, it's named *The Teammates*.

They have terrific brethren. Examples flourish throughout the Major League parks.

Willie Mays is represented at Oracle Park in San Francisco by an image of his swing that marked a total of 660 home runs. Josh Gibson has a similar statue at Nationals Park in Washington DC, indicating his clout that reached mythical status for the Homestead Grays.

Tom Seaver's statue outside Citi Field shows the legendary right-hander right before he released the ball, when his knee went so low it hit the dirt. It's a hallmark image that Mets fans remember fondly of the pitcher who won three Cy Young Awards. Jackie Robinson's statue at Dodger Stadium shows No. 42 sliding into home; Ernie Banks readies his batting stance at Chicago's Wrigley Field; and, in Kansas City, George Brett prepares to crush the ball outside Kauffman Stadium.

It's a challenge for sculptors. They must fulfill their artistic vision while satisfying the discernment of those who saw the players exemplifying their craft hundreds of times, either at the ballpark or on television.

In his landmark 1952 essay "Monuments and Memorials," Jean Labatut, a leading architect of the twentieth century, defines the benchmarks for artistic and architectural analysis in this area.[1] Labatut's paradigm dictates that artistic works are conduits for education about the past. "Words, customs, methods of reasoning, and techniques may vary, but art is the easiest channel for understanding; through the arts we can become easily acquainted with other times and other peoples and with other people in our own time," explains Labatut.[2]

This is particularly true of baseball, a sport fueled by the power of nostalgia, memory, and lore combined with history. These hallmarks are evident during a home game at Fenway Park as one is immersed in excitement pulsating throughout Red Sox Nation, some of whose members may have spent so much time at this Boston landmark they could find their way around it blindfolded.

Fenway Park's statues highlight the ballpark's magical, timeless aura as a link to the past; Red Sox fans take great comfort in knowing that they are at the same stadium, perhaps sitting in the same seats, where previous generations of their families witnessed Boston's finest ballplayers. A teenaged fan from Needham going to a Sunday afternoon game after morning mass at St. Joseph Parish might be able to trace his clan's loyalty back to his great-great-grandfather, the son of Irish immigrants, who saw his first game during the ballpark's inaugural year of 1912 when he was a teenager himself.

Red Sox narratives are embedded in the team's transgenerational fandom, indeed. A thirteen-year-old Jewish fan from Brookline will know about Ted Williams's exquisite season of 1941, Carlton Fisk's home run in Game Six of the 1975 World Series, and the joyous World Series championship in 2004 as well as he knows his haftorah when he ascends to the bema at Temple Ohabei Shalom for his bar mitzvah ceremony.

Afterward, he will deliver a speech explaining his Torah reading and the applicability of Judaic tales, figures, and lessons from ancient times to the present day. It would not be surprising to hear him speak about the suffering of Red Sox fans and compare it to the plight of Jews searching for meaning and wandering in the desert before achieving fulfillment. Community, faith, and hope would likely be the cornerstones of the speech. His party might include the Red Sox emblem on his cake.

Labatut calls attention to the importance of consumers as well as the artists: "Our understanding and enjoyment of a work of art depend (1) on the radiating power or quality of the work of art itself and (2) on the quality of our power of reception."[3] If we assume that the statues are fine representations of their subjects, the responsibility then falls on the fans to stop, observe, and perceive what the sculptor attempted to convey. The intangible nexus joining the statues is a quiet dignity.

Yastrzemski's statue does not show him at bat preparing for a pitch or following through a swing. Rather, he's doffing his cap during his last at bat in a show of respect to the fans who showered the eighteen-time All-Star with a downpour of affection during his Red Sox tenure, which began in 1961 and ended in 1983 with 3,419 hits, a .285 batting average, and an MVP Award, in addition to the Triple Crown Award.

Summarizing the deep-seated relationship between Yaz and Red Sox fans, it depicts him neither smiling nor grimacing; his visage shows a quiet, almost graceful appreciation that Red Sox Nation recognized his greatness, composure, and endurance.

A stellar ballplayer whose time in the Major Leagues spanned six American presidencies, Yaz was a loyal workhorse who stayed with the team for his entire career. Peers are few but notable. Cases in point: Bob Gibson and the Cardinals, Mike Schmidt and the Phillies, George Brett and the Royals, Johnny Bench and the Reds, Mickey Mantle and the Yankees, Bob Feller and the Indians, Tony Gwynn and the Padres, and Robin Yount and the Brewers.

At the statue's unveiling in 2013, Yastrzemski underscored the emotional impact at seeing the representation outside Fenway Park's right-field boundary. "I'm deeply honored to stand before you today, seeing this statue in front of the place I called home for 23 years," said the American League leader in batting average three times, runs scored three times, and hits twice. "This statue means as much to me as being inducted into the Hall of Fame and having my number retired."[4]

The *Teammates* statue shows Williams, Pesky, Doerr, and DiMaggio with their bats resting on their shoulders, presumably engaging in conversation before a game. Their outstanding play led to the American League title in 1946, and their continuing bond after retirement inspired sports journalist David Halberstam to write the 2003 book *The Teammates: A Portrait of Friendship*, a bestseller that inspired the statue's name.

It's another quiet moment, abundant with anticipation rather than reflection.

One can imagine the foursome chatting about their opponents, discussing pitchers, and sharing insights as they get ready to take batting practice. Where Yastrzemski's statue depicts the slugger at the end of his career, the *Teammates* statue shows four baseball heroes—two of them Hall of Famers (Williams and Doerr) in their prime.

Antonio Tobias Mendez created the Yastrzemski and *Teammates* statues, part of a strong baseball portfolio. Orioles fans traversing Camden Yards will recognize Mendez's work representing their gloried chronicles in statues of Brooks Robinson, Frank Robinson, Jim Palmer, Earl Weaver, Eddie Murray, and Cal Ripken Jr. Like Yastrzemski, his statue of Nolan Ryan outside Globe Life Field in Arlington shows the powerful hurler tipping his hat to the fans as they enter.

But Mendez's artistic contributions go beyond baseball—he created the statue of Don Shula in Miami, for example—and further than sports to represent a wide swath of American icons. Mendez has contributed public art showcasing Davy Crockett at the Tennessee state capitol in Nashville; Teddy Roosevelt at the Theodore Roosevelt Inaugural National Historic Site in Buffalo, New York; Thurgood Marshall on Lawyers Mall at the Maryland State House in Annapolis; U.S. senator Arthur H. Vandenberg at McKay Tower in Grand Rapids, Michigan; and Danny Thomas at the St. Jude Children's Hospital in Memphis.

Working on his two statues for the Red Sox involved research at Fenway Park, examination of the players' attributes, and a meeting with one of his subjects. Mendez recalls:

"The Red Sox invited a handful of sculptors who had done work for other baseball parks. Their original request for the *Teammates* statue was to base it on the cover photo for Halberstam's book, which shows the four players kneeling. The original photo had Rudy York, who was cropped out."

Mendez's other proposal was to have them interacting while waiting for batting practice.

"I was given a year and a half to create the statues. With the *Teammates* statue, when I was doing my research, I took a flight to Boston from Maryland, where I live, and read *The Teammates* on the way. While going through the photo archives at Fenway, they asked if I wanted to meet Pesky, but I had to keep the project a secret. I sat with him in the stands for a game. The Red Sox had brought someone from the Minors to fill in for shortstop that evening and Johnny was in the stands taking notes on the player. The Red Sox told him that I was doing a research paper on Halberstam's book for a university.

"I asked him what he saw in the player. He said, 'I don't like how he's flipping the ball in a double play and not looking at the second baseman.' Pesky saw that I had the book in my hand, and he said, 'It's a great book.' Then he baited me to see what I knew. As a fan of baseball, I don't remember statistics but I remember stories. He asked me the last year Williams hit .400 for the season. I answered, 'It was the year before you came up to the Majors.'

"There was a handicapped fan who saw that I had an all access pass and asked why I had it. I thought she was going to spoil it. A staffer grabbed me, took me down on the field, and gave me a camera because I wanted to get ideas from the players at batting practice."[5]

Ted Williams's statue has an equally quiet portrayal. Instead of the Splendid Splinter in his batting pose demonstrating offensive dominance that resulted in a .344 career batting average, the statue shows him putting a cap on the head of a young boy with cancer.

It's artistic testimony to the relationship between the Red Sox and the Jimmy Fund. Williams had been a vigorous advocate, often visiting Boston Children's Hospital to be with kids facing unimaginable horrors but only on the condition that the media not be forewarned. He didn't want to be noticed, and certainly not praised, for private time with young cancer patients and their families, though public appearances were necessary to raise awareness and money.

Franc Talarico was the sculptor. At the unveiling, Talarico admitted that he was not a baseball fan, so he had done some research, reading about Williams and talking to people who knew him. "This is a classic Greek pose," explained the Scranton-born sculptor. "And I chose that pose because I feel it's almost like a warrior with a club, and yet with the sensitivity of placing the hat on the little kid's head."[6]

It's identical to a statue that Talarico had done for the Ted Williams Museum & Hitters Hall of Fame in Hernando, Florida. After the museum closed in 2006, its statue went to City of Palms Park in Fort Myers—the spring training site for the Red Sox—where it stayed until 2012, when the team moved spring training operations to JetBlue Park.

Less than a week after Williams died in 2002, Boston mayor Thomas Menino and a city council member, Rob Consalvo, proposed that a statue of the slugger would properly honor his exploits.

Citing Williams's military record and the work with the Jimmy Fund, Menino said, "He gave so much back, and that's why it would be a fitting tribute."[7]

Two years later, Williams's surviving compadres from the *Teammates* statue—Pesky and Doerr—unveiled Talarico's interpretation before a game against the Yankees on April 16, 2004.

Armand LaMontagne designed two statues that were at the Ted Williams Museum. One depicts Williams sitting on a bench; it got moved to the Splendid Splinter, a bed and breakfast in Vermont owned by Williams's daughter Claudia. LaMontagne's original wood statue of Williams after swinging the bat now stands in the National Baseball Hall of Fame Museum in Cooperstown, New York, thanks to Red Sox owner Jean Yawkey donating it in 1985. Polar Park—home of the Worcester Red Sox—houses the bronze replica.

Labatut suggests that memorials and monuments do more than simply fill space in an aesthetically positive fashion, though that is a part of their appeal: "They exist primarily for emotional and intellectual reasons and not for mere physical service."[8]

Placement matters as well. "Air space" is the term that Labatut uses. "Then that architectural air space becomes the living memorial or monument, whatever the physical function of the space involved—a circulation area in a room, in a small garden or park, in a playground or library, in a civic center or hospital, in a church or an industrial plant, even in a museum if by its character the museum is not a mausoleum where works of art are too often buried alive," Labatut writes.[9]

Indeed, baseball players memorialized at the Baseball Hall of Fame will prompt a different reaction among visitors paying homage there than at a ballpark.

Statues of Lou Gehrig, Roberto Clemente, and Jackie Robinson stand alongside each other in the Hall of Fame lobby, forming a welcoming trio for visitors to the Cooperstown shrine. Each player suffered tragedy, marking baseball as a sport with both poignant agonies and astonishing feats; the Ted Williams and Babe Ruth statues are posed in their batting stances in the atrium where the inductees' plaques are on the walls.

They represent the best in baseball. It's quite possible that the statues combined with the exhibits, information, and academic atmosphere will provoke curiosity among the Hall of Fame's visitors to learn more about the players by watching documentaries and reading their biographies. The same analysis applies to the statues that were at the now defunct Williams museum in Florida.

But ballpark statues have a deeper value—the emotional hold rooted in the tribal nature of sports. Williams et al. belong to New England. Period. The offerings of Talarico and Mendez emphasize that precept for Red Sox fans and remind visitors of the players' importance to civic pride. Pesky did not spend his entire Major League career with the Red Sox, but fans cannot separate them any more than Giants rooters will relinquish their loyalties to—and the legacies of—Willie Mays and Willie McCovey, who both spent some time with other teams.

Statues are just one aspect of art's power in sports, though. "There is no Frigate like a Book," wrote Emily Dickinson in her poem by that title, well known to AP English students. Dickinson's missive describes the power to impact the reader's imagination and emotions. Baseball fans saw this in the early 1970s, when Roger Kahn's *The Boys of Summer* jump-started nostalgia for Brooklyn Dodgers fans still mourning the team's vacating Ebbets Field for Los Angeles after the 1957 season.

The same goes for film.

What man hasn't teared up when Gale Sayers—played by Billy Dee Williams—asks his teammates to please ask God to love Brian Piccolo in *Brian's Song* or when Kevin Costner's character, Ray Kinsella, asks his dad to have a catch at the end of *Field of Dreams*?

Certain baseball photographs have become iconic, too. Pirates fans smile and laugh at the Associated Press photos of Bill Mazeroski heading toward home plate after hitting a game-winning home run in the bottom of the ninth inning of the seventh game of the 1960 World Series.

Baseball fans of any team loyalty can appreciate Nat Fein's photo for the *New York Herald Tribune* revealing the heartbreaking frailty of fifty-three-year-old, cancer-stricken Babe Ruth supporting himself with a bat as he gazes at the enormity of Yankee Stadium during a day in his honor just two months before he died in 1948. It won the Pulitzer Prize.

But a statue has a permanence that other art forms don't. One can keep a book on a shelf or refrain from searching for films and photographs online. Ballpark statues are pervasive. Labatut writes, "There always will be monuments giving precise information as to place and time. Both are inevitable footprints of an era."[10]

So true. For Red Sox fans, Fenway Park's statues honor players whose footprints are as mammoth as those in the accounts of Boston-area natives John Adams in helping form an independent nation, Tip O'Neill in guiding the Democratic Party when he was Speaker of the House of Representatives, Oliver Wendell Holmes Jr. in writing Supreme Court decisions, and fictional TV surgeon Charles Emerson Winchester III in treating wounded soldiers at the 4077th Mobile Army Surgical Hospital during the Korean War.

"The need and demand for memorials and monuments will always exist," writes Labatut. "A reasonable answer will arise from people who, always asking for memorials and monuments, demand neither modern

Baalbeks nor golden calves—who want something greater, more spiritual, and more human, something nearer their hearts, their homes, and their communities, an expression of monumentality in the scale of their own time."[11]

What Mendez, Talarico, and LaMontagne accomplished are terrific cultural contributions to the legacy of the Red Sox that may be joined in years to come with statues of Carlton Fisk's jumping to will the ball toward the right side of the foul pole; David Ortiz's mighty swing that sent 541 balls over the fence; and Jim Rice's presence at the plate, whether preparing for a pitch or after swatting any one of his 2,452 hits.

Great players inspire. Their statues remind us why, long after they have left the field.

PART 6

Voices of the Fans

17

Go Sox!

The Fans Speak Out

Baseball is generational yet timeless.

Nowhere is this precept more palpable than at the three oldest ballparks in the Major Leagues; two belong to teams that have lineage dating back to the latter part of the nineteenth century.

A baby boomer grandfather from Pasadena with season tickets to the Dodgers' home games takes his ten-year-old grandson to Dodger Stadium—which debuted in 1962—and talks about Orel Hershiser breaking Don Drysdale's scoreless consecutive innings record; Sandy Koufax's four no-hitters, including the perfect game against the Cubs; Maury Wills's stolen-base record; Steve Garvey's batting prowess; and Fernando Valenzuela's legendary rookie season.

A Generation X married couple from Evanston ventures to Wrigley Field on Opening Day with tickets behind home plate, purchased by the husband along with a Ryne Sandberg jersey. They're birthday gifts for his wife because their first date happened at a 1984 Cubs game when they were first-year students at Northwestern University.

They recall '84 with pride, nostalgia, and pain. The Cubs made their first postseason appearance since the playoffs were created in 1969 but lost to the San Diego Padres. Before that, you'd need to go back to the 1945 World Series for the team's most recent opportunity in the postseason.

Originally called Weeghman Park, Chicago's North Side stadium opened in 1914. Fenway Park predates it by two years, though the Red Sox history began with their first game at Huntington Avenue Grounds in 1901 when the team was called the Americans. But Fenway, Major League Baseball's oldest ballpark, though full of nobility, may be considered obsolete when measured by modern standards.

What was cutting edge during the early twentieth century has long since been surpassed in materials, aesthetics, and engineering. The sight-lines at Fenway Park are obstructed by support poles in certain areas, something that is not a problem at Petco Park in San Diego, Oracle Park in San Francisco, or PNC Park in Pittsburgh.

There's also the money factor. Modern stadiums have more opportunities for deep-pocketed patrons willing to pay top dollar for luxury suites. Plus, like their counterparts at Dodger Stadium in Los Angeles, Yankee Stadium in the Bronx, and Wrigley Field in Chicago, the Red Sox are leaving millions of dollars on the table by not offering stadium naming rights to a corporation. Such a transaction could be an eight-figure deal for the Red Sox coffers.

Boston may one day have a different home for the Red Sox. But that's not a new idea at all. For example, a 1958 proposal for a new stadium in Norwood was revealed to be a potential site for a National Football League team should the league expand or an owner want to transplant his operation to the Boston area.[1] Alternatively, college football teams would have a feasible site for their contests with a Norwood stadium.

The Red Sox, too.

General Manager Joe Cronin dismissed the idea, though he acknowledged the ongoing bane of the limited parking around Fenway Park. The Norwood proposal solved this dilemma with spaces for fifteen thousand cars. There was also talk of a spur line being created for fans who wanted to travel by train. But the location had an additional lure. "For the Red Sox, the location is a natural due to their tremendous number of fans south of Boston," stated a spokesperson. "Providence has always been a Sox stronghold."[2]

The Norwood stadium was conceived as the centerpiece of a complex on Route 1, in the vicinity of Route 128 and next to Norwood Airport. Planned features included a gymnasium, indoor pool, handball courts, golf driving range, offices, and stores. Parents could put their kids in a nursery or playroom while they tended to knocking down pins in the bowling alley housing 102 lanes. A retractable roof was described, but there were no solid plans when the renderings were revealed on April 1, 1958.[3]

Another groundbreaking proposal did have a detailed design for such an invention.

In 1962 Massachusetts governor John Volpe created the Greater Boston Stadium Authority to research possibilities for a new facility. Three years later, Philadelphia architect Vincent Kling unveiled his proposal for a stadium in the South Station area to be shared by the Red Sox and Patriots with a trailblazing amenity—the first stadium with a retractable roof.

Additionally, Kling's design included one hundred private suites, a parking garage with three thousand spaces, and a companion arena for indoor sports. Kling claimed, "Just walking into this stadium will generate a sense of excitement in the sports fan. His seat in the stadium will be closer to the action than in any other stadium yet planned."[4]

Alas, neither stadium was to be. But even if the day happens when the Red Sox have a new home, landmark status protects Fenway Park from being demolished. Red Sox fans keep the legendary ballpark on Jersey Street alive as well, not only through purchases of tickets, merchandise, and apps but also through memories, chronicles, and lore that get passed down to successive generations as a birthright.

Devotion is as resonant today as it was in the days of Nuf Ced McGreevy and the Royal Rooters.

Gabrielle Starr is the editor of *Bosox Injection* and a reporter covering the Sox for the *Boston Herald*. She estimates her attendance at Fenway Park totals at least two hundred games, a conservative figure.

"I am a third-generation Bostonian, so I grew up hearing many stories about the pain of endless defeat. My great-uncle is 104 years old and was born in June 1918, so he does not remember the 1918 championship, but he's lived the 86-year drought. His brother, my father's father, was also a great fan of the Sox, and would pull my father out of school for special occasions. They attended the 1967 World Series, for what would be Carl Yastrzemski's only multi-homer postseason game of his career.

"Having grown up with so much heartbreak, my father was scared to let me watch their 2004 postseason run. I was 11 when the Sox Reversed the Curse (always capitalized), and it was such a stunning and momentous occasion. I truly don't think it will ever be paralleled by a Boston sports event, though the 2013 championship comes close, due to the fact that it was won at Fenway (the first in 95 years) and was so important to the city after the Marathon Bombing months before.

"I remember that the day after the Red Sox won the 2004 World Series, my mother came home from her office downtown and described the city. She told us that people were walking around in a blissful daze, with men and women wearing Red Sox shirts under their blazers and caps on their heads."[5]

David Starr is Gabrielle's father, a rabbi whose first game at Fenway Park was Game Two in the 1967 World Series. The Red Sox won 5-0. The 2004 World Series title resonates because of his family history.

"As a second-generation Bostonian, it meant a lot. My family immigrated to Boston from Eastern Europe before World War I, a time coincidentally of the Red Sox becoming a winning franchise. My surviving uncle was born here in Boston in 1918. So, the family/Sox congruence felt very real to me.

"There are other great sports towns so I can't compare Boston with St. Louis or Pittsburgh, for example. Boston feels like a midsize city with a big city self image based on its history and its famous educational and cultural institutions like Harvard. But it's also pretty inbred, dotted with urban ethnic neighborhoods. College sports isn't that big of a deal here probably because there aren't major universities in terms of sports programs competing at the highest level (with the possible exception of BC/BU in hockey), though that hasn't prevented cities like Philly from being crazy about city school basketball.

"Maybe sports don't have to compete against the attractions that one might find in a larger more cosmopolitan city. And the fact that we've been blessed with marquee players—Williams, Russell, Orr, Bird, Brady—makes a huge difference.

"Certainly in the past two decades the intertwining levels of support and success [have] been amazing, and unprecedented. What's sad is that for all of the sports mania we associate with Boston[,] it enjoyed the greatest dynasty in the history of pro sports—the Celtics of Russell and Auerbach from 1957 to 1969, eleven titles in thirteen years—and that franchise went quite underappreciated—probably because the blackness of the team clashing with the whiteness of much of the city—given the magnitude of their greatness."[6]

Clayton Trutor grew up in Burlington, Vermont. He has a PhD in U.S.

history from Boston College, teaches at Norwich University, writes for SB Nation, and chairs the Vermont chapter of the Society for American Baseball Research. He coedited the SABR book *Overcoming Adversity: Baseball's Tony Conigliaro Award* with Bill Nowlin. He selects Conigliaro as one of his two favorite Red Sox figures.

"I'd like to have had dinner with either Harry Agganis or Tony Conigliaro. I'd have liked to have known what it felt like to be the hometown hero on the Olde Towne Team. They both died so young and so tragically, I'd also like them to both know that they were remembered and loved."[7]

Eric Burckhardt grew up in Peabody. He has followed the Red Sox since he was seven years old, in 1974.

"I believe Boston fans' loyalty stems from the region's long, deep-rooted, vibrant history dating back to the *Mayflower* landing at Plymouth Rock and the Puritans settling in the area. The Boston Tea Party and the Revolutionary War led to the beginning of America's independence.

"Boston's fan base is also one comprised of a unique regional makeup. New England consists of six states whose largest metropolitan area is Greater Boston: Massachusetts, Maine, Vermont, New Hampshire, Rhode Island, and Connecticut. Fans in this region also must be a little tougher than most just by geography. Everything from brutally cold Opening Days and April baseball to snow-covered fans and fields at December football games."[8]

Joshua Krumholz is a lawyer who grew up in New Jersey as a diehard Mets fan.

"When we moved to Boston in 1988, I had already decided that I was all in on the Sox (after delicate negotiations with my wife, who remains to this day an ardent Yankee[s] fan—she grew up in Long Island). Our kids were raised as Sox fans. I did so because, back then, there was no ESPN or the Internet, so to keep up with your team, you really needed to rely on box scores. I was way too big a fan for that, knew we would be in Boston for the duration, and I liked the Sox anyway because I hated the Yankees, so I was all in.

"I would say that I was a normal baseball fan until 2003. That was the first time I got a taste of how the Sox could steal your soul, which they indisputably did. I am still flummoxed as to why Grady Little did not take Pedro [Martínez] out of that game.

"So then 2004 rolls around and I am fully in the camp that they can't win. No way, I am no sucker. My kids told me to have faith when they were down one, then two, then three. And I thought, poor naïve kids. When it finally happened, I did not have the decades of scars that others had, but I felt like I could celebrate by their side because I fully understood what it meant to them."[9]

John Bennett estimates that he's seen close to four hundred Red Sox games in Fenway Park. But his dedication has taken him on the road to see the team play in thirteen other stadiums plus the London series in 2019. He has seen at least one game at Fenway in every postseason series since the 1990 ALCS, in addition to the 1999 All-Star Game.

The 2004 World Series had a tremendous impact on him.

"It was cathartic—that whole week with the comeback against the Yankees. I was there for Game One of the World Series against the Cardinals when David Ortiz and Mark Bellhorn hit massively important home runs that landed right near where I was sitting in the right-field stands. This was the first World Series game I had ever attended, after holding tickets for three other World Series games in past years that never happened for one reason or another.

"So, a lot of it was personal for me, but there was also a lot of it that was a shared experience with thousands of people. You can never underrate the power of a shared experience. Part of my joy was a sense which I call 'relieved happiness.' This is a type of happiness you feel when something does NOT happen—in this case, that the team did not blow it this time.

"However, another part of it was a sense of peace. This was the goal of being a fan all my life—to finally get there. And the goal had been achieved. I have experienced a lot with the Red Sox since then, but in a way everything since 2004 has been an anti-climax.

"I was watching the end of Game Four with my mother. She was 69 at the time and had followed the team on and off since the days of Ted Williams. When the last out was made, I said, 'It was time.' I got up and gave her a little hug."[10]

Larry Ruttman saw his first Red Sox game in 1936, a home game against the Yankees. His father took him. Ruttman, ninety-one, shares his insights on the bonds between the Red Sox and their fans:

"My favorite player is Ted Williams, by far. I saw him play many times. The first time was in 1940, again with my father. In the second game of a twin bill against the Chisox, I recall clearly at age nine, Ted's topspin line single to right in the ninth inning of the nightcap, followed by Double XX's (Jimmie Foxx) walk off homer out by the flagpole in deep center. When I got to UMass, I went to the *New York Times* archive in the library to make sure that wasn't a figment of my overheated imagination. It wasn't. It taught me the value of fact checking.

"The players know how much the fans love, respect, and inspire them to rise above themselves. That creates a mutual loyalty, which, in a fraught era, is life enhancing."[11]

Bill Nowlin has written dozens of books about the Red Sox. He's been going to Red Sox games since 1957, when he was twelve years old. Nowlin estimates his Fenway Park attendance at fifty or more games a year in the past few years—excluding the pandemic-shortened season of 2020, when he saw twenty-two games—and all eighty-one home games in 2022. But he's also seen a dozen or so Red Sox games in Japan, England, and spring training in the Dominican Republic, in addition to road trips in the United States and Canada. During 2020, he saw the team play in Buffalo. Nowlin summarizes being a Red Sox fan in one word: diehard.

"I was at the pennant-clinching game in 1967, the final two World Series games in 1975, and the 'Bucky Dent game' in 1978, when the Red Sox lost the pennant to the Yankees. I was only four years old and we didn't have a TV in 1949 when they managed to lose that pennant to the Yankees, too.

"I watched the final games of 1986 on TV—as I did in 2003 when the Red Sox lost the final game of the ALCS.

"When the Red Sox finally won it—after the never-done-before come-from-behind-zero-games-to-three ALCS in 2004—I took off for the Kenmore Square area near Fenway to celebrate with thousands of others who had done the same. Each of the next three or four mornings when I woke up, I found myself questioning, 'Did that really happen? Did the Red Sox *really* win the World Series?' Yes, they had. But it took a long time to sink in. When they won it again in 2007, I found myself trying to telepathically communicate with Red Sox fans everywhere: 'Stay humble. Let's not get full of ourselves.'"[12]

Scott Melesky grew up in Wolcott, Connecticut, and now lives in Glendale, California. He has been a sports journalist for twenty-three years and has contributed to nine books. He has been a member of SABR for four years and has seen the Red Sox in person for thirty-six consecutive years and forty overall at Fenway Park, New York City, Los Angeles, San Diego, Anaheim, and Milwaukee. He also attended Game Five of the 2018 World Series in person. His favorite player was Carl Yastrzemski.

"Yaz was the consummate professional superstar that I idolized as a child and I emulated as an adult. He was so stoic. And I loved his batting stance, which I tried to imitate with limited success. Yaz hit for average and power. He was so talented both offensively and defensively. He had a great throwing arm. Yaz worked so hard and made the game look easy.

"I was lucky to see him play once, during the first Red Sox game that I saw in person. They lost to the A's 12–5, but I was so excited to see Yaz pinch-hit for Gary Allenson in the bottom of the ninth inning. On the first pitch, he hit a long fly ball to deep center field off pitcher Keith Atherton before it was caught by Dwayne Murphy.

"Though it would be recorded as an innocuous out by the statisticians that day, it was a moment that I have cherished my entire life as I got to see my baseball hero bat in person. It was such a thrill for me."[13]

Gary Stockbridge is a baseball coach. He ran the Tri-Valley Baseball Camp for nearly twenty-nine years (1978–2007) in nine different towns: Franklin, Medfield, Medway, Framingham, Blackstone, East Taunton, Holliston, Stoughton, and Foxboro. He also coached in high school and college for almost fifty years, from 1976 to 2018—Medfield High School, Babson College, Boston College, and Medway High School—in addition to coaching at the Ted Williams Camp in Lakeville, Massachusetts, for three years in the 1970s.

"My favorite experience there was 1978 when I had a chance to meet [Ted Williams]. I heard from the coaches that Ted was coming that morning on his way north to fish like he did every summer. I ran to the public phone booth and called my wife to bring my son to the camp.

"As I am waiting for her, Ted pulls in at the exact same time she arrived. I couldn't believe my good luck. I introduced myself and he was nice enough to sign my baseball and pinch my two-year-old's cheek. At the camp, we were broken into teams. I had a yellow shirt and a young teenage player as an assistant. Each coach had this arrangement and when it came time to move to the next field, we'd march as a team to the designated field.

"A rather unsavory middle-aged coach with his fifteen-year-old assistant was adjacent to my group. That 'yellow shirt' was a great young man who was from Canada. The kid had been to the camp when he was younger. He was a mulatto kid and the coach was barking at him all the time.

"So, when the time came to change fields, the bigoted coach yells out, 'Hey half-breed, get those bags over here!' Out of the corner of my eye was Teddy Ballgame walking across the field within hearing distance.

"Ted didn't run, but I noticed he picked up his gait briskly, went right up to that offending coach and read him the riot act! He dressed him up and down! Ted was half Mexican and to see him defend the young Canadian was awesome. Ted was more than just a great player, he was a great human. That was a side not everyone had a chance to see given his reputation for being a bit gruff, but I saw it in person. He's my hero in more ways than baseball."[14]

James D. Smith III lived in Boston from 1976 to 1985, doing pastoral ministry in Dorchester and doctoral studies at Harvard. Jim and his wife, Linda, have San Diego roots, celebrating that both Bobby Doerr and Ted Williams (a San Diego native) played for the original 1936 Padres in the Pacific Coast League. Jim's father, J.D., saw them at Lane Field.

"Bobby Doerr, nicknamed 'The Silent Captain,' was my favorite Sox player: 1936 Padre, his number one retired at Fenway, Baseball Hall of Famer who 'played hard but retired with no enemies,' vital Christian married to wife Monica for over 60 years. She had MS, and I saw the loving care he offered her. So inspiring! We met several times, but I'd also include visits with Ted Williams and Joe Wood (at his New Haven home) among my favorites. Most memorable time at Fenway? It was Yaz's last game on October 2, 1983. I sat with family in the center field bleachers' front row. After the game, he ran around the field and, passing us, looked up smiling and waved.

"In 2004 (back in San Diego), our delight at the Sox's World Series sweep of the St. Louis Cardinals was heightened by calls from Boston old timers in our church—and SABR members who'd met for meetings in the basement and elsewhere during our years there."[15]

Donna Cohen's family has season tickets dating back five generations.

"Thanks to my grandfather, Irving Rodman, who started the tradition over 60 years ago, our family is a five-generation season-ticket holder family," she reports. "He probably never expected it would become a legacy and for sure, he never expected that the least sports savvy of all his grandchildren (me) would create a business advancing and promoting baseball or that I would attend most home games. When in town, I can be seen at three-quarters of the games watching from our family seats. Out of town, I attend our team's games in New York, Chicago, and California.

"I can still hear my grandfather yelling at the television when I was a little girl: 'You're a bum!' I thought the players lived inside his television set. Until one day, I went to Fenway Park with him. I was nine years old, dressed in my blue and green best suit. Remember the days when fans dressed for the games? Oh, I felt so grand.

"We walked through the dungeon-like corridors with cement-filled walls, up the ramp, and headed toward the fifth row at Field Box 59. It was just like *The Wizard of Oz*. TECHNICOLOR! The green of the grass, the white of the bases, the music, the people, 'Ladies and Gentlemen, Boys and Girls, Welcome to Fenway Park' boomed over the loudspeaker. That was the day I fell in love with baseball and although I live elsewhere, I call Field Box 59 at Fenway Park home.

"Where else can you go where you have an intimate, personal bond with 38,000 people you never met? We sing together, we dance together, we cheer together, and we cry together. My daughter said it best during a Q/A with the Red Sox: 'I just want to thank you. I know that there are three times when my whole family will get together. Bar Mitzvahs, holidays, and Red Sox Games.' The Boston Red Sox is a Cohen family value.

"My favorite player? Each and every player of the minor leagues, all of them who grind it out every day hoping to make it to the bigs.

"The first game played after the Boston Marathon Bombing was the greatest game I ever saw live at Fenway Park. The city was devastated[,] looking for a safe haven, community, and a semblance of normalcy. The Red Sox did not disappoint. The Opening Ceremony acknowledged the tragedy, loss, and surge of volunteers and public servants coming together and provided a place to start the healing process. We all remember the infamous statement of David Ortiz during the ceremony. I can't tell you the score, but I can tell you the game played that day was the greatest game I've ever been to at Fenway Park!"[16]

Originally from Narragansett, Rhode Island, and currently living in Acton, Massachusetts, John Pearson went with his parents to a double-header against the Tigers on July 31, 1975, when he was eight years old. The Red Sox won both games. It was his first Fenway Park experience.

"Grandparents and parents pass their love for the teams down to their children and grandchildren—connecting generations in a way that few other things can. For many years I would have said the greatest game I saw at Fenway was Game Four of the 2004 ALCS where Dave Roberts stole second base and the Red Sox went on to beat the hated Yankees.

"But now, I'd say Game Two of the 2013 ALCS was the greatest, which I attended with our (then) 11-year-old son. With the Sox already down 1 game to 0 in the series to Detroit and trailing 5–1 in the 8th inning, David Ortiz hit a grand slam that literally sent the right fielder over the fence and into the bullpen. Fenway went crazy with 38,000 people screaming, hugging, and jumping. If Ortiz doesn't hit that homerun, the Sox likely lose that game, lose the series, and don't win the World Series. But he did!

"The World Series victory in 2004 was one of the most emotional moments of my life. I cried harder than I've ever cried, and it surprised me. Up until the last out, I didn't believe they would win. Thirty-plus years of agony including 1975, 1978, 1986, and 2003 was washed away in an instant. I also thought of my father who was born in November 1918, a life-long Red Sox fan, and passed away before seeing them win a World Series.

"After the game, at 1:00 a.m. Eastern, I drove the 45 minutes from Acton to Fenway Park. Even though the team played that game in St.

Louis, I wanted to be part of whatever celebration was happening and be close to Fenway Park."[17]

Joe LeBritton grew up in Shrewsbury, Massachusetts. He went to Fenway Park for the first time in the summer of 1961, when he was seven years old.

"The greatest Red Sox game I ever saw was on June 1, 1974, from the front row seats next to the dugout. Luis Tiant pitched a five-hit shutout against the White Sox. The Red Sox won 8-0. Yastrzemski went three-for-three and had three RBI[s]. It was really fun to see all the players up close.

"If I could have dinner with any Red Sox player, it would be Jim Lonborg to talk about his pivotal role on the Impossible Dream team of 1967, how the pennant was won and what might have been versus the Cardinals in the World Series."[18]

Mel Seibolt estimates that he's been to more than two hundred games at Fenway Park since his first, in 1964 with his Brookline Little League team. One of those games was Game Six of the 1975 World Series because of luck connected with romance.

"On October 21, 1975, I get a call from my girlfriend in the early afternoon. 'Are we doing anything tonight?' she asks. I thought she wanted to go to a movie.

"'Wanna go to the game?'

"'What game?' I asked.

"'The Red Sox,' she replied.

"'Are you kidding me?' I answered.

"I picked her up at her aunt and uncle's house in Brookline. Her aunt met me at the door. She says, 'The tickets are on top of the refrigerator, sit where you want.' Sit where you want? I didn't realize what that meant until I picked up a stack of tickets with an elastic band around them. The tickets were for both the sixth and seventh games. I didn't want to think of how they were obtained, although it was believed that her uncle was heavily involved with sports betting in the Greater Boston Area long before it became legal! Don't ask, don't tell.

"I knew the park fairly well. I picked seats four rows behind the Cincinnati dugout. We sat in the middle of some of their season ticket holders. They were very nice. Some had been here for several days because of the rainouts. Two of them told me that they had called their office to tell their bosses that they weren't coming back until the series ended.

"We parked on the street (Brookline Avenue) fairly close to the park. Under the same circumstances today, those spaces would be restricted. The atmosphere was 'electric.' We were facing elimination. The game was one of ebbs and flows. Freddie Lynn hits a three-run homer in the first inning. Reds tie it in the fifth and go ahead by three with two runs in the seventh and one in the eighth.

"Behind three runs in the bottom of the eighth, Bernie Carbo hits a two-out, pinch-hit home run to tie it.

"The park erupted. In all my years coming to Fenway, I had never witnessed that kind of fan response to a home run. That was, until Fisk's home run in the 12th. Fisk's was more memorable, but to me, we never get to a 12th inning without Bernie Carbo.

"After the game, we went to our favorite Chinese restaurant, the Golden Temple, for a bite to eat. The restaurant was packed from patrons celebrating the game. The next day, of course, it was front page news on the *Boston Globe* and *Boston Herald* and all that anyone was talking about.

"My favorite Red Sox moment: May 28, 1971. Red Sox vs. A's. Sonny Siebert (8-0) vs. Vida Blue (10-1). What a night! It was the first time Dick Williams returned to Fenway since being fired by the Sox in '69. Largest crowd at Fenway in several years. Two Sox home runs, both by Rico Petrocelli. Three home runs by Oakland—Reggie Jackson, Sal Bando, Dave Duncan. Sox win 4-3.

"I took my mother to the game. What made it my favorite moment was the enjoyment that my mother experienced that night. She was ecstatic. My mother was an avid Red Sox fan all her life. So much so, I included this fact, at length, in my eulogy at her funeral."[19]

Barbara Mantegani's first Red Sox game was the father-son game in 1962.

"We sat behind the Red Sox dugout and watched team captain Carl Yastrzemski play catch with his son," she recalls. "My greatest memory is the seventh inning. When the Red Sox called for a reliever, they sent the baseball golf cart out to the bullpen, and the cart—which as we know had a baseball cap shaped roof—pulled up to the mound and the hugest human being I had ever seen at that point in my young life, Dick Radatz, aka The Monstah, got out and walked onto the mound. I think we won the game, but for me it didn't matter, because I saw The Monstah in person.

"My favorite player of all time is Tony Conigliaro. He was so amazing and the comparisons to Williams early in his career were not terribly far-fetched in my humble opinion.

"And the most important thing to this young Italian girl whose name was always mispronounced and mocked: he was ITALIAN. And gorgeous. And multitalented since he was also an amazing singer and was in a group. And then there was that misplaced Jack Hamilton fastball and the world changed. Yes, they upgraded the batting helmet after that, but you still never know when a player's career could be cut short.

"To this day whenever someone refers to a young player as 'the next [fill in the name of a Hall of Famer],' I think of Tony C. When I heard that he had passed away I took the rest of the day off and went home."[20]

Baseball represents a long-standing link between fathers and sons, most evident in popular culture with the ending scene in *Field of Dreams*. But the maternal influence ought not be dismissed. Amy Polacko took her son, Max Nadoraski, to his first baseball game at Fenway Park when he was nine months old.

Amy: "I always tell him that we spent more time in the bathroom changing his diapers than we did watching the game! He was most enamored by the announcer and perked up every time he spoke."

Max: "I can't say I remember that game—but I do remember some other memorable ones when I was really young! The Red Sox staff picked me to dance with Wally on the home dugout during the seventh inning stretch. We sang 'Take Me Out to the Ballgame' and threw peanuts out into the crowd. Sometimes I'd leave school early, my mom would pick me up and we'd head to Boston for a game!"

Amy: "When Max was 10, someone gifted us tickets to a private Fanatics dinner with David Ortiz and 10 other people in Boston. We joke about this night all the time! David came over to introduce himself and said, 'Who is this?' to Max, but he was totally awestruck. He panicked, forgot his name and said 'Uhhhh.' We had to go to the bathroom so I could try to calm Max down before returning to the event.

"I have to admit I had not realized we were going to spend two hours with David in an intimate horseshoe dinner setting, but he was absolutely amazing! He was very down to earth and spent a lot of time talking to Max directly about baseball. He burst out laughing with that famous Big Papi roar when Max gave him a photo of his David Ortiz Halloween costume. We took photos with David and when he drove away in his white Range Rover, Max was waving goodbye to him. I'll never forget that he thought David could see him through the tinted windows. It was cute."

Max: "It was cool to see David and he was even friendlier than I thought he would be! I couldn't believe I was there. I knew it was a once in a lifetime experience. My hands were trembling when he was talking to me during dinner about Kirby Puckett and how he got the number 34. I gave him a photo of me dressed as him for Halloween with my phone number on it but he hasn't called yet! I have the bat he signed hanging up in my bedroom with all my Red Sox memorabilia and will give it to my kids someday."

Amy: "If I could pick any Red Sox player from history or the present with whom to have dinner, it would be Jim Rice. Not only was he an outstanding player for the Red Sox, where he spent his entire career, but he is a class act. I'm so glad he made it into the Hall of Fame on the last ballot. The video of him rescuing a young boy who was hit by a line drive during a 1982 game against the Chicago White Sox has always stayed with me. Rice knew that someone had to get the boy medical attention immediately since paramedics would take too long reaching him. His quick action saved the boy's life and he continued to work with many children's charities after retirement. We need more Jim Rices in our world today!"

Max: "Well, my dreams came true when I had dinner with David Ortiz. I can't imagine anyone else being as funny and kind. But if I had to pick a second player to have dinner with, it would be Carlton Fisk. I love the way he 'waved the ball fair' in the 12th inning of Game 6 of the 1975 World Series. Maybe he can teach me how to do that too."[21]

Karl Lindholm is seventy-eight years old and an emeritus dean of Middlebury College. He's been a Red Sox fan since birth, attending approximately fifty Red Sox games at Fenway Park and fifty games on the road. He estimates that he's seen another twenty or more Minor League games in Pawtucket, Worcester, and Portland.

In 2019 a friend gave Lindholm the chance to fulfill a dream of every Red Sox fan—throwing out the first pitch at Fenway Park. The friend won the opportunity and four tickets to a Red Sox game courtesy of a charity auction to benefit Greater Boston PFLAG, an education and advocacy group that supports LGBTQ families and individuals. He was very happy he didn't "bounce it."

"My dad was born in Waltham, the son of immigrant Swedes who worked in the watch factory there. He was a great athlete at Waltham High (football, principally) and is in their Hall of Fame. He passed down his love for the Sox, part of the American ritual of fathers playing catch with sons. Teaching high school in Maine and Cleveland, I spent five summers in Cambridge in the early '70s taking classes at Harvard, walking to Sox games, crossing the Charles, and sitting in the bleachers.

"The greatest Red Sox game I ever saw was Game Four of the 1975 World Series in Cincinnati, when Luis Tiant threw 163 pitches in the rain for a complete game and a 5–3 victory. The game ended on a nice over-the-shoulder catch by Fred Lynn on a blast by Ken Griffey.

"I think my favorite Red Sox player is Pedro Martínez. He was so good and for a few years he was the best ever, unhittable, and he played with both elan and ferocity. He had a good time out there. I tried never to miss a game (on TV) that he pitched. Artistry. Fast ball rides in to righty hitters, breaking ball down and away, change floats in on the fastball trajectory, all thrown with an identical motion, arm slot. Brilliant. Plus, he was a player of color, dark-skinned, and he offset some of the Red Sox' unfortunate history with race.

"How do I summarize being a Red Sox fan? Bone deep, unavoidable."[22]

Mark Peloquin estimates his Fenway Park attendance to be around one hundred games.

"Northeastern cities are very densely populated and have diverse populations," he notes. "It is difficult to come up with something in common with your neighbor sometimes. That is when sports come in handy. I lived in Boston for 10 years. I remember getting on the bus and total strangers started talking about the game. It was a neutral subject that we could all celebrate or commiserate with each other.

"When the Red Sox won the World Series in 2004, it was redemptive. All of a sudden, the team I rooted for my whole life wasn't a punch line."[23]

Howard Homonoff went to his first Red Sox game at Fenway Park in 1967. Since then, he's seen approximately one hundred home games and another forty to fifty away games.

"As a sports fan for over 50 years, Yaz's 1967 season is the single most heroic season-long performance I've ever seen," Homonoff recalls. "Taking a moribund franchise and completely reviving it with incredible clutch hitting and fielding and a Triple Crown for a team that had no idea how to win prior to this season.

"Other players I have loved have been more physically talented, especially Fred Lynn, Mookie Betts, Roger Clemens, and in terms of hitting certainly David Ortiz. But likely because I was an impressionable young kid, 1967 massively shaped my thinking, even beyond 2004.

"I can say that the greatest experience of going to games was Patriots Day. I went several times with friends during high school. 11:00 a.m. start to the game, and in those days the game would be over by 1:30 p.m. or even earlier. We would watch the whole game, then run as fast as we could from Fenway to the Prudential Center which was where the Boston Marathon would finish. I saw Bill Rodgers win his Marathon in 1975, which was a stunning upset at the time."[24]

Ron Kercheville is a Texan, but his Red Sox roots run deep because of a family connection.

"I guess you could say I've been a Red Sox fan since 1946," he recalls. "Not because I was born that year, but because my dad, Bob Kercheville, attended the World Series that year between the Red Sox and the Cardinals. As I grew up in the small town of San Marcos, Texas, I heard him tell stories of his trip to the World Series and those stories made me a fan for life.

"My dad got that opportunity because one of his good friends that he grew up with in an even smaller town—Kyle, Texas—was a pitcher for the Red Sox. Cecil 'Tex' Hughson. It seems Tex had purchased not one but TWO new Cadillacs that year and wanted one of them to be back in

Kyle. So, dad and three others were provided tickets to the games and transportation on the team train between Boston and St. Louis.

"I discovered baseball cards around 1954 and I was thrilled with each Red Sox player I got. I've been a devoted fan of the BoSox and even continue to collect baseball cards to this day. My collection includes every Red Sox card for every year since 1949. It was a thrill as an adult to find cards of players that I idolized when I was a kid!

"I am happy to say I have successfully passed on the Red Sox gene to both of my sons (Greg and Brandon) and a grandson (Jackson). Go Sox!"[25]

John Tierney has been going to Fenway Park for more than fifty years. He was a sophomore at MIT and dating the woman who later became his wife when they went to their first Red Sox game, in 1972. He estimates that they've attended around three hundred home games. Because he grew up in the New York area, his favorite player of all time is Mickey Mantle. He factors Mantle into a tale regarding the so-called curse that plagued Red Sox fans for decades.

"My wife (Kathy) and I feel as though we contributed to the breaking of the so-called 'Curse of the Bambino.' Game Seven of the Yankees series in 2004 was played on October 20, which is Mickey Mantle's birthday. I took Kathy out to eat before the game but took an out of the way detour after dinner to the nearby town of Sudbury. We stopped in front of a large old farmhouse, where I pointed out to my wife that the house had been owned by Babe Ruth when he played for the Red Sox.

"I told her that the two of us were there to convince Ruth's spirit to renounce the curse. I also suggested that we talk with Mantle's spirit, because I believed that Mantle could convince Ruth that the 2004 Red Sox team was more in line with Mantle and Ruth's personalities than the dull, drab 2004 Yankees. My wife stared at me in disbelief, and we sat there in silence for a good 15 minutes.

"We drove home, and as they say, the rest is history."[26]

Notes

Introduction

1. The shows existed in the same fictional universe, according to an episode from each show. A 1983 episode of *Cheers* features the sister of Carla Tortelli announcing that she's going to St. Eligius to give birth. A 1985 episode of *St. Elsewhere* has a scene with three doctors having a drink at Cheers and interacting with Carla, Norm Peterson, and Cliff Clavin. But an earlier *St. Elsewhere* episode contradicts this same-universe theory. Dr. Jack Morrison takes his young son to the Bull & Finch Pub, which was the model for the bar in *Cheers*. A banner outside mentions this, and Dr. Morrison asks the boy if he wants to go where everybody knows his name, a reference to the *Cheers* theme song. *Cheers*, "Little Sister, Don't Cha," Paramount Television, aired October 13, 1983, on NBC; *St. Elsewhere*, "Cheers," MTM Television, aired March 27, 1985, on NBC; *St. Elsewhere*, "Hello, Goodbye," MTM Television, aired May 16, 1984, on NBC.

1. April 15, 2013

1. "David Ortiz: 'This Is Our Fucking City,'" NESN, accessed January 6, 2023, https://www.youtube.com/watch?v=AoTnGa-Dckw.
2. John Zaremba, "Bomb Expert: Attack," *Boston Herald*, April 16, 2013, 12.
3. Hurley was reportedly a mile from the finish line when the bombs exploded. Bauman and Hurley had a daughter who was born in July 2014. They married a few months later, in November. In 2016 Hurley ran the marathon and Bauman waited for her at the finish line. A year later, they divorced. A family spokesperson related a statement to the *Hollywood Reporter*: "Jeff and Erin have decided that it is best to move forward as friends. Though their relationship has changed, their admiration, love and mutual respect for each other will never waver. They are dedicated to loving and parenting their daughter, Nora, and ask for privacy." Pamela McClintock, "Couple at Center of Upcoming Boston Marathon Bombing Romance Film to Divorce," *Hollywood Reporter*, February 8, 2017, https://

www.hollywoodreporter.com/news/general-news/real-couple-portrayed
-boston-marathon-bombing-movie-stronger-divorce-973007/.

4. Bauman and Arredondo appeared before Game Six of the Stanley Cup
Finals. The Chicago Blackhawks won the game 3-2 and, in turn, the Stanley
Cup. In this appearance, Bauman used a walker for support as he rose to
stand on his prosthetic legs. Bauman wrote in his book that "Carlos waved
the Boston Strong flag as I raised my right hand and waved to the crowd.
They went bah-nanas. They were ready. I had given as much as I could."
Jeff Bauman with Bret Witter, *Stronger* (New York: Grand Central Publish-
ing, 2014), 182.

5. "'Did They Get It Right? I Think That's an Impossible Question for a Survivor,'" *Boston Globe*, December 16, 2016, B14.

6. *St. Elsewhere*, "In Sickness and in Health," MTM Productions, aired February 8, 1984, on NBC.

7. President Franklin Delano Roosevelt to Judge Kenesaw Mountain Landis,
January 15, 1942, National Baseball Hall of Fame and Museum, https://
baseballhall.org/discover-more/stories/short-stops/keep-baseball-going.

8. Sarah Schweitzer and Evan Allen, "Joining Sorrow—the Joy of Coming
Together Again," *Boston Sunday Globe*, April 21, 2013, A1.

9. Mike Scandura, "Ortiz Is a Hit in Pawtucket," *Boston Sunday Globe*, April
12, 2013, D6.

10. Mike Scandura, "Ortiz Shows Progression in His Rehab," *Boston Globe*,
April 14, 2013, C7.

11. Ortiz retired after the 2016 season with 2,472 hits, 541 home runs, and a
career average of .286. The Baseball Hall of Fame inducted him in 2022.

12. Michael Silverman, "Buchholz Starting to Find Rhythm," *Boston Herald*,
April 21, 2013, B17.

2. Never Give Up!

1. Prov. 19:17.

2. 1 John 3:17.

3. 1 Cor. 9:7.

4. Brynner won the Tony Award for portraying the king of Siam in *The King
and I*. He received a special Tony Award in 1985 for his more than 4,600
performances in the role. In the *Good Morning America* interview, Brynner
talked about how he had wanted to make a commercial when he learned
the severity of his illness. Part of the excerpt used by the American Cancer
Society went, "Now that I'm gone, I tell you: Don't smoke. Whatever you
do, just don't smoke." "Yul Brynner's Posthumous Message," United Press

International, *Los Angeles Times*, February 20 1986, https://www.latimes
.com/archives/la-xpm-1986-02-20-ca-10075-story.html.

5. Herbert Black, "Jimmy Fund Marks 15th Year," *Boston Sunday Globe*,
November 24, 1963, A40.

6. Maria Karagianis, "William S. Koster, at 72, a Founder of Jimmy Fund,"
Boston Globe, October 2, 1978, 14.

7. "Braves Champs Last Night, for Little Jimmy in Hospital," *Boston Sunday
Globe*, May 23, 1948, C1.

8. "'Cancer Jimmy' Sees, Roots Braves to Win," *Boston Daily Record*, May 24,
1948, 5.

9. "'Jimmy' Thrilled as He Sees Tribe Win Game for Him," *Boston Daily
Globe*, May 24, 1948, 7. This article says that Jimmy went with his father,
but an article the previous day reported that Jimmy's doctor had okayed
the outing as long as a nurse accompanied him. "Braves Champs Last
Night for Little Jimmy in Hospital," C1. The *Boston Daily Record* stated that
a doctor and a nurse went with Jimmy, who stayed for the first game and
six innings of the second game. John Gillooly, "Braves Sweep Pair from
Cubs, 8–5, 12–4," *Boston Daily Record*, May 24, 1948, 46.

10. "Marblehead Game to Benefit 'Jimmy,'" *Boston Daily Globe*, May 27, 1948, 25.

11. "Boston Angler, 2, Steals Show at Ayer Trout Derby," *Boston Daily Globe*,
May 31, 1948, 1.

12. "Milton Merchants, Linehans to Play for Jimmy Fund," *Boston Daily Globe*,
June 16, 1948, 23; "Milton Merchants Play Linehan Club to Aid Jimmy
Fund," *Boston Evening Globe*, June 18, 1948, 27.

13. "Brookline Arranges 'Jimmy Fund' Night," *Boston Daily Globe*, June 24,
1948, 25.

14. "First Service Command Nine Helps 'Jimmy' Fund," *Boston Evening Globe*,
July 1, 1948, 26.

15. "Somerville Bans 'Benefit' Carnival as a 'Nuisance,'" *Boston Daily Globe*,
July 2, 1948, 1.

16. Vern Miller, "Braves Line Up Grid Game for Jimmy Fund," *Boston Sunday
Globe*, August 15, 1948, 31.

17. Vern Miller, "Fans Boo Pro Gridders in Braves Field Charity Game," *Boston
Sunday Globe*, August 22, 1948, 32.

18. Julian Beaumont, "He Started the Public Worrying about a Boy," *Boston
Sunday Globe*, October 24, 1948, A29. Theater executives began the Variety
Club in 1928.

19. Beaumont, "He Started the Public Worrying about a Boy," A29.

20. Ted Ashby, "The Amazing Jimmy Fund," *Boston Evening Globe*, May 31, 1951, 27.

21. "Citations Given at Luncheon of Trustees of Jimmy Fund," *Boston Evening Globe*, January 19, 1953, 3.

22. "Red Sox Replace Braves," *Barre (VT) Daily Times*, April 10, 1953, 2; "Red Sox to Aid in Jimmy Fund," *Boston Daily Globe*, April 11, 1953, 4.

23. Hy Hurwitz, "Williams Dinner Nets $125,000 for Fund—Kennedys Give $50,000," *Boston Daily Globe*, August 18, 1953, 1.

24. "Ted's Speech," *Boston Daily Globe*, August 18, 1953, 6.

25. Virginia Bright, "Ted Williams, Youngsters' Friend," *Boston Sunday Globe*, January 22, 1956, A28.

26. Cassidy Lent, email to author, November 18, 2022.

27. Hy Hurwitz, "Ted Heads Jimmy Fund: Plan to Expand Cancer Fight across U.S. Told by Williams," *Boston Daily Globe*, June 29, 1956, 1.

28. William Coltin, "Braves' Bat Boy of 49 Long Friend of Cripples," *Boston Sunday Globe*, July 21, 1957, 41. Howard explained that he had been a Braves bat boy in 1954 and recalled that the *Newburyport Daily News* spearheaded a "community drive" to raise money so he could travel to see the team during spring training in Bradenton, Florida.

29. Black, "Jimmy Fund Marks 15th Year," A40.

30. Herbert Black, "Jimmy Fund to Expand Cancer Center," *Boston Globe* (morning edition), December 10, 1963, 20. The assassination of President John F. Kennedy, a Boston-area native, on November 22 caused the event to be rescheduled from its original date of November 25. "Jimmy Fund Banquet Postponed," *Boston Globe* (morning edition), November 23, 1963, 9.

31. Neil Singelais, "Sox Go to Bat for 'Jimmy,'" *Boston Sunday Globe*, August 6, 1972, 60.

32. Singelais, "Sox Go to Bat for 'Jimmy,'" 60.

33. Singelais, "Sox Go to Bat for 'Jimmy,'" 60.

34. "History of Dana-Farber Cancer Institute," Dana-Farber Cancer Institute, accessed August 6, 2023, https://www.dana-farber.org/about-us/history-and-milestones.

35. Ernie Roberts, "The Jimmy Fund Is His Life," *Boston Evening Globe*, July 23, 1975, 48.

36. Larry Whiteside, "Jimmy Fund: 30 Years of Aiding Kids," *Boston Sunday Globe*, May 29, 1975, 7.

37. Maria Karagianis, "William S. Koster, at 72, a Founder of Jimmy Fund," *Boston Globe*, October 2, 1978, 14.

38. "History of Dana-Farber Cancer Institute."

39. Dan Shaughnessy, "Jimmy Fund Gets 50th Anniversary Gift: 'Jimmy,'" *Boston Sunday Globe*, May 17, 1998, A1.

40. Shaughnessy, "Jimmy Fund Gets 50th Anniversary Gift," A1.

41. Michael Vega, "Pregame Festivities a Winner, Too," *Boston Globe*, April 9, 2013, C3.

42. Katheleen Conti and Jon Chesto, "Lucchino to Head Jimmy Fund," *Boston Globe*, April 21, 2016, C6.

43. Thomas Farber, telephone interview by author, November 15, 2022.

44. Lynn MacLeod, email to author, March 18, 2023.

45. Lisa Patti, email to author, December 15, 2022.

3. A Chance to Excel

1. Ted Williams and John Underwood, *The Science of Hitting* (New York: Simon and Schuster, 1971; repr. Touchstone, a division of Simon and Schuster, 2013), 10.

2. Ted Williams, Induction Speech, National Baseball Hall of Fame and Museum, Cooperstown NY, July 25, 1966, https://www.youtube.com/watch?v=Yi8ukM_NCf4.

3. "Paige Thumbs Down Idea," *The Sporting News*, August 13, 1942, 8.

4. Baseball historian Glenn Stout authored a comprehensive article about the tryout. Glenn Stout, "Tryout and Fallout: Race, Jackie Robinson and the Red Sox," *Massachusetts Historical Review* 6 (2004): 11–37, available at https://glennstout.com/tryout-and-fallout-race-jackie-robinson-and-the-red-sox/.

5. Press release, Office of the Commissioner, Major League Baseball, February 9, 1971, BL-175.2003, Folder 1, Document_1971_02_09A, National Baseball Hall of Fame and Museum, Cooperstown NY, https://baseballhall.org/discover-more/digital-collection/1529.

6. Joseph Durso, "Paige Is First Star of Old Negro Leagues to Be Selected for Hall of Fame," *New York Times*, February 10, 1971, 52.

7. Jack Lang, "'Proud to Be in It!'" *The Sporting News*, February 20, 1971, 42.

8. "Satchel Named to 'Regular' Hall of Fame," United Press International, *Chicago Defender*, July 8, 1971, 32.

9. Joe Williams, "Old Satch Belongs in the Hall," *New York World-Telegram and Sun*, February 5, 1964, 28.

10. "Sports People: Honoring Satchel," *New York Times*, June 13, 1982, S7.

11. "Satchel Paige Signs Contract with Cleveland," Associated Press, *Chicago Tribune*, July 8, 1948, 49.

12. Ray Gillespie, "Satch Signs '150th' Pact, Cuts Another Year from His Age," *The Sporting News*, February 20, 1952, 25.

13. "Satch Pays Off for Proof He Played in '26," Associated Press, *Chicago Tribune*, August 24, 1948, 22.

14. Dan Daniel, "How Old Is Satchel? Well, That's a Guess," *New York World-Telegram*, July 22, 1948. A photocopy of this article with the date handwritten is in Satchel Paige's file in the National Baseball Hall of Fame and Museum's A. Bartlett Giamatti Research Center. A copy of the newspaper is on microfilm at the Library of Congress, but that edition does not have this article, so it probably appeared in another edition that was never archived. Joel Mota, email to author, April 10, 1923.

15. Wendell Smith, "Only Color Barred Him from Majors," *Pittsburgh Courier*, January 25, 1947. The newspaper and date are estimated from a photocopy of this obituary found in Gibson's Baseball Hall of Fame file. It uses the same font as the *Courier*, which was published weekly. Smith's title at the *Courier* was sports editor, which appears in the byline. Gibson died on January 20, 1947; January 25 was a publication date that year. A page number does not appear on the photocopy. The title is unreadable, so the subtitle is used for the purpose of this endnote. Only the national edition of the *Courier* from January 25 is available on microfilm at the Carnegie Library of Pittsburgh, but that edition does not have this article, so it probably appeared in another edition that was never archived.

16. Dave Anderson, "A Folk Hero for Cooperstown," *New York Times*, February 6, 1972, S5. Sam Bankhead, a teammate of Gibson and Paige in the Mexican League, praised the backstop's defense: "As a catcher he sometimes threw guys out stealing without getting out of his crouch" (S5).

17. The HBO roster of Black history docudramas includes *The Josephine Baker Story*, *Don King: Only in America*, *The Tuskegee Airmen*, and *Introducing Dorothy Dandridge*. They were part of HBO's overall commitment to original programming; other dramas highlighting recent and historical events included *And the Band Played On*, *From the Earth to the Moon*, *Without Warning: The James Brady Story*, *Barbarians at the Gate*, and *Dead Ahead: The Exxon "Valdez" Disaster*.

18. Anthony Castrovince, "MLB Adds Negro Leagues to Official Records," Major League Baseball, accessed October 16, 2022, https://www.mlb.com/news/negro-leagues-given-major-league-status-for-baseball-records-stats; James Wagner, "Baseball Reference Adds Negro Leagues Statistics, Rewriting Its Record Book," *New York Times*, June 15, 2021, updated

September 7, 2021, https://www.nytimes.com/2021/06/15/sports/baseball
/baseball-reference-negro-leagues.html. As an example, Baseball Reference shows that seven of the top ten MLB batting averages in 1927 now
belong to Negro Leaguers. There were seven Negro Leagues between 1920
and 1948 with varying years of existence: Negro National League (I), Eastern Colored League, American Negro League, East-West League, Negro
Southern League, Negro National League (II), Negro American League.

4. Songs of the Sox

1. *The Godfather Part II*, directed by Francis Ford Coppola (Paramount Pictures, 1974).
2. Dave Egan, "Nuf Ced McGreevey [*sic*] Plaque Proposed," *Boston Daily
   Record*, February 8, 1943, 33.
3. Egan, "Nuf Ced McGreevey [*sic*] Plaque Proposed," 33.
4. "'Nuf Ced' McGreevy Dies," *Boston Evening American*, February 3, 1943, 28.
5. "McGraw Obdurate," *Boston Daily Globe*, October 7, 1904, 4.
6. "They're in the Lead," *Boston Daily Globe*, September 25, 1897, 7. John
   "Honey Fitz" Fitzgerald was a future mayor of Boston. In 1917 he became
   a grandfather to John F. Kennedy, another future politician—congressman,
   senator, and president.
7. "They're in the Lead," 7.
8. "They're in the Lead," 7.
9. "Outplayed by Boston," *Baltimore Sun*, September 25, 1897, 6.
10. "The Ball Field," *Baltimore Sun*, September 25, 1897, 4.
11. "Boston Rooters Own the Town," *Boston Daily Globe*, September 25, 1897,
    7.
12. "Nervy Nick," *Boston Daily Globe*, September 28, 1897, 5.
13. "Hurrah for Boston," *Baltimore Sun*, September 27, 1897, 6.
14. "Great Victory for the Birds," *Baltimore American*, September 26, 1897, 9,
    quoted in "Even Money," *Boston Daily Globe*, September 27, 1897, 5.
15. Egan, "Nuf Ced McGreevey [*sic*] Plaque Proposed," 33.
16. "Tessie," Rooter's Souvenir, 1903 World Series, Boston Public Library,
    Michael T. "Nuf Ced" McGreevy Collection, last accessed August 6,
    2023, https://www.digitalcommonwealth.org/search/commonwealth:
    sf2688186.
17. Erik Van Rheenen, "The Spin Rate: 'Tessie' by Dropkick Murphys," Pitch-
    erList, May 31, 2022, https://www.pitcherlist.com/the-spin-rate-tessie-by
    -dropkick-murphys/.

18. The Beatles returned two weeks later to perform on the February 23, 1964, episode of *The Ed Sullivan Show*.

19. Jeremy Siegel, "The Unlikely Story of How 'Dirty Water' Became a Fenway Anthem," *Morning Edition*, WGBH, April 14, 2022, https://www.wgbh.org /news/local-news/2022/04/14/the-unlikely-story-of-how-dirty-water -became-a-fenway-anthem.

20. "Music Legend: Neil Diamond on New Album & Hitting the Road," *Today*, NBC, October 20, 2014, https://www.youtube.com/watch?v=4fJ6pbPi_qI.

21. Stephanie Vosk, "Another Mystery of the Diamond, Explained at Last," *Boston Sunday Globe*, "City Weekly," May 29, 2005, 1.

22. Ian Browne, "How 'Sweet Caroline' Became a Fenway Hit," Major League Baseball, January 21, 2021, https://www.mlb.com/news/sweet-caroline-red -sox-fenway-park-history; Ian Browne, "Fenway Park's Anthem Started Innocuously," Major League Baseball, April 17, 2013, https://www.mlb.com /news/fenway-parks-anthem-started-innocuously/c-45075964.

23. Matthew Leimkuehler, "How Neil Diamond's 'Sweet Caroline' Became Iowa State's Inescapable Celebration Song," *Des Moines Register*, September 7, 2018, https://www.desmoinesregister.com/story/entertainment /music/2018/09/07/sweet-caroline-iowa-state-cyclones-athletics-football -basketball-neil-diamond-cyhawk-boston-redsox/1211156002/.

24. Abby Hoffman, "Sweet Caroline: A History of Pitt's Sing-Along Tradition," *Pitt News*, October 24, 2014, https://pittnews.com/article/4019/arts-and -entertainment/sweet-caroline-a-history-of-pitts-sing-along-tradition/.

25. "Yankees Pay Tribute to Boston," YES Network, accessed January 4, 2023, https://www.youtube.com/watch?v=VlrbWwxHETM.

5. Hi Neighbor!

1. "Our Story: 1905," Narragansett Beer, accessed January 13, 2023, https:// www.narragansettbeer.com/our-story.

2. "Our Story: 1920 to 1933," Narragansett Beer, accessed January 13, 2023, https://www.narragansettbeer.com/our-story.

3. "Our Story: 1935," Narragansett Beer, accessed January 13, 2023, https:// www.narragansettbeer.com/our-story.

4. *Hi-Neighbor! The Story of the Narragansett Brewing Company*, Rhode Island PBS special, May 25, 2022, https://www.pbs.org/video/hi-neighbor-the -story-of-the-narragansett-brewing-company-qgexgz/.

5. Curt Gowdy with Al Hirshberg, *Cowboy at the Mike* (Garden City NY: Doubleday, 1966), 110.

6. Donna Halper, email to author, February 5, 2023.

7. Red Sox clubhouse manager Johnny Orlando told Gowdy before the game that it would be the last one for Williams. But Orlando requested that the broadcaster not say anything. When Williams hit the home run, Gowdy forgot to keep silent about it during his call: "A home run for Ted Williams in his last time at bat in the Major Leagues!" "Ted Williams Homers at His Last at Bat—Curt Gowdy Announces," YouTube, accessed February 4, 2023, https://www.youtube.com/watch?v=Rl6cOMQ4xkc; "Curt Gowdy Interview, Part 2 of 6, EmmyTVLegends.org," Curt Gowdy, interviewed by Marvin Wolf, Boston, Massachusetts, May 19, 2000, Television Academy Foundation, https://interviews.televisionacademy.com/interviews/curt -gowdy?clip=46342#interview-clips, 17:27–19:08.

8. "Curt Gowdy Interview, Part 2 of 6," 12:36–13:34.

9. Jerry Lisker, "Cool Hand Curt among the Egomaniacs," *Sunday News* (New York), September 17, 1972, 106.

10. "Our Story: 1981," Narragansett Beer, accessed January 13, 2023, https:// www.narragansettbeer.com/our-story.

11. *Hi-Neighbor!* PBS special.

12. *Hi-Neighbor!* PBS special.

13. "Our Story: 2005," Narragansett Beer, accessed January 13, 2023, https:// www.narragansettbeer.com/our-story.

14. *Hi-Neighbor!* PBS special.

15. Brian Schade, emails to author, November 9, 2022, August 13, 2023.

16. Jim Crooks, email to author, January 30, 2023. Crooks is Narragansett's vice president of sales and marketing. In addition to providing color and background on Narragansett, he was an invaluable conduit in providing responses from Mark Hellendrung to the author's questions.

6. Where Red Sox History Began

1. "Baseball Gossip," *Boston Evening Record*, May 8, 1901, 7.

2. "First Home Game of New Nine," *Boston Daily Advertiser*, May 9, 1901, 8.

3. W. S. Barnes Jr., "American Team Inaugurates Its Season with an Overwhelming Defeat of the Athletics," *Boston Morning Journal*, May 9, 1901, 10.

4. "With not a single hitch to mar the event—from the perfect weather conditions down to the proper outcome of the game from a home standpoint—the day was a notable one in Boston baseball." "Boston Americans Cheered to Victory by 11,000 Rooters," *Boston Post*, May 9, 1901, 1. In another account, "the weather was all the most ardent rooter could

desire." "Eleven Thousand See Collins' Team Beat the Athletics, 12 to 4,"
Boston Herald, May 9, 1901, 8.

5. "Boston Americans Cheered to Victory by 11,000 Rooters," 1.

6. "Athletics Open Boston's Grounds, but Are Beaten," *Philadelphia Inquirer*,
May 9, 1901, 6.

7. Fred Schuld, "Charles Somers," Society for American Baseball Research,
Baseball Biography Project, accessed December 27, 2022, https://sabr.org
/bioproj/person/charles-somers/.

8. "Boston Americans Cheered to Victory by 11,000 Rooters," 1

9. "Boston Americans Cheered to Victory by 11,000 Rooters," 1.

10. "A New Right Fielder," *Louisville Courier-Journal*, May 20, 1895, 2.

11. Collins led both leagues in home runs and total bases in 1898.

12. "To Hold Collins," *Boston Daily Globe*, March 1, 1901, 4.

13. "Somers' Claim," *Boston Sunday Globe*, March 3, 1901, 1.

14. "Collins Talks," *Boston Sunday Globe*, March 10, 1901, 7.

15. "Never Dangerous," *Fall River Daily Herald*, August 10, 1896, 6.

16. "Lajoie Signs with American League," *New York Times*, March 21, 1901, 7.

17. "Eleven Thousand See Collins' Team Beat the Athletics, 12 to 4," 8.

18. "American League Opening," *Boston Traveler*, May 9, 1901, 6. The major
sources for the play-by-play summary in this chapter were the detailed
accounts in the *Boston Post* and *Philadelphia Inquirer*.

19. "Athletics Open Boston's Grounds, but Are Beaten," 6.

20. "Eleven Thousand See Collins' Team Beat the Athletics, 12 to 4," 8.

21. "Boston Americans Cheered to Victory by 11,000 Rooters," 1.

22. Barnes, "American Team Inaugurates Its Season with an Overwhelming
Defeat of the Athletics," 10. It's implied in the *Philadelphia Inquirer* article
that Hemphill advanced: "Boston's last run was made in the seventh on
Hemphill's double, Jones' out and Collins' hit." "Athletics Open Boston's
Grounds, but Are Beaten," 6.

23. Barnes, "American Team Inaugurates Its Season with an Overwhelming
Defeat of the Athletics," 10.

24. The analysis does not include 1898, when Freeman batted .364 for the
Washington Senators but played in only twenty-nine games.

25. "Young to Play in Boston," *Boston Evening Transcript*, March 9, 1901, 5.

7. Reel Red Sox

1. "Red Sox Call Up Outfielder, 3d Baseman from Minors," *Boston Evening
Globe*, August 29, 1950, 34.

2. Piersall's book also provided the story for the August 18, 1955, episode of CBS's anthology series *Climax!* Tab Hunter played Piersall.

3. Hy Hurwitz, "'Fear Strikes Out' Dramatic, but It's Rough on Facts," *Boston Daily Globe*, February 11, 1957, 9.

4. Jerry Kellar, "Jimmy Piersall Still Crazy after All These Years," *Wilkes-Barre Times Leader*, August 24, 1994, B1, https://www.timesleader.com/archive /848064/jimmy-piersall-still-crazy-after-all-these-years-the-kid-wanted -an-answer.

5. Jimmy Piersall with Richard Whittingham, *The Truth Hurts* (Chicago: Contemporary Books, 1984), 30–31.

6. "Jimmy Piersall," *SportsCentury*, ESPN, August 17, 2000. It's unclear whether Ginsberg and Kell were talking about the same incident.

7. *Happy Days*, "You Go to My Head," Paramount Television, aired October 1, 1974, on ABC. The reference to *Fear Strikes Out* is logical. During the show's early episodes in its eleven-season run beginning on January 15, 1974, writers and producers used several hallmarks of the mid- to late 1950s as story fodder, including atomic bomb shelters, Howdy Doody, the second Eisenhower-Stevenson presidential election, and the quiz show scandal.

8. Roger Birtwell, "Boudreau Thinks Well of Rookie Shortstop," *Boston Evening Globe*, April 1, 1952, 44.

9. During spring training, manager Lou Boudreau addressed Piersall's potential at shortstop: "In a year or two, Jim Piersall will become the Red Sox shortstop for the next eight or 10 years." Still, Boudreau expressed a let's-see-what-happens approach when he said that he hadn't yet determined whether to keep Piersall with Boston or send him back to the Minors for seasoning. Birtwell, "Boudreau Thinks Well of Rookie Shortstop," 44.

10. Jim Piersall and Al Hirshberg, *Fear Strikes Out: The Jim Piersall Story* (Boston: Little, Brown, 1955), 5.

11. David Germain, "Bambino's Curse Blesses Lovers," Associated Press, *Berkshire Eagle*, April 8, 2005, D5.

12. Forrest Hartman, "Funny 'Fever Pitch' Scores a Romantic Home Run," in "Calendar: April 8–15, 2005," *Reno Gazette-Journal*, April 8, 2005, 74.

13. Christopher Smith, "Farrelly Brothers' 'Fever Pitch' Makes It over the Plate," *Bangor Daily News*, April 15, 2005, C11.

14. Carina Chocano, "Love Steps to the Plate," in "Calendar," *Los Angeles Times*, April 8, 2005, A22.

15. Chris Nashawaty, "'The Town' Director Ben Affleck Talks Filming in Fenway Park, Being a Local Hero, and Why He Won't Run for Office," *Enter-*

tainment Weekly*, September 7, 2010, https://ew.com/article/2010/09/07/ben-affleck-the-town-interview/.

16. "Interview: The Post-Credit Podcast Sits Down with Jon Hamm," *The Post-Credit Podcast*, BroBible, May 4, 2022, https://brobible.com/culture/article/jon-hamm-the-town-legacy.

17. Titus Welliver, "Titus Welliver on Ben Affleck & Getting to Film 'the Town' inside Fenway Park," *The Rich Eisen Show*, NBC Sports Audio, Sirius XM, June 22, 2021, https://www.youtube.com/watch?v=vF041Dmb9oc.

18. Wesley Morris, "With New Film, Affleck Ties Boston Knot Tighter," *Boston Globe*, September 15, 2010, A1.

19. Joe Neumaier, "Affleck Shines as Man of Steal," *Daily News* (New York), September 17, 2010.

20. Christy Lemire, "'The Town' Further Reveals Affleck's Talent," Associated Press, *Journal Tribune Weekend* (York County ME), September 25, 2010, C7.

21. Ty Burr, "DeLillo's 'Game 6' Is Painfully Good," *Boston Globe*, March 10, 2006, D7.

8. The Ballad of Sam "Mayday" Malone

1. Sports bars: *Cheers*, "Bad Neighbor Sam," Paramount Television, aired November 15, 1990, on NBC; street address: *Cheers*, "The Stork Brings a Crane," Paramount Television, aired November 2, 1989, on NBC; Melville's Seafood Restaurant: *St. Elsewhere*, "Cheers," MTM Television, aired March 27, 1985, on NBC.

2. "Cy Young of skirt chasers": *Cheers*, "Executive Sweet," Paramount Television, aired November 10, 1988, on NBC; Miss Tennessee: *Cheers*, "How to Marry a Mailman," Paramount Television, aired October 19, 1989, on NBC; a thousand women: *Cheers*, "The Improbable Dream: Part 1," Paramount Television, aired September 21, 1989, on NBC.

3. Some sources count the ninety-minute finale as three episodes, for a series total of 275.

4. *Cheers*, "Give Me a Ring Sometime," Paramount Television, aired September 30, 1982, on NBC.

5. *Cheers*, "Indoor Fun with Sammy and Robby," Paramount Television, aired February 22, 1990, on NBC.

6. *Cheers*, "Hot Rocks," Paramount Television, aired March 16, 1989, on NBC.

7. *Cheers*, "Take Me Out to the Ball Game," Paramount Television, aired March 26, 1992, on NBC.

8. Saul Steinberg, *View of the World from 9th Avenue*, cover art, *New Yorker*, March 29, 1976.

9. *Cheers*, "The Tortelli Tort," Paramount Television, aired October 14, 1982, on NBC.

10. *Cheers*, "The Boys in the Bar," Paramount Television, aired January 27, 1983, on NBC.

11. *Cheers*, "Endless Slumper," Paramount Television, aired December 2, 1982, on NBC.

12. *Cheers*, "The Heart Is a Lonely Snipehunter," Paramount Television, aired January 10, 1985, on NBC.

13. A second-season episode uses a life-size cardboard cutout of Foxx to represent T-Bone Scappagione, a recently deceased peer of Coach. *Cheers*, "Coach Buries a Grudge," Paramount Television, aired February 16, 1984, on NBC.

14. *Cheers*, "Don Juan Is Hell," Paramount Television, aired December 12, 1985, on NBC.

15. *Murphy Brown*, "You Say Potatoe, I Say Potato: Part 1," Warner Bros. Television, aired September 21, 1992, on CBS; *Murphy Brown*, "You Say Potatoe, I Say Potato: Part 2," Warner Bros. Television, aired September 21, 1992, on CBS.

16. *Cheers*, "They Called Me Mayday," Paramount Television, aired December 1, 1983, on NBC.

17. *Cheers*, "Strange Bedfellows: Part 2," Paramount Television, aired May 8, 1986, on NBC.

18. *Cheers*, "No Contest," Paramount Television, aired February 17, 1983, on NBC.

19. *Cheers*, "Woody for Hire, Meets Norman of the Apes," Paramount Television, aired January 7, 1988, on NBC.

20. *Cheers*, "Bar Wars," Paramount Television, aired March 31, 1988, on NBC.

21. Thomas Boswell, "Hitting Their Stride: Boggs, Once a Boring Hitter, Is Living More Dangerously," *Washington Post*, syndicated to *Los Angeles Times*, August 2, 1987, https://www.latimes.com/archives/la-xpm-1987-08-02-sp -906-story.html.

22. *Cheers*, "Cheers Fouls Out," Paramount Television, aired September 27, 1990, on NBC; *Cheers*, "Where Have All the Floorboards Gone?" Paramount Television, aired November 7, 1991, on NBC.

23. *Cheers*, "Little Carla, Happy at Last: Part 1," Paramount Television, aired October 15, 1987, on NBC; *Cheers*, "Little Carla, Happy at Last: Part 2," Paramount Television, aired October 22, 1987, on NBC.

24. Howard Rosenberg, "Why the Nielsen Jeers for 'Taxi' and 'Cheers'?" *Los Angeles Times*, December 15, 1982, part VI, 1.

25. Rosenberg, "Why the Nielsen Jeers for 'Taxi' and 'Cheers'?," part VI, 9.

26. Phil Rosenthal, "A Toast to 'Cheers' on Episode No. 200[:] Once Low-Ranked Show Reaches Rare Milestone," *Orlando Sentinel*, November 8, 1990, https://www.orlandosentinel.com/news/os-xpm-1990-11-08-9011070185-story.html.

27. Brandon Tartikoff and Charles Leerhsen, *The Last Great Ride* (New York: Turtle Bay Books, 1992), 164.

28. Gary Deeb, "Despite Abysmal Ratings, 'Cheers' to Run Next Fall," *Sacramento Bee*, March 11, 1983, 43.

9. A Little Roller up along First

1. *Baseball Night in New York: Living Room Edition*, SNY, May 20, 2020, https://www.youtube.com/watch?v=ja61pOpiQfg.

2. *E:60*, "Behind the Bag," ESPN, October 25, 2011, https://www.youtube.com/watch?v=oUP_iyxazPM (no longer available).

3. 1986 World Series, Game Six, aired October 25, 1986, on NBC, https://www.youtube.com/watch?v=7ujwjqIldwU.

4. *E:60*, "Behind the Bag."

5. *1986 Mets: The Movie*, "Bill Buckner about That Ground Ball," accessed September 21, 2022, https://www.youtube.com/watch?v=hG2tOBp-CqM.

6. *Baseball Night in New York.*

7. Leigh Montville, "Buckner's Story Is Painfully Familiar," *Boston Globe*, October 24, 1986, 60.

8. Thomas Boswell, "It Hurts to Watch Buckner," *Washington Post*, October 25, 1986, B1.

9. Hal Bock, "Buckner Plays with Much Pain," Associated Press, *Columbus (GA) Ledger*, October 24, 1986, A13.

10. Bock, "Buckner Plays with Much Pain," A13.

11. Montville, "Buckner's Story Is Painfully Familiar," 60. Buckner's determination to play through pain was inherent. In August 1977, after Buckner had been particularly effective in the batter's box, Cubs manager Herman Franks said, "Lord knows where we'd be if we had him healthy all season. He's probably playing at no more [than] 50 percent. I'd just like to have him at 90 percent next year. You should see this guy getting ready for a game. He rides that bike in there and does all kind of exercises. Then he goes in, and Tony (Trainer Garofalo) tapes him here to here." Richard Dozer, "Buckner's Hot Bat Keeps Cubs Afloat," *The Sporting News*, August 27, 1977, 13.

12. *The Rich Eisen Show*, October 17, 2017, https://www.youtube.com/watch?v=SpU_7YbPuCI.
13. *The Odd Couple* has been great fodder for Hollywood. There was a TV movie reuniting Jack Klugman as Oscar and Tony Randall as Felix in 1993. A Black cast starred in *The New Odd Couple*, which aired during the 1982–83 season on ABC. CBS revived the premise in 2015. This version starred Matthew Perry as Oscar and Thomas Lennon as Felix. CBS canceled it in 2017. The original play by Neil Simon debuted in 1965. Walter Matthau and Jack Lemmon starred in the 1968 movie and its 1998 sequel, *The Odd Couple II*. In 1975 ABC's Saturday morning cartoon *The Oddball Couple* featured a sloppy dog and a tidy cat.
14. Amalie Benjamin, "Buckner's Appearance Marks End of an Error," *Boston Globe*, April 9, 2008, 40.
15. Benjamin, "Buckner's Appearance Marks End of an Error," 40.
16. *E:60*, "Behind the Bag."
17. *E:60*, "Behind the Bag."
18. Jeff English, "Bill Buckner," Society for American Baseball Research Baseball Biography Project, accessed September 21, 2022, https://sabr.org/bioproj/person/bill-buckner/.
19. *Rich Eisen Show*, October 17, 2017.
20. *E:60*, "Behind the Bag."

10. Hope for Tomorrow

1. Tom Fitzgerald, "Park a Bruin, Esposito a Ranger in Five-Man 'Shocker,'" *Boston Globe*, November 8, 1975, 1.
2. John Powers, "Espo Fumes over 'Coldness,'" *Boston Sunday Globe*, November 9, 1975, 1.
3. Leigh Montville, "Espo Always the Garbageman," *Boston Sunday Globe*, November 9, 1975, 94.
4. Fred Lynn, *MLB's 20 Greatest Games, #1—1975 World Series Game 6 Reds vs. Red Sox*, "Lynn on Crashing into Outfield Wall," MLB Network, May 22, 2011, https://www.youtube.com/watch?v=K9ay6wddb34. Padding appeared on the outfield walls the following year.
5. Bob Ryan, "Reds Saw Game Drop Right into Evans's Glove," *Boston Globe*, October 22, 1975, 26.
6. Dwight Evans, *Red Sox Stories*, Boston Red Sox, NESN, redsox.com, April 30, 2006, https://www.youtube.com/watch?v=-DYROsNOCnQ; Tom Catlin, LinkedIn message to author, March 25, 2023.

7. Harold Friend, "Mickey Mantle's Most Significant Catch," Bleacher Report, March 6, 2010, https://bleacherreport.com/articles/357816 -mickey-mantles-most-important-catch.

8. Earl Lawson, "Fisk Knew It Was Gone as Soon as It Left Bat," *Cincinnati Post*, October 22, 1975, 26.

9. "Carlton Fisk's Iconic 1975 Home Run and the Rat That Changed Television," *The Sporting News*, Mass Live, April 19, 2012, https://www.masslive .com/redsox/2012/04/carlton_fisks_iconic_1975_home.html.

10. Desmond Ryan, "'Rocky': Tale of Loser Is Winner," *Philadelphia Inquirer*, December 22, 1976, 34.

11. Out of Sight, Baby

1. Lou Connelly, "Tony: 'I Had No Chance . . . ,'" *Boston Herald Traveler*, August 19, 1967, 1.

2. Connelly, "Tony: 'I Had No Chance . . . ,'" 1.

3. The Red Sox needed space for their acquisition, so they bumped right-hander Galen Cisco to their Triple-A team, the Toronto Maple Leafs; George Smith, who had been sidelined since getting injured in spring training, went to the Triple-A Phoenix Giants.

4. Henry McKenna, "Yaz, Siebern Lift Sox, 12–11," *Sunday Herald Traveler*, August 20, 1967, sec. 2, 1; Clif Keane, "Rodgers Loses Glove, Sox Win, 12–11," *Boston Sunday Globe*, August 20, 1967, 59.

5. Fred Campa, "Tony C Anxious to Get In on 'Kill' (World Series)," *Boston Record-American*, August 28, 1967, 35.

6. Harold Kaese, "Chisox Bid Top for Harrelson," *Boston Globe* (morning edition), August 29, 1967, 23.

7. Larry Claflin, "Sox to Start Harrelson," *Boston Record-American*, August 30, 1967, 56. The other right fielders were Jim Landis, George Thomas, and José Tartabull.

8. Bill Liston, "Biggest Win—Williams," *Boston Herald Traveler*, September 19, 1967, 42.

9. Larry Claflin, "Sox Erupt for 3 Runs in 9th to Topple Tigers Again, 4–2," *Boston Record-American*, September 20, 1967, 64.

10. Henry McKenna, "Sox Do It Again, 5–4," *Boston Herald Traveler*, September 21, 1967, 45.

11. Bill Liston, "Nearly a Dark Night—Williams," *Boston Herald Traveler*, September 23, 1967, 13.

12. Tim Horgan, "Who'll Buy Champagne? Yaz, Natch," *Sunday Herald Traveler*, October 1, 1967, sec. 2, 1.

13. Gillette advertisement, *Boston Herald Traveler*, October 2, 1967, 8.

14. TWA advertisement, *Boston Herald Traveler*, October 2, 1967, 4.

15. Filene's advertisement, *Boston Herald Traveler*, October 2, 1967, 5.

16. Lechmere advertisement, *Boston Herald Traveler*, October 2, 1967, 7.

17. "Right Out of Sight," *Boston Globe* (morning edition), October 2, 1967, 10.

18. Fred Ciampa, "Weeping Conigliaro Consoled by Yawkey," *Boston Record-American*, October 2, 1967, 33.

19. Larry Claflin, "Yaz Wins Triple Crown, Tops RBIs, Hits, Ties HRs," *Boston Record-American*, October 2, 1967, 35.

20. Jimmy Cannon, "Williams Made Sox into Champs," *Boston Record-American*, October 3, 1967, 38.

21. Joe Cashman, "Koufax Analyzes Sox, Cardinals Strong Points," *Boston Record-American*, October 3, 1967, 36.

22. Larry Claflin, "Red Sox 3–2 Underdog," *Boston Record-American*, October 3, 1967, 48.

23. Carl Yastrzemski, "'We'll Still Win It in Six,'" *Boston Globe* (morning edition), October 5, 1967, 1.

24. Jim Lonborg, "Javier's Hit Was 'Like Seeing a Train Wreck,'" *Boston Herald Traveler*, October 6, 1967, 1.

25. Jack Clary, "Briles Not That Tough, Scott Says," *Sunday Herald Traveler*, October 8, 1967, sec. 2, 1.

26. Carl Yastrzemski, "Yes, Briles Threw at Me," *Boston Sunday Globe*, October 8, 1967, 1.

27. Jack Clary, "Tired Gibson Beat the Red Sox, Wants to Head Home," *Boston Herald Traveler*, October 9, 1967, 38.

28. Clary, "Tired Gibson Beat the Red Sox, Wants to Head Home," 38.

29. Will McDonough, "Lonborg Longs for Long Rest," *Boston Globe* (morning edition), October 9, 1967, 23.

30. Jim Lonborg, "Lonborg Tells How He Won THE Game," *Boston Herald Traveler*, October 10, 1967, 1.

31. Larry Claflin, "Lonborg Series Record," *Boston Record-American*, October 10, 1967, 52.

32. Bill Liston, "Back to the Green Monster, and Credit Foy, Yips Yaz," *Boston Herald Traveler*, October 10, 1967, 45.

33. Liston, "Back to the Green Monster, and Credit Foy, Yips Yaz," 45.

34. Clif Keane, "The Red Sox Come Back," *Boston Globe* (morning edition), October 10, 1967, 1.
35. Lou Connelly, "Rico Shows Sox His Vitamin Sock," *Boston Herald Traveler*, October 12, 1967, 48.
36. George Sullivan, "We'll KO Gibson in Five—Scott," *Boston Herald Traveler*, October 12, 1967, 49.
37. "Series Sidelights," *Boston Globe* (morning edition), October 13, 1967, 48.
38. John Gillooly, "Red Sox Fans Roar Tribute to Losers," *Boston Record-American*, October 13, 1967, 86.
39. Red Smith, "A Grand Ride to Finish Line," *Boston Globe* (morning edition), October 13, 1967, 50.
40. D. Leo Monahan, "Never Lost Faith in Myself—Lonborg," *Boston Record-American*, October 13, 1967, 87.
41. State Street Bank and Trust Company advertisement, *Boston Record-American*, October 14, 1967, 35.
42. Star Markets advertisement, *Boston Record-American*, October 14, 1967, 12.
43. Al Hirshberg, "Red's Sour View of Boston Team—'Lucky,'" *Boston Herald Traveler*, October 13, 1967, 1.
44. "Red Sox Give Yaz Left Field," *Boston Globe* (morning edition), October 14, 1967, 1.

12. Worthy Rivals

1. "American League," *New York Times*, May 8, 1903, 10. Newspapers often had their own scorers, leading to differing statistics. In the *Boston Daily Globe* account, Dinneen gave up five hits. "In Fine Form," *Boston Daily Globe*, May 8, 1903, 5.
2. "Highlanders Fight to the Last Ditch but Lose Pennant," *Evening World* (New York), October 10, 1904, 1.
3. T. H. Murnane, "Boston Wins Again," *Boston Daily Globe*, October 11, 1904, 1.
4. Melville E. Webb Jr., "'Royal Rooters' Happy," *Boston Globe*, October 11, 1904, 1.
5. Ed Cunningham, "Red Sox Sell Babe Ruth to Yanks for More than $100,000," *Boston Herald*, January 6, 1920, 1.
6. Nick Flatley, "Ruth Deal Foreshadows Sale of Red Sox," *Boston American*, January 6, 1920, 9.
7. "New York Manager Says Ruth Has Signed New Contract—Hockey," *Boston Evening Transcript*, January 6, 1920, 20.
8. "Sale of Babe Ruth Stirs Storm among Hub Fans," *Boston Traveler*, January 6, 1920, 1.

9. "Sale of Babe Ruth Stirs Storm among Hub Fans," 1.
10. Eddie Hurley, "Looking 'Em Over," *Boston Evening Record*, January 6, 1920, 10.
11. "Ruth Claims Deal No Surprise to Him," *Boston Herald*, January 6, 1920, 18.
12. Paul H. Shannon, "Red Sox in Deal for .300 Hitter," *Boston Post*, January 6, 1920, 14.
13. Paul H. Shannon, "Sale of Ruth Stirs Up Fans," *Boston Post*, January 7, 1920, 10.
14. *The Curse of the Bambino*, HBO Sports, aired as an episode of *Sports of the 20th Century*, September 16, 2003, on HBO.
15. "Bucky Dent's HR in the AL East Playoff Game," Major League Baseball, accessed December 24, 2022, https://www.youtube.com/watch?v=0tl7xW4Oxo0.
16. "Yankees vs. Red Sox . . . Red Sox vs. Yankees," The Connecticut Forum, February 17, 2005, https://www.youtube.com/watch?v=-x-RiVawtqk.
17. Ray Fitzgerald, "So, Just How Bad Was It?" *Boston Globe*, September 8, 1978, 21.
18. Peter Gammons, "Sox Err 7 Times; NY Zeroes In, 13-2," *Boston Globe*, September 9, 1978, 21.
19. Dan Shaughnessy, "Mueller Slams Dramatic Homer, 11-10," *Boston Sunday Globe*, July 25, 2004, 1.
20. *Reverse of the Curse of the Bambino*, HBO Sports, aired as an episode of *Sports of the 20th Century*, December 10, 2004, on HBO.
21. 2004 World Series, Game Four, aired October 27, 2004, on FOX, https://www.youtube.com/watch?v=RAshX7IJfyc.

13. A Man Called Yastrzemski

1. In 1952 Williams played in six games in April. The following year, he returned to the Red Sox in early August and played in thirty-seven games.
2. Bob Holbrook, "Yaz, Bob It's Yaz," *Boston Globe* (morning edition), March 1, 1961, 31.
3. Bob Holbrook, "Yaz Takes Dad's Advice," *Boston Sunday Globe*, March 26, 1961, 63.
4. Bob Holbrook, "Yaz Takes Ted Tip, Gets 4 Hits," *Boston Globe* (morning edition), March 18, 1961, 13.
5. Bob Holbrook, "Doerr Sizes Up Sox Rookies," *Boston Sunday Globe*, September 17, 1961, 68.
6. Will McDonough, "Yaz Spectacular in Sox 10-9 Win," *Boston Globe* (morning edition), March 30, 1967, 29.
7. Harold Kaese, "Mrs. JFK, Son Saw One-Hitter," *Boston Globe* (morning edition), April 15, 1967, 19.

8. Joe Cashman, "Yaz Greatest Left Fielder Billy Martin Ever Saw," *Boston Record-American*, August 8, 1967, 32.

9. "Williams Calls Yaz 'Greatest,'" *Boston Globe* (morning edition), October 6, 1967, 28.

10. Carl Yastrzemski, "Batters' Nemesis . . . the Slider," *Boston Globe*, October 7, 1967, 1.

11. 125 *Congressional Record* (House, September 14, 1979) (remarks of Rep. Silvio Conte and Rep. Joe Moakley).

12. "A Resolution in Honor of Carl Yastrzemski of the Boston Red Sox," 125 *Congressional Record* (Senate, September 14, 1979) (introductory remarks by Sen. Ted Kennedy).

13. Murray Chass, "Yastrzemski Gets 3000th on Single," *New York Times*, September 13, 1979, C23.

14. Peter Gammons, "Yaz Hits 3000," *Boston Globe*, September 13, 1979, 1.

15. Larry Whiteside, "At 36, Yaz's Most Explosive Night . . . ," *Boston Evening Globe*, May 20, 1976, 25.

16. Whiteside, "At 36, Yaz's Most Explosive Night . . . ," 25.

17. Whiteside, "At 36, Yaz's Most Explosive Night . . . ," 25.

18. Jack Craig, "TV Replay Doesn't Show Lee Injury," *Boston Globe*, May 22, 1976, 19. According to this article, "Velez then arrived and began to pull Yaz, after which a veritable torrent of bodies poured over them, especially Yaz. This is when he apparently suffered his leg injury."

19. Parton Keese, "Yaz's 2 Homers Help Red Sox Down Yanks, 8-2, after Brawl," *New York Times*, May 21, 1976, 46.

20. Craig, "TV Replay Doesn't Show Lee Injury," 19.

21. Sen. Ted Kennedy, "A Resolution in Honor of Carl Yastrzemski of the Boston Red Sox," S. Res. 232, 98th Cong. (September 28, 1983).

22. Steve Marcus, "Regrets, He's Had a Few," *Newsday*, January 11, 1989, 110.

23. Paul Clerici, "Yastrzemski's Number Retired at Fenway's Yaz Day," *Walpole (MA) Times*, August 10, 1989, 15.

24. "Yastrzemski Undergoes Heart Bypass Surgery in Boston," Associated Press, ESPN.com, August 19, 2008, https://www.espn.com/mlb/news/story?id=3542769.

14. Tom Seaver's Last Hurrah

1. ABC later fared better with a trio of shows reflecting baby boomers who grew up in the 1960s. The ensemble drama *thirtysomething* captured the angst of "young urban professionals" in their thirties living in the

Philadelphia area. The "yuppie" drama aired for four seasons—1987 to 1991—pairing nicely with the network's *The Wonder Years*, which recounted the growing pains of Kevin Arnold from age twelve to seventeen as he navigated first crushes, tough teachers, and middle-class life in an unnamed suburban town. *The Wonder Years* aired from 1988 to 1993 and took place twenty years before that time frame. *China Beach* was a critically acclaimed, Emmy-winning, one-hour drama based on a real U.S. Army hospital during the Vietnam War. ABC aired it from 1988 to 1991.

2. Predating the tsunami of nostalgia that flooded popular culture were two 1981 songs about baseball. Terry Cashman's "Talkin' Baseball" covered notable people and events from the 1950s to the 1980s. Cashman later recorded several versions specific to a team's history. Steve Goodman's "A Dying Cub Fan's Last Request" represented the hopelessness of Cubs fans, which wasn't fully quashed until the team's 2016 World Series title.

3. Mike Lupica, "Camelot's Back at Shea," *Daily News* (New York), December 17, 1982, C28.

4. Steve Wulf, "It Was a Terrific Homecoming," *Sports Illustrated*, April 18, 1983, 36.

5. "Sox Make Pitch," *Herald and Review* (Decatur IL), January 21, 1984, 16.

6. Steve Richards, "Deals Helped in '67, '75," *Boston Globe*, June 30, 1986, 31.

7. Justin Barrasso, "Roger Clemens Reflects on All He Learned from Tom Seaver," *Sports Illustrated*, September 4, 2020, https://www.si.com/mlb/2020/09/04/tom-seaver-roger-clemens.

8. Dan Shaughnessy, "A Tip of the Hat," *Boston Globe*, July 2, 1986, 67.

9. Larry Whiteside, "Seaver Off to Good Start, 9-7," *Boston Globe*, July 2, 1986, 67.

10. Dan Shaughnessy, "Smarting Sox Swept," *Boston Sunday Globe*, October 5, 1986, 57.

11. "Injury to Knee Ligament Puts Seaver on Sideline," Associated Press, *Sacramento Bee*, October 17, 1986, C3.

12. Al Nipper, telephone interview by author, August 31, 2022.

13. Bill Madden, "Seaver Cut Loose," *Daily News* (New York), November 4, 1986, 32.

14. "Red Sox, Yankees Say No to Seaver," *New York Times*, December 8, 1986, C2.

15. Jim Corbett, "Seaver Answers Ailing Mets' Call," Gannett News Service, *Sunday Star-Gazette* (Elmira NY), June 7, 1987, 17.

16. Joseph Durso, "Strawberry Is Back in Lineup," *New York Times*, June 12, 1987, D17.

17. Jim Corbett, "Some Improvement, Some Doubts," *Daily Times* (Westchester NY), June 17, 1987, 33.

18. Joseph Durso, "'Mediocre' Pitching Shakes Up Seaver," *New York Times*, June 21, 1987, S4.

19. Jack Lang, "'No Pitches Left in This Arm,'" *Daily News* (New York), June 23, 1987, 52.

20. "Tom Seaver Day, July 24, 1988," Sportschannel, last accessed August 27, 2022, https://www.youtube.com/watch?v=Qcf1NEMlCGA.

21. *The Andy Griffith Show*, also called *Andy of Mayberry* in syndication, had initially aired on CBS and spawned the spinoff *Mayberry R.F.D.*

22. The October 4–10, 1986, issue of *TV Guide* featured Andy Griffith and Lucille Ball with the caption "Two Old Favorites Return to Series TV." ABC's *Life with Lucy* starred the iconic comedienne in her fourth sitcom. Ball hadn't appeared in the format on a regular basis since 1974. Though her nostalgia factor was undeniable, the ABC show didn't make it past Thanksgiving. NBC aired *Matlock* until 1992, then ABC took custody. It aired for three more seasons, ending in 1995.

15. Location, Location, Location

1. Robert Foster, "Douse That Sign" (letter to the editor), *Boston Evening Globe*, May 15, 1974, 26.

2. Richard C. Greenhalgh, "Citgo Sign: Boston's Best," *Boston Evening Globe*, October 1, 1976, 20.

3. Walter Guertin, letter to the editor, *Boston Globe*, October 12, 1976, 21.

4. Warren Thayer, letter to the editor, *Boston Globe*, October 12, 1976, 21.

5. Anne D. Kenney, letter to the editor, *Boston Globe*, October 12, 1976, 21; Mark Vershbow, letter to the editor, *Boston Globe*, October 12, 1976, 21.

6. Christina Robb, "City Lights Turn on the City," *Boston Globe: Calendar*, August 25, 1977, 1.

7. Gary Langer, "Turning Off Kenmore Square Signs," *Boston Globe*, July 30, 1979, 16.

8. Robert Campbell, "A Movement Is Afoot to the Return of a Crown Jewel? Switch Boston's Garish, Glorious Citgo Sign Back On," *Boston Sunday Globe*, April 6, 1980, 234.

9. Robert Campbell, "A Fossil, It Sits There, a Sign of Its Time and, Sadly, Ours," *Boston Globe*, June 21, 1982, 1.

10. Robert Campbell, "A Magnificent Seven," *Boston Globe Magazine*, August 22, 1982, 13.

11. Frances Bragg, letter to the editor, *Boston Globe*, January 21, 1983, 18.

12. Irene Sege, "Boston's Citgo Sign Is Given a Reprieve," *Boston Globe*, November 17, 1982, 29.

13. Joanne Ball, "Keeping Up with the Citgo Sign," *Boston Globe*, January 12, 1983, 17.

14. Nicholas M. Buck, letter to the editor, *Boston Globe*, January 24, 1983, 9.

15. John T. Lu, letter to the editor, *Boston Globe*, January 24, 1983, 9.

16. Sarah Darwin, letter to the editor, *Boston Globe*, January 24, 1983, 9.

17. "Citgo Sign-Off," *Boston Globe*, January 25, 1983, 20.

18. Marcia Myers, the commission's executive director, explained, "To force the owner to maintain such a sign, to pay rent for its space, taxes and other permits, and in this case of the Citgo sign, to operate it, is, we conclude, an unreasonable burden." Joanne Ball, "It's No Go for Citgo 'Landmark,'" *Boston Globe*, January 26, 1983, 17.

19. Anndee Hochman, "A Sign Blinks Once More in Kenmore Sq.," *Boston Globe*, August 11, 1983, 22.

20. Peter J. Howe, "Jewels of the Night Skyline Enter '90s in Glowing Health," *Boston Globe* (Metro Region edition), December 31, 1989, 21.

21. "Hands Off the Citgo Sign," *Boston Globe*, October 9, 2006, A6.

22. D. P. Pare, "Citgo Sign Is No Cultural Treasure" (letter to the editor), *Boston Globe*, October 11, 2006, A10.

23. Jack Nicas, "On the Bench," *Boston Globe*, July 22, 2010, B1.

24. Alison Frazee, email to author, November 12, 2022.

25. Bruce Wells, email to author, September 15, 2022.

26. Spencer Buell, "The Citgo Sign Will Not Be an Official Landmark," *Boston Magazine*, November 29, 2018, https://www.bostonmagazine.com/news/2018/11/29/citgo-sign-landmark-veto/; Spencer Buell, "The Citgo Sign Will (Probably) Finally Become a Landmark," *Boston Magazine*, November 14, 2018, https://www.bostonmagazine.com/news/2018/11/14/citgo-sign-will-probably-become-landmark/.

27. Frazee email.

28. Madhri Yehiya, "Students Express Disapproval as New Kenmore Square Building Slowly Covers Iconic Citgo Sign," *Daily Free Press* (independent student newspaper at Boston University), October 21, 2021, https://dailyfreepress.com/2021/10/21/students-express-disapproval-as-new-kenmore-square-building-slowly-covers-iconic-bu-citgo-sign/.

29. Warren Thayer, email to author, November 11, 2022.

30. Eddie Bruckner, email to author, April 9, 2023.

31. Arthur Krim, telephone interview by author, November 12, 2022.

16. Of Sluggers and Statues

1. Jean Labatut, "Monuments and Memorials," in *Forms and Functions of Twentieth-Century Architecture*, vol. 3, ed. Talbot Hamlin (New York: Columbia University Press, 1952), 521.
2. Labatut, "Monuments and Memorials," 523.
3. Labatut, "Monuments and Memorials," 522.
4. Steve Silva, "Yaz Statue Unveiled at Fenway," Boston.com, September 13, 2022, https://www.boston.com/sports/extra-bases/2013/09/22/yaz_statue_unveiled_at_fenway/.
5. Antonio Tobias Mendez, telephone interview by author, November 4, 2022.
6. Doug Fernandes, "Williams Statue Unveiled," *Boston Herald-Tribune*, April 16, 2004, https://www.heraldtribune.com/story/news/2004/04/16/williams-statue-unveiled/28800521007/.
7. Scott S. Greenberger and Alice Gomstyn, "City Proposes Williams Statue," *Boston Globe*, July 10, 2022, B2.
8. Labatut, "Monuments and Memorials," 523.
9. Labatut, "Monuments and Memorials," 523.
10. Labatut, "Monuments and Memorials," 521.
11. Labatut, "Monuments and Memorials," 532.

17. Go Sox!

1. NFL expansion didn't happen. The American Football League debuted in 1960 with the Boston Patriots as a charter team. They played in Nickerson Field, Fenway Park, Alumni Stadium, and Harvard Stadium. The Patriots called Foxboro Stadium their home from 1971 to 2001. Since 2002, they've played at Gillette Stadium.
2. "60,000-Seat Stadium Planned," *Boston Evening Globe*, April 1, 1958, 1.
3. "Big Sports Stadium Planned in Norwood," *Boston Daily Globe*, February 27, 1958, 1; "60,000-Seat Stadium Planned," 1.
4. Will McDonough, "'No Time to Waste on Something Puny,'" *Boston Globe* (morning edition), July 1, 1965, 2.
5. Gabrielle Starr, email to author, January 8, 2023.
6. David Starr, email to author, January 26, 2023.
7. Clayton Trutor, email to author, December 3, 2022.
8. Eric Burckhardt, email to author, November 27, 2022.
9. Joshua Krumholz, email to author, November 28, 2022.
10. John Bennett, email to author, December 19, 2022.

11. Larry Ruttman, email to author, July 26, 2022.

12. Bill Nowlin, email to author, July 27, 2022.

13. Scott Melesky, email to author, December 9, 2022.

14. Gary Stockbridge, email to author, November 19, 2022.

15. James Smith, email to author, December 24, 2022.

16. Donna Cohen, email to author, January 22, 2023.

17. John Pearson, email to author, January 16, 2023.

18. Joe LeBritton, email to author, December 13, 2022.

19. Mel Seibolt, email to author, January 17, 2023.

20. Barbara Mantegani, email to author, January 27, 2023.

21. Amy Polacko, email to author, January 29, 2023.

22. Karl Lindholm, email to author, February 13, 2023.

23. Mark Peloquin, email to author, March 17, 2023.

24. Howard Homonoff, email to author, March 26, 2023.

25. Ron Kercheville, email to author, March 20, 2023.

26. John Tierney, email to author, December 8, 2022.

Selected Bibliography

Appel, Marty. *Slide, Kelly, Slide: The Wild Life and Times of Mike "King" Kelly, Baseball's First Superstar*. Lanham MD: Scarecrow Press, 1996.

Ballou, Bill. *Behind the Green Monster: Red Sox Myths, Legends, and Lore*. Chicago: Triumph Books, 2009.

Bradlee, Ben, Jr. *The Kid: The Immortal Life of Ted Williams*. Boston: Little, Brown, 2013.

Cataneo, David, with contributions by Linda Householder. *Tony C: The Triumph and Tragedy of Tony Conigliaro*. Nashville TN: Rutledge Hill Press, 1997.

Connelly, Michael. *Fenway 1946: Red Sox, Peace, and a Year of Hope*. Lanham MD: Lyons Press, 2020.

Crehan, Herb. *The Impossible Dream: 1967 Red Sox, Birth of Red Sox Nation*. South Orange NJ: Summer Game Books, 2016.

Flavin, Dick. *Red Sox Rhymes: Verses and Curses*. New York: HarperCollins, 2015.

Gitlin, Martin. *The Ultimate Boston Red Sox Time Machine Book*. Lanham MD: Rowman & Littlefield, 2020.

Halberstam, David. *The Teammates: A Portrait of Friendship*. New York: Hyperion, 2003.

Latchford, Jennifer, and Rod Oreste (for the Boston Public Library and the Boston Red Sox). *Red Sox Legends*. Charleston SC: Arcadia, 2007.

Leavy, Jane. *The Big Fella: Babe Ruth and the World He Created*. New York: HarperCollins, 2018.

McAdam, Sean. *The Franchise: Boston Red Sox—A Curated History of the Sox*. Chicago: Triumph Books, 2022.

Montville, Leigh. *The Big Bam: The Life and Times of Babe Ruth*. New York: Doubleday, 2006.

———. *Ted Williams: The Biography of an American Hero*. New York: Doubleday, 2004.

Petrocelli, Rico, and Chaz Scoggins with Bill Nowlin. *Tales from the 1967 Red Sox Dugout: A Collection of the Greatest Stories Ever Told from the Impossible Dream Season*. New York: Sports Publishing, 2021.

Piersall, Jim, and Al Hirshberg. *Fear Strikes Out*. Boston: Little, Brown, 1955.

Prime, Jim, and Bill Nowlin. *Amazing Tales from the Boston Red Sox Dugout: A Collection of the Greatest Red Sox Stories Ever Told*. New York: Sports Publishing, 2002.

Remy, Jerry, and Nick Cafardo. *If These Walls Could Talk: Stories from the Boston Red Sox Dugout, Locker Room, and Press Box*. Chicago: Triumph Books, 2019.

Shaughnessy, Dan. *The Curse of the Bambino*. New York: Dutton, 1990.

Stout, Glenn. *Fenway 1912: The Birth of a Ballpark, a Championship Season, and Fenway's Remarkable First Year*. Boston: Houghton Mifflin Harcourt, 2011.

Stout, Glenn, and Richard A. Johnson. *Red Sox Century: The Definitive History of Baseball's Most Storied Franchise, Expanded and Updated*. Boston: Houghton Mifflin Harcourt, 2005.

Tiant, Luis, with Saul Wisnia. *Son of Havana: A Baseball Journey from Cuba to the Big Leagues and Back*. New York: Diversion Books, 2019.

Whalen, Thomas J. *When the Red Sox Ruled: Baseball's First Dynasty, 1912–1918*. Chicago: Ivan R. Dee, 2011.

Williams, Ted, and John Underwood. *The Science of Hitting*. New York: Simon and Schuster, 1971.

Yastrzemski, Carl, and Gerald Eskenazi. *Yaz: Baseball, the Wall, and Me*. New York: Doubleday, 1990.

Index

Adair, Jerry, 113, 121, 122
Affleck, Ben, 71–72
Affleck, Casey, 71
Agee, Tommie, 116
Allenson, Gary, 196
Alley, Kirstie, 85
Alomar, Sandy, 151
Amaro, Rubén, 117
The American Sportsman, 49
Amorós, Sandy, 106
Anderson, Bill, 49
Anderson, Sparky, 103
Andrews, Mike, 19, 113, 114–15
The Andy Griffith Show, 165
Argo, 73
Arizona Diamondbacks, 44
Arliss, 94
Armas, Tony, 160
Armbrister, Ed, 103
Arredondo, Carlos, 5
Arroyo, Bronson, 140
Associated Press, 5, 71, 73, 90,
    161, 185
Atherton, Keith, 196
Atlanta Braves, 7, 113

"Babe Ruth's Curse," 42
Backman, Wally, 75, 88
Bailey, Andrew, 10
Balboa, Rocky, 110–11
Baltimore Orioles, 119, 137, 160, 181

Baltimore Orioles (nineteenth cen-
    tury), 54–55, 58
Banacek, 76
Bando, Sal, 201
Barfield, Jesse, 159
Barnes, W. S., Jr., 55, 61
Barrett, Marty, 87–88
Barrymore, Drew, 68, 70–71
Bauman, Jeff, 4–5, 7, 10
Bayer, Chris, 89
Baylor, Don, 158, 160
Bean, Billy, 81
The Beatles, 41, 46, 72, 155
Beattie, Jim, 137
Belafonte, Harry, 29
Bell, George, 160
Bellhorn, Mark, 140, 194
Bench, Johnny, 104–5, 151
Bengtson, Phil, 152
Bennett, Dennis, 122
Bennett, John, 194
Benny, Jack, 31–32, 71
Berg, Peter, 6
Bergman, Steven, 42
Berkeley Building, 175
Bernhard, Bill, 59–61
Berra, Yogi, 83, 106–7
Betts, Mookie, 205
Beverly Hills 90210, 95
Bible verses, 4, 11
The Big Chill, 155

Bigelow Cleaners, 175

Billingham, Jack, 103

Billings, James, 57

Birmingham Black Barons, 65–66

Blue, Vida, 201

Bluford, Guion, 28

Boggs, Wade, 74, 84–85, 87–88

Borbón, Pedro, 104

Bosox Injection, 191

"Boston Accent," 54

Boston Americans, 37, 57

Boston Beaneaters, 38, 57, 61

Boston Braves: Babe Ruth ends career
with, 134; Jackie Robinson plays
against, in Major League debut, 27;
and Jimmy Fund, 12–13, 14, 15, 23;
and Narragansett sponsorship of
radio broadcasts, 45–46; and "Nuf
Ced" McGreevy, 38, 40

Boston Bruins, 5, 78, 85, 101–2, 113

Boston Celtics, 48, 85, 129, 158, 162

Boston City Council, 27

Boston College, 192, 193, 196

Boston Common, 72, 76

Boston Edison, 168

Boston Garden, 49, 102, 162

Boston Harbor, 3

Boston Marathon, 3–6, 44, 191, 205

Boston Police Department, 3, 7–8

Boston Preservation Alliance, 170

Boston Public Library, 37

Boston Red Sox: and Boston Marathon bombing, 3–10; and *Cheers*,
76–86; and Citgo Sign, 167–77;
fans of, 189–206; and Huntington Avenue Grounds, 54–64; and
Jimmy Fund, 11–24; in movies,
65–75; and Narragansett beer,

45–53; and 1967 American League
East pennant, 120–22; 1967 team,
101–11; rivalry of, with New York
Yankees, 129–44; in songs, 37–44;
and statues, 178–88; and World
Series (1975), 101–11. *See also specific players*

Boston Symphony Orchestra, 175

Boston Tea Party, 193

Boston University, 174, 192

Boston Yanks, 13–14

Boswell, Thomas, 85, 90

Bouton, Jim, 117

Boyd, Oil Can, 74, 90, 161, 176

Boyer, Ken, 116

The Boys of Summer (Kahn), 185

BP, 172, 175

Bradshaw, Terry, 95

Brady, Tom, 44, 192

The Brady Bunch, 94–95

Brandon, Bucky, 116, 117

Brett, George, 179

Briles, Nelson, 123

Brock, Lou, 122–23, 125

Brockton Rox, 97

Brohamer, Jack, 137

Brooklyn Bridegrooms, 40

Brooklyn Dodgers, 14, 26–27, 112, 185

Brown v. Board of Education of Topeka,
30, 112

Bruckner, Eddie, 175

Brynner, Yul, 11

B. Schade Brewing Company, 51

Buchholz, Clay, 9, 10

Buck, Joe, 142

Buckner, Bill, 69, 75, 87, 89–94, 96–97

Buckner, Jody, 96–97

Buddin, Don, 83

Index

Buffalo Bisons, 56
Buford, Don, 116
Buhner, Jay, 93
Burckhardt, Eric, 193
Burgess, Smoky, 116
Burgmeier, Tom, 138
Burke, Glenn, 81
Burleson, Rick, 103, 105, 136, 149, 151
Burr, Ty, 75
Burrows, James, 76, 85

Cain, Lorenzo, 9, 10
California Angels: and Bill Buckner, 96; and Frank Malzone, 83; and Jack Hamilton, 69, 114-15; and Jimmy Piersall, 67; 1967 season of, 120-21; and 1986 American League playoffs, 74, 89, 90, 161
Campanella, Roy, 30
Campbell, Bill, 137
Campbell, Krystle Marie, 3
Canadian American Association of Professional Baseball, 97
Cannon, Jimmy, 121
Carbo, Bernie, 105, 110, 201
Carlton, Steve, 157
Carolina League, 145
Carrigan, Bill, 40
Carter, Gary, 75, 88-89
Cash, Norm, 118
Cashen, Frank, 163
"Centerfield," 156
Cepeda, Orlando, 123, 127
Cervantes, Alfonso J., 126
Chambers, Diane, 68, 80-81
Chambliss, Chris, 138, 151
Chaney, Darrel, 103
Charles River, 41

Charlestown MA, 46, 72-73
Chávez, Hugo, 170
Chech, Charlie, 62
Cheers: controversial subject matter in, 79-82; depiction of Yankees fans in, 78; description of, 76; and exterior of Bull & Finch Pub, 77; Nielsen ratings for, 85-86; Red Sox in dialogue in, 82-84
Chesbro, Jack, 130
Chicago Blackhawks, 101
Chicago Cubs, 13, 27, 96
Christensen, John, 89
A Christmas Story, 141
Cincinnati Reds, 102-8
Citgo Sign: artwork for, 167, 175; as Boston landmark, 168-71, 173-74; and Citgo company history, 171-72; comparison of, to other oil company names and logos, 172-73; and energy crisis, 168; history of, 171-73; origins of, 167; and public opinion, 167, 169
Cities Service, 167. *See also* Citgo Sign
City of Palms Park, 183
Clark, Petula, 29
Clarke, Horace, 117
Clarke, Lenny, 135
Clavin, Cliff, 79
Clemens, Roger, 87-88, 159, 161
Clemente, Roberto, 184
Cleveland Indians, 12, 27, 28, 31, 67, 107, 147
Cleveland Lake Shores, 56
Cleveland Naps, 61-62
Cleveland Spiders, 56, 58, 61
Clinton, Lou, 83
Cobb, Ty, 132

Cohen, Donna, 198-99
Colavito, Rocky, 116
Collier, Sean, 4
Collins, Jimmie, 57, 59-60, 62, 131
Collins, John, 126
Collins, Tim, 9-10
Columbus Senators, 56, 67
Combs, Earle, 134
Conant, William, 57
Concepción, Dave, 107
Conigliaro, Tony, 69, 114, 116, 117, 121, 128
Conroy, Wid, 130
Consalvo, Rob, 183
Cooper, Cecil, 103
Cooperstown NY, 26, 183-84
Copley Square, 4
Cosell, Howard, 95
Costanza, George, 93
Coughlin, James "Jem," 72
Coyle, Harry, 108
Crawford, Steve, 160
Criger, Lou, 59-60
Crime Story, 165
Crockett, Davy, 181
Cronin, Joe, 28, 46, 67, 190
Cross, Lave, 59
Crow, Aaron, 9
Cuellar, Mike, 156
Culver, George, 119
Curb Your Enthusiasm, 91-94, 97
Curse of the Bambino, 42

Damon, Johnny, 140
Damon, Matt, 71, 139
Danson, Ted, 76, 91
Darcy, Pat, 105, 107-8
Dark, Alvin, 13, 116

David, Larry, 91-93
Davis, Ed, 6, 7
Delock, Ike, 83-84
Dent, Bucky, 79, 135, 139
Detroit Tigers, 27, 121
Diamond, Neil, 42, 44
Dickinson, Emily, 184-85
Dillard, Steve, 150
DiMaggio, Dom, 178, 181
DiMaggio, Joe, 82-83, 106
Dinneen, Bill, 40, 129, 130-31
"Dirty Water," 41-42
DiSarcina, Gary, 8
Doby, Larry, 27
Dodger Stadium, 94, 179, 190
Doerr, Bobby, 125, 146, 178, 181, 183, 197
Doherty, Henry Latham, 172
Don't Look Back, 31
"Don't Walk the Hawk," 42
Dorchester MA, 46, 72-73, 105
Dorsey, Joseph, 114
Dougherty, Patsy, 130
Dowd, Tommy, 59-60
Dow Jones Industrial Average, 109
Downey, Robert, Jr., 74
Downing, Al, 117
Doyle, Denny, 103, 105, 151, 158
Drago, Dick, 105, 137
Drew, Stephen, 9, 10
Dropkick Murphys, 40-41
Drysdale, Don, 94, 189
Duffy, Frank, 138
Duncan, Dave, 201
Dunphy, Don, 48
Dykstra, Lenny, 87

Eastern League, 65
Eastwick, Rawly, 105

Ebbets Field, 185
Eckersley, Dennis, 138
Egan, Dave, 37, 40
Eighteenth Amendment, 45
Eisenhower, Dwight, 154
Eisenstadt, Alfred, 26
Elberfeld, Kid, 130
Elliott, Bob, 13
Ellsbury, Jacob, 9–10
Empire Oil & Refining, 172
Escobar, Alcides, 10
Esposito, Phil, 101–2
Eutaw House, 39
Evans, Dwight, 87–88, 103–7, 110

Fallon, Jimmy, 68–70
Fall River Indians, 58
Falstaff Brewing Company, 49
Farrell, John, 9
FBI, 4, 5, 7–8, 72
Fear Strikes Out, 65–68
Fein, Nat, 185
Felice, Jason, 157
Fenway Park: and All-Star Game
    (1999), 194; Bill Buckner throws out
    first pitch at, 96; and fans, 197–99,
    206; Jackie Robinson tryout at,
    27–28; and Little Fenway, 175; and
    Patriots Day, 3, 44, 199; and statues,
    178–88; in *Stronger*, 5; in *The Town*,
    71–73; and World Series (1975),
    102–8, 111; and Yawkey Way name
    change, 28. *See also* Green Monster
Fernández, Tony, 160
Ferris, Hobe, 59–60, 131
Ferris Bueller's Day Off, 155
Fever Pitch, 68–71
Figueroa, Ed, 139

Filene's, 120
Finley, Charlie, 116
Fire Department of New York, 6
Fisk, Carlton, 48, 102–3, 106–10, 135,
    137–38, 201
Fitzgerald, John, 38, 39
Flood, Curt, 124, 127
Florida Marlins, 141, 165
Flynn, Doug, 156
Ford, Betty, 81
Ford, Gerald, 6
Fort Myers FL, 183
Fortune 500, 28
Fort Wayne IN, 49
Foster, George, 104, 107, 157
Foulke, Keith, 142
Foxx, Jimmie, 82–83, 195
Foy, Joe, 114, 124
Francona, Terry, 140
Francouer, Jeff, 9
Frazee, Alison, 170–71
Frazee, Harry, 78, 101, 131–34
Freeman, Buck, 59–61, 62
Fregosi, Jim, 114
Fultz, Dave, 60

Galvin, Frank, 141
Game of the Week, 47–48
Game 6, 74–75
Ganzel, John, 130
Garciaparra, Nomar, 141
Gardner, Wes, 89
Garfield, James A., 6
Garvey, Steve, 189
Gehrig, Lou, 134, 153, 184
Geier, Phil, 58
General Mills, 33
Gerard, Lou, 108

Gerónimo, César, 103–4, 107
Get Smart, 126
Getz, Chris, 10
Giants Stadium, 94
Gibson, Bob, 122, 123, 125–26
Gibson, Josh, 26, 32–33, 178
Gibson, Russ, 113, 118–19
Giles, Brian, 157
Ginsberg, Joe, 67
Gionfriddo, Al, 106, 108
Gomes, Jonny, 9–10
Gone Baby Gone, 71, 73
Good Will Hunting, 71
Gordon, Alex, 10
Gossage, Goose, 136
Gossett, Lou, Jr., 31
Gowdy, Curt, 16, 45–49
Grand Rapids Furniture Makers, 56
Great Brinks Robbery, 93
Greater Boston PFLAG, 204
Greater Boston Stadium Authority, 191
Green, Pumpsie, 27–28, 47, 112
Green Acres, 174
Green Monster, 79, 83, 104, 176
Griffey, Ken, 103–6, 204
Griffith, Clark, 131
Grillli, Steve, 150
Grote, Jerry, 164
Grove, Lefty, 158
Guidry, Ron, 138
Gyllenhaal, Jake, 5

Halberstam, David, 181, 182
Hall, Jimmie, 115
Halper, Donna, 46–47
Hamilton, Jack, 69, 114, 202
Hancock, Garry, 138–39
Hansen, Ron, 116

Happy Days, 67
Hardin, Jim, 119
Harrell, Pauline Chase, 168
Harrelson, Ken "Hawk," 42, 116–17, 122, 124
Hassler, Andy, 137, 138
Hatfield, Fred, 65
Hayden, Jack, 59–60
Heath, Jeff, 13
Heep, Danny, 88
Hegan, Mike, 117
Hemphill, Charlie, 59–60
Henderson, Dave, 88
Henderson, Steve, 156
Henneberry, David, 8
Hernandez, Keith, 75, 88, 89
Herrera, Kelvin, 10
Hershiser, Orel, 189
Hodge, Ken, 101
Hodges, Gil, 164
Hogan, Chuck, 71
Holmes, Tommy, 13
Homestead Grays, 178
Homonoff, Howard, 205
Horlen, Joe, 116
Hornby, Nick, 68
Horton, Willie, 118, 149
Hosmer, Eric, 9
Houk, Ralph, 150
Howard, Elston, 27, 114, 124, 125, 147, 158
Howard, Mike, 157
Howard, Sam, 16
Hoyt, Waite, 134
Hubert H. Humphrey Metrodome, 160
Hughes, Dick, 125, 156
Hughson, Cecil "Tex," 205
Huntington Avenue Grounds, 38, 54–62, 129, 189

Hurley, Eddie, 132–33
Hurley, Erin, 4, 5
Hurst, Bruce, 74

Inside Sports, 81
International League, 27, 31
Iowa State University, 43
Isabella Stewart Gardner Museum, 93

Jackson, Reggie, 136, 138, 201
Jack Trice Stadium, 43
Jenkins, Fergie, 149
JetBlue Park, 183
Jeter, Derek, 93, 140
Jethroe, Sam, 27–28
Jimmy Fund: and Carl Einar Gus-
    tafson, 18–19; and Charles A. Dana
    Foundation, 18; and Children's
    Cancer Research Foundation, 12,
    14, 17, 18; and Children's Medical
    Center, 12; creation of, 11–12; and
    Dana-Farber Cancer Institute, 18,
    19–20; and Dan Shaughnessy, 18,
    22; in *Fever Pitch*, 69; fundraising
    events for, 13–18, 23–24; and Joe
    Cifre, 14; and Larry Lucchino, 19;
    and Lisa Patti, 22–23; and Lynn
    MacLeod, x, 20–22; and Mike
    Andrews, 19; naming of, 12; and
    Norman Jaffe, 18; and Ralph
    Edwards, 12, 14; and Sidney Far-
    ber, 15, 18, 21, 24; and Sidney Far-
    ber Cancer Center, 18, 22; and Ted
    Williams, 15–16, 17, 23, 183; and
    Thomas Farber, 20; and Variety
    Club of New England, 11–12, 14, 15;
    and William Koster, 12, 18
Johnson, Alex, 149

Johnson, Ban, 38, 56, 129
Johnson, Cliff, 159
Johnson, Darrell, 105
Johnson, Elliot, 10
Johnson, Walter, 132
Jones, Boisfeuillet, 17
Jones, Charlie, 60
Jones, Dalton, 118, 123, 126
Josephson, Duane, 116

Kaat, Jim, 156
Kahn, Roger, 185
Kaline, Al, 118, 157
Kansas City Athletics, 31, 112, 116, 148
Kansas City Cowboys, 129
Kansas City Monarchs, 27
Kansas City Royals, 9–10, 96, 139
Kauffman Stadium, 179
Keaton, Michael, 74
Kelly, Matt, 40
Kelso, Bill, 115
Kenmore Square, 168–70, 173, 176
Kennedy, Caroline, 42–43
Kennedy, Jacqueline, 42
Kennedy, John (baseball player), 27, 117
Kennedy, John F. (U.S. president), 6,
    42–43, 46, 153–54
Kennedy, Ted, 15, 148–49, 151
Kercheville, Ron, 205–6
Kilfoyl, John, 56
Killebrew, Harmon, 121
Killilea, Henry J., 56
King, Edward, 168
King, Martin Luther, Jr., 28–29
King, Stephen, 155
Kingman, Dave, 157
The Kinks, 41
Kirk, Paul, 30

Kleinow, Red, 130–31
Kling, Vincent, 191
Knight, John, 58
Knight, Ray, 75, 88–89
Knoop, Bobby, 113, 114, 115
Koosman, Jerry, 164
Kottaras, George, 10
Koufax, Sandy, 121, 123, 157, 189
Kovalchuk, Brian, 49
Krim, Arthur, 175
Kruh, David, 42
Krumholz, Joshua, 193–94
Krupa, Charles, 5
Kuhn, Bowie, 29, 30
Kyle TX, 205–6

Labatut, Jean, 179–80, 183–84, 185, 186
LaChance, George, 130
Lachemann, Rene, 31
Lajoie, Nap, 37, 58–59
LaMontagne, Armand, 183–84, 186
Lamp, Dennis, 157
Landis, Bill, 128
Landis, Kenesaw Mountain, 7
Langston, Mark, 161
Larsen, Don, 107
Late Night with Conan O'Brien, 70, 152
Late Night with David Letterman, 110, 152
Late Night with Jimmy Fallon, 70
Late Night with Seth Meyers, 54
Lavagetto, Cookie, 48
Lazzeri, Tony, 134
LeBec, Carla Tortelli, 77, 82
LeBritton, Joe, 200–201
Lechmere, 120
Lee, Bill "Spaceman," 151
LeFlore, Ron, 149, 150
Lehane, Dennis, 71

Lemieux, Mario, 153
Lemon, Bob, 136
Lincoln, Abraham, 6
Lindholm, Karl, 203–4
Lindo, Delroy, 32
Little, Grady, 194
Little World Series, 27
Lloyd, Harold, 94
Lochhead, Harry, 60
Lofton, Kenny, 140
Lolich, Mickey, 118, 121
Lombardi, Vince, 152
Lonborg, Jim, 116, 120, 121, 122, 123, 125, 126, 128, 200
Long, Herman, 129
Lord, Lee, 53
Los Angeles Angels, 146
Los Angeles Dodgers, 78, 96, 112
Los Angeles Lakers, 129
Louis, Joe, 48
Louisiana Purchase, 131
Louisville Colonels, 56, 57, 65–66
Lu, Lingzi, 3
Lyle, Sparky, 113
Lynn, Fred, 79, 83, 103–5, 136, 138–39, 201, 205
Lyons, Steve, 158
Lyric Stage, 42

Mackey, Biz, 30
Malden, Karl, 66
Malone, Sam "Mayday," xv, 68, 76–86
Malzone, Frank, 83
Manfred, Rob, 33
Manhattan, 41, 74, 172, 176
Mantegani, Barbara, 201–2
Mantle, Mickey, 32, 93, 106, 152, 156–57, 206

Marathon Day, 3-4
Marblehead High School, 13
March on Washington, 29
Marino, Dan, 94
Maris, Roger, 78, 123, 124, 134, 148, 152
Marotte, Jean Gilles, 101
Martin, Billy, 107, 147
Martin, Dean, 32
Martin, Pat, 101
Martínez, Pedro, 194, 204
Maryland State House, 181
The Mary Tyler Moore Show, 11
Masi, Phil, 13
Massachusetts Energy Office, 168
Massachusetts General Hospital, 4
Massachusetts Institute of Technology (MIT), 4, 175, 206
Mathewson, Christy, 37, 61, 158
Mattingly, Don, 87
Maxvill, Dal, 124
Mays, Willie, 32, 48, 106-7, 149, 178, 184
Mazeroski, Bill, 185
Mazzilli, Lee, 88
McCarver, Tim, 123
McClendon, Lloyd, 157
McCovey, Willie, 184
McDermott, Jerry, 170
McDougald, Gil, 106, 107
McEnaney, Will, 105
McGinnity, Joe, 61
McGraw, John, 37, 38, 40
McGreevy, Michael "Nuf Ced," 37-40, 127, 142, 191
McGuire, Jim Deacon, 131
McHale, Kevin, 85
McKinley, William, 6
McLain, Denny, 118

McNamara, John, 89, 90, 159-60, 161-62
Meacham, Bob, 158
Meeks, Lindsey, 68
Melesky, Scott, 196
Melville's Seafood Restaurant, 76
Memorial Stadium, 119, 128, 137
Mendez, Antonio Tobias, 181-82, 184, 186
Menino, Thomas, 3, 183
Meyers, Seth, 54
Miami Marlins, 31
Middlebrooks, Will, 9
Mientkiewicz, Doug, 142
Miles, Kevin, G., 4
Millar, Kevin, 141
Miller, Rick, 149
Milwaukee Braves, 15, 46
Minneapolis Millers, 146
Minnesota Twins, 113, 119-21, 141, 148
Mirabelli, Doug, 140
MIT. *See* Massachusetts Institute of Technology (MIT)
Mitchell, Kevin, 75, 89
Mitchell, Paul, 5
Mobile AL, 31
Monboquette, Bill, 47
Montreal Expos, 17
Montreal Royals, 27
"Monuments and Memorials" (Labatut), 179-80
Moore, Norma, 66
Morehead, Dave, 47
Moret, Roger, 104-5
Morgan, Joe, 103-6
Morse, Joseph, 16
Moustakas, Mike, 9-10
Muchnick, Isadore, 27

Mueller, Bill, 141
Munson, Thurman, 135–36, 138, 151
The Munsters, 41
Murcer, Bobby, 153
Murphy, Bob, 47
Murphy, Dwayne, 196
Murphy Brown, 84
Murray, Eddie, 181
Musial, Stan, 32, 146, 148, 149
"My Maryland, My Maryland," 39

Nadoraski, Max, 202–3
Napoli, Mike, 10
Narragansett Beer, 45–53
Narragansett RI, 199
National Baseball Hall of Fame and
    Museum, 26, 29–31, 164, 183–84
Nationals Park, 178
Nava, Daniel, 9–10
NBC: Cheers, 85–86; Game of the Week,
    47–48; Seinfeld, 91; Wednesday
    Mystery Movie, 76; World Series
    (1975), 102, 108; World Series
    (1986), 89, 165
Negro Leagues, 26–27, 29–30, 33
Nelson, Craig T., 155
Nettles, Graig, 136, 151
Newark Eagles, 30
New Britain CT, 77
Newcombe, Don, 48
New England League, 58
New Sweden ME, 21, 22
New York Comic Con, 42
New York Giants, 27, 38, 112
New York Mets, 67, 74–75, 161–63
New York Rangers, 101
New York Yankees: and Babe Ruth
    trade, 131–35; as Highlanders, 129;

and Seinfeld, 93; and "Sweet Caro-
line," 44; World Series titles of, 78,
134, 137. See also Red Sox-Yankees
rivalry
Nichols, Reid, 158
Nipper, Al, 163
Nolan, Gary, 103
Nomo, Hideo, 47
Norman, Dan, 156
Norman, Fred, 103
Norris, Jack, 101
Northeastern University, 54
Northrup, Jim, 118
Norwood Airport, 190
Norwood MA, 190
Nowlin, Bill, 193, 195–96

Oakland Athletics, 149
O'Brien, Conan, 70, 152
The Odd Couple, 95–96
Oil and Gas Historical Society, 172
Ojeda, Bobby, 87–89
O'Neill, Tip, 84, 185
Orr, Bobby, 78, 192
Ortiz, David: Achilles heel injury of,
8; and Boston Marathon bombing,
3, 5, 8, 10, 199; fan memory of, 199,
202–3, 205; home runs of, 9, 186;
Jeff Bauman, 5; and Minnesota
Twins, 8; and New York Yankees,
140, 141; and Pawtucket Red Sox,
8; signing of, with Boston Red Sox,
8; and World Series, 9, 194
Osborne, Bobo, 146
Osco, 127
Owen, Spike, 87–88

Pabst, 49

Pacific Coast League, 31
Paige, Satchel, 12, 26-27, 29, 30-33
Palmer, Jim, 181
Pantusso, Ernie "Coach," 77, 82
Pappas, Milt, 156
Parent, Freddy, 59-60, 130
Park, Brad, 101
Parker, Wes, 94
Parnell, Mel, 47, 71
Patrick, Deval, 3
Patriots Day, 3-4
Patriots Day (film), 5-6
Pawtucket Red Sox, 8-9
Pearson, John, 199-200
Pedroia, Dustin, 9
Peloquin, Mark, 204-5
Peninsula Grays, 31
Pepitone, Joe, 93-94, 147
Pérez, Salvador, 9, 10
Pérez, Tony, 103-4, 107
Perini, Lou, 15, 16
Perkins, Anthony, 66
Pesky, Johnny, 178, 181, 182, 183
Peterson, Norm, 77, 80, 104
Petrocelli, Rico, 103, 104, 105, 114, 115, 117, 119, 122, 125, 126, 128
Petróleos de Venezuela, 170, 172
Philadelphia Athletics, 40, 54, 57-61, 112, 129
Philadelphia Phillies, 27, 51, 58, 157
Philley, Dave, 66
Piazza, Mike, 7
Pickering, Joe, Jr., 42
Piersall, Jimmy, 65-69
Piniella, Lou, 138, 151, 163
Pink, Mary, 43
Piscopo, Joe, 152
Pittsburgh PA, 33

Pittsburgh Penguins, 153
Pittsburgh Pirates, 37, 61, 129-30
Pittsburgh Steelers, 95
Podres, Johnny, 106
Polacko, Amy, 202-3
Ponzi, Charles, 93
Portland Beavers, 31
Poulsen, Ken, 113
Powers, Doc, 60
Prince of Thieves (Hogan), 71
Prohibition, 45, 50
Puckett, Kirby, 203
Puleo, Charlie, 157

Raleigh Capitals, 145
Ramirez, Hanley, 5
Randolph, Willie, 138, 148
Ratelle, Jean, 101
Reagan, Ronald, 6
Red Sox-Yankees rivalry: and American League East playoff (1978), 79, 135-38, 195; and Babe Ruth trade, 131-35; and "Boston Massacre," 137-38; in *Cheers*, 77-78; in *Fever Pitch*, 68-69; in 1967, 116-17; origins of, 129, 135; and pennant race (1904), 130-31
Reese, Pee Wee, 106
Reese, Rich, 120
Reichardt, Rick, 115
Related Beal, 173
Remy, Jerry, 136, 139, 154
Renner, Jeremy, 72-73
Rentería, Édgar, 142
Repoz, Roger, 115
Reverse of the Curse of the Bambino, 141
Rice, Jim, 74, 83, 87, 136, 150, 186, 203
Richard, Martin, 3

The Rich Eisen Show, 93
Richert, Pete, 128
Rickey, Branch, 27
Ripken, Cal, Jr., 181
Riverfront Stadium, 104
Rivers, Mickey, 136, 151
Roberts, Dave, 150, 199
Robinson, Bill, 117
Robinson, Brooks, 107, 181
Robinson, Frank, 28, 128
Robinson, Jackie, 27-28, 33, 112, 178, 184
Rocky, 110-11
Rodgers, Bill, 205
Rodgers, Bob "Buck," 114, 115
Rodriguez, Alex, 140
Rodríguez, Aurelio, 150
Rohr, Bill, 147
Rojas, Minnie, 114
Romine, Kevin, 159, 160
Roosevelt, Franklin, 6, 7, 27
Rose, Pete, 103, 105
Ross, David, 9
Royal Rooters, 37-39, 191
Russell, Jim, 13
Ruth, Babe: curse of, 42, 87, 105, 206; honored at Yankee Stadium, 185; as Red Sox player, 83, 131-34; referenced in *61**, 153; trade of, to Yankees, 78, 101, 131-35
Ruttman, Larry, 194-95
Ryan, Jack, 62

Sain, Johnny, 12, 16
Saltamachia, Jarrod, 5, 9
Sambito, Joe, 160
Sancta Maria Hospital, 114
Sandberg, Ryne, 189
San Diego Chargers, 153

San Diego Padres, 189
San Diego Padres (Pacific Coast League), 197
San Francisco Giants, 112, 115
Santana, Rafael, 88
Santiago, José, 117, 120-22, 126
Saturday Night Live, 70, 152
Schiraldi, Calvin, 74-75, 88-89
Schoendienst, Red, 123, 127
Scott, George, 83, 115, 117-20, 122, 124, 125, 126, 128, 138, 139
Scranton Red Sox, 65
Scully, Vin, 89, 162
Seattle Mariners, 31, 42, 160
Seaver, Tom: achievements of, 156; and Boston Red Sox, 158-63; and Chicago White Sox, 157-58; and Cincinnati Reds, 156; and COVID-19, 165; death of, 165; knee surgery of, 163; last game of, 161; last victory of, 160; and Lewy body dementia, 165; and New York Mets, 156-57, 159, 162, 163-64; no-hitter of, 157, 165; retirement of, 164; and return to Shea Stadium (2008), 164; and *Sports Illustrated*, 155; statue of, 178-79; three hundredth victory of, 158-59; and Tom Seaver Day, 164; uniform number of, retired, 164; and World Series (1969), 156; and World Series (1973), 156
Seibolt, Mel, 200
Seinfeld, 91
Seitz Brewing Company, 51
Selbach, Kip, 130
Seybold, Socks, 60
Shannon, Mike, 123, 125

Shea Stadium, 74, 87, 90, 166
Sheffield, Gary, 140
Shell Oil, 172
Shields, James, 9
shiva, 92
Siebern, Norm, 115, 117, 119
Siebert, Sonny, 201
Sierra, Rubén, 140-41
The Silver Slipper, 40
Sinatra, Frank, 71, 109
Sinden, Harry, 102
Sisk, Doug, 157
Sisler, George, 132
Skowron, Moose, 93, 115
Smart, Maxwell, 126
Smith, Bubba, 95
Smith, Charley, 147
Smith, Jim, 197-98
Smith, Mayo, 118
Smith, Reggie, 113, 114, 115, 118, 119, 122, 123, 124, 128
Snider, Duke, 107
Snyder, Jimmy "The Greek," 122
Soden, Arthur, 57
Solomon, 68
Somers, Charles, 56-57, 62
Southworth, Billy, 12, 18
Spahn, Warren, 13, 158
Sparma, Joe, 156
Speaker, Tris, 132
Spielberg, Steven, 110
Sports Illustrated, 69, 155
Sprowl, Bobby, 138
Stahl, Chick, 59-60
Stahl, Jake, 40
The Standells, 41
Stanfield, Fred, 101
Stanky, Eddie, 13, 116

Stanley, Bob, 75, 89, 138
Stanley Cup, 102, 113
Stapleton, Dave, 90
Star Markets, 127
Starr, David, 192
Starr, Gabrielle, 191-92
Star Trek, 29, 128
State Street Bank and Trust Company, 127
statue(s): of Carl Yastrzemski, 179-80; *The Teammates*, 178, 181-82, 183; of Ted Williams, 183
Stearnes, Turkey, 30
Steinberg, Charles, 43
Steinberg, Saul, 78
Steinbrenner, George, 163
Stengel, Casey, 153
Stephenson, Jerry, 115, 123
St. Louis Browns, 27, 31, 132
St. Louis Cardinals, 70, 122-28, 163, 198, 200
St. Louis Perfectos, 61
Stockbridge, Gary, 196-97
Strawberry, Darryl, 88
Sullivan, Marc, 160
Suttles, Mule, 30
"Sweet Caroline," 42-44, 69
Symphony Hall, 175

Talarico, Franc, 183-84, 186
Tampa Bay Rays, 9
Tartabull, Danny, 93
Tartabull, José, 114, 118
Tartikoff, Brandon, 85
Tarver, La Schelle, 89
TD Garden, 4, 7
The Teammates (Halberstam), 181, 182
The Teammates (statue), 178, 181-82

Ted 2, 42
Ted Williams Camp, 196–97
Ted Williams Museum & Hitters Hall of Fame, 183
"Tessie," 40–41
Texas Rangers, 148
Thayer, Warren, 174
Third Base (bar), 37
Thomas, George, 117
Thompson, Hank, 27
Thompson, Jason, 150
Thornton, Jerry, 141
Tiant, Luis, 103–4, 139, 200, 204
Tidewater Tides, 164
Tierney, John, 206
Tiger Stadium, 118–19, 150
Tillman, Bob, 116
Tobey, Amy, 43
Toledo Blue Hens, 26
Torgeson, Earl, 13
Toronto Blue Jays, 97, 139, 159
Torrez, Mike, 135
The Town, 71–73
Tresh, Tom, 116–17, 147
Tri-Valley Baseball Camp, 196
Truman, Harry 12
Trutor, Clayton, 192–93
Tsarnaev, Dzhokar, 4, 7–8, 44
Tsarnaev, Tamerlan, 4, 5, 8
Turn-Style, 127
TWA, 120
Twin Towers. *See* World Trade Center
"Twist and Shout," 155

Underwood, Blair, 32–33
Union Park, 39
United Flight 93, 6–7
University of Pittsburgh, 43–44

Upshaw, Willie, 159
Urich, Robert, 84
U.S. House of Representatives, 6, 148

Vadnais, Carol, 101
Valenzuela, Fernando, 189
Val Perry Trio, 42
Vancouver Canucks, 102
Varitek, Jason, 140
Veale, Bob, 156
Veeck, Bill, 27
Vélez, Otto, 151
Victorino, Shane, 9
Vietnam War, 108–9, 168
View of the World from 9th Avenue, 78
Virgil, Ozzie, 27, 146
V-J Day, 26
Vollmer, Clyde, 47
Volpe, John, 127, 191

Wagner, Honus, 40
Wahlberg, Mark, 6
Walker, Moses Fleetwood, 26
Walker, Weldy, 26
Walsh, Marty, 173–74
Wang, Devin, 5
Washington Senators, 17, 54–55, 59, 61, 132
Waterbury CT, 65
Watertown Police Department, 7–8
The Way It Was, 48
WBZ, 45
Weaver, Earl, 181
Weaver, Robert, 29
Weeghman Park, 189
Welliver, Titus, 72
Wells, Bruce, 175
Werhas, Johnny, 115

Wertz, Vic, 106

West, Jerry, 95

Western League, 56

Wheaties, 33

Whitaker, Steve, 117

White, Bill, 135

White, Roy, 117

Willhite, Nick, 114

Williams, Bernie, 93, 140

Williams, Claudia, 183

Williams, Dick, 113, 117–19, 121, 123, 201

Williams, Joe, 30–31

Williams, Marvin, 27–28

Williams, Ted: batting skill of, 25–26, 32, 145, 179; and Carl Yastrzemski, 145, 147, 148; and *Cheers*, 78, 79; and City of Boston Korean War Medal, 15; fan memory of, 195, 197, 201; Hall of Fame induction speech of, 26, 28, 29, 33; and Jimmy Fund, 15–16; and Korean War, 15, 25, 46, 145, 185; last at bat of, 47; *The Science of Hitting*, 25–26; statues of, 178, 181–83; and Ted Williams Camp, 196–97; and Variety Club of New England's Distinguished Service Medal, 15; and Washington Senators, 25; and World War II, 15, 25, 145

Williams, Walt, 116

Williamson, Mykelti, 32

Wills, Maury, 189

Wilson, Earl, 47, 118–19

Wilson, Mookie, 75, 88–90, 92

Winfield, Dave, 94

Winters, Mike, 140

Wise, Rick, 107

The Wizard of Oz, 198

WJAR, 45

WNAC, 45

Wood, Joe, 197

Worcester Red Sox, 183

World Series: (1903), 40, 61, 126; (1918), 70, 137, 191–92; (1919), 131; (1946), 88, 126, 135, 142; (1947), 106; (1948), 12; (1954), 107; (1955), 106; (1960), 185; (1965), 121; (1966), 48; (1967), 17, 88, 102, 122–28, 142, 147, 191, 192, 200; (1969), 48, 107; (1972–74), 48; (1975), 48, 88, 102–8, 111, 135, 179–80, 195, 200–201, 204; (1986), 41, 69, 74–75, 87–88, 96, 135, 161–63, 165, 195; (1989), 7; (2004), 41, 42, 70, 96, 141–42, 192, 194, 195–96, 198, 199, 205, 206; (2007), 96, 142, 196; (2013), 10, 142, 191; (2018), 142, 196

World Trade Center: attack on (1993), 6; attack on (2001), 6, 7, 10

World War I, 192

World War II, 6, 7, 26, 154, 177, 178

Wrightman, Ben, 68–71

Wrigley Field, 179, 189

Wuhl, Robert, 94

Wyatt, John, 115, 121

"Yankee Doodle," 39

Yankee Stadium, 116–18, 139, 141, 150–51, 153, 158

Yastrzemski, Carl: and American League East playoff (1978), 136, 138; and Baseball Hall of Fame, 151; career statistics of, 180; and *Cheers*, 83; fan memory of, 196, 200, 205; and Gold Glove, 147; hitting for the cycle, 47; and Minor Leagues, 145–46; and 1967 season,

Yastrzemski, Carl (*cont.*)
  115–21, 125, 127, 128, 147, 191; and
  1976 season, 149–51; retirement
  of, 147, 151–52; rookie season of,
  145–48, 153–54; statue of, 178, 180–
  81; and Ted Williams, 145–48, 152;
  three thousandth hit of, 148–49;
  and Triple Crown, 79; and World
  Series (1967), 121–25, 127; and
  World Series (1975), 103, 105
Yastrzemski, Carl, Sr., 146
Yawkey, Jean, 183
Yawkey, Tom, 17, 27–28, 121

Yawkey Way, 28
Yeager, Chuck, 28
York, Rudy, 182
Yost, Ned, 9–10
Young, Cy, 30, 37, 40, 54, 59, 60–62,
  76
Young, Steve, 153

Zachry, Pat, 156
Zanussi, Joe, 101
Zauchin, Norm, 47
Zenith, 120
Zimmer, Don, 138